Annals of Information Systems

Volume 14

For further volumes, go to
http://www.springer.com/series/7573

David Schuff · David Paradice · Frada Burstein ·
Daniel J. Power · Ramesh Sharda
Editors

Decision Support

An Examination of the DSS Discipline

Editors
David Schuff
Department of Management Information Systems
Temple University
Philadelphia, PA 19122, USA
david.schuff@temple.edu

David Paradice
Department of Risk Management/Insurance, Real Estate and Business Law
Florida State University
Tallahassee, FL 32306-1110, USA
paradice@fsu.edu

Frada Burstein
Monash University
Caulfield East, VIC 3145, Australia
frada.burstein@infotech.monash.edu.au

Daniel J. Power
Department of Management
University of Northern Iowa
Cedar Falls, IA 50614-0125, USA
daniel.power@uni.edu

Ramesh Sharda
Department of Management Science and Information Systems
Oklahoma State University
Stillwater, OK 74078, USA
ramesh.sharda@okstate.edu

ISSN 1934-3221 e-ISSN 1934-3213
ISBN 978-1-4419-6180-8 e-ISBN 978-1-4419-6181-5
DOI 10.1007/978-1-4419-6181-5
Springer New York Dordrecht Heidelberg London

Printed on acid-free paper

Springer is part of Springer Science+Business Media (www.springer.com)

Preface

The origin of this volume came while planning the 2009 International Conference on Decision Support Systems. The theme of that 2-day conference was "Assessing Today and Envisioning Tomorrow." We wanted to summarize where the field had been and generate ideas regarding where it was going. The meeting brought together representatives from both academia and industry, and covered topics ranging from the earliest group decision support systems to new methods of managing emergency medical respons e to the future of telepresence.

The notion of looking both backward and forward to put the field of Decision Support Systems into perspective also seemed a great subject for a volume of the Annals of Information Systems series. This volume reflects some of the best papers from that event.

The first paper, "GDSS: Past, Present, and Future," is a summary of a panel discussion led by Paul Gray (Claremont Graduate University), and joined by Bob Johansen (the Institute for the Future), Jay Nunamaker (University of Arizona), Jeff Rodnman (Polycom, Inc.), and Gerald R. Wagner (University of Nebraska). The paper starts with Gray's interesting history of group decision-making systems, starting with Churchill's War Room during World War II and ending with the University of Arizona's GDSS facilities. The next section includes a discussion by Johansen regarding how GDSS systems can facilitate leadership by supporting foresight, insight, and action. Nunamaker's section addresses the escalating need for support of global teams, citing continued outsourcing, an increasingly competitive environment, and pressure to reduce costs related to travel. He also discusses the challenges of working in global teams and provides recommendations for how to make them more effective. In the fourth section, Wagner takes an entrepreneurial perspective, discussing the development and commercialization of several DSS and GDSS systems in which he was involved, including the Interactive Financial Planning System (IFPS), Vision Quest, WebIQ, and the follow-on to IFPS called Planners Lab. Finally, Rodman gives an overview and history of telepresence, and presents his vision for the future in this space.

The second paper is titled "Reflections on the Past and Future of Decision Support Systems: Perspective of Eleven Pioneers." This paper reports the reflections of a number of people who have been active in the DSS field since its inception, including a timeline and a description of major events. Dan J. Power (University of Northern Iowa), Frada Burstein (Monash University), and Ramesh Sharda (Oklahoma State University), all well-established and respected researchers in the DSS field in their own rights, document the commentary provided in these interviews. Interestingly, these pioneers of the field were generally more interested in talking about the future than they were about reminiscing about the past.

Sean Eom's (Southeast Missouri State University) paper, titled "The Intellectual Structure of Decision Support Systems Research (1991–2004)," uses author co-citation analysis to determine the major areas of study in the field. The paper is interesting for both its methodology and its findings. Eom constructed his data set from most frequently cited 1% of papers, and his analysis revealed six major areas: group support systems, model management, foundations, DSS evaluation, user interfaces, and multiple criteria DSS and negotiation support systems.

The fourth paper focuses on a topic that has received increasing emphasis in the last few years. In "Ethical Decision Making and Implications for Decision Support" John R. Drake (Eastern Michigan University), Dianne J. Hall (Auburn University), and Teresa Lang (Columbus State University) examine decision making processes in ethical contexts. They adapt Jones' issue contingent model of ethical decision making and fold in theories by Rest and Kohlberg to develop DSS design implications. Their approach provides a blueprint to build systems that could be the basis for measurable progress in the area of decision support in situations involving ethical concerns.

The fifth paper illustrates the global nature of our field. James Pick (University of Redlands) investigates web and mobile spatial decision support in "Web and Mobile Decision Support as Innovations: Comparison of United States and Hong Kong, China." Fourteen business and government organizations are studied in this paper, with most of them being assessed as having achieved a middle stage of adoption/diffusion of this technology. None of the organizations were found to be in an advanced stage. The research provides an interesting, multinational look at a rapidly emerging technology that is not always accepted without resistance.

Chapter 6, titled "Knowledge Management Capability in Education," was written by Jeremy Hodges (Embry-Riddle Aeronautical University) and Ronald Freeze (Emporia State University). Hodges and Freeze present a case study where a Knowledge Management Capability Assessment (KMCA) instrument was validated within a Department of Defense educational organization. This extends their previous work, where the instrument was developed and testing in the manufacturing industry. The application to this new setting yields several interesting insights, including that basic knowledge capabilities are consistent across industries.

Our seventh paper is written by a trio of researchers from Ben-Gurion University. Meira Levy (also from Deutsch Telekom Laboratories), Nava Pliskin, and Gilad Ravid collaborated to write "Knowledge Warehouse for Decision Support in Critical Business Processes: Conceptual Modeling and Requirements Elicitation." This paper is particularly timely, since it considers the dynamic and often unpredictable characteristics of today's business environment. The authors combine a knowledge warehouse conceptual model with information that decision makers in critical business processes own. Their goal is to enable rational decision transparency. Their design science approach opens the door to new research in DSS in an important way.

The eighth paper in this volume, titled "Agent-based Modeling and Simulation as a Tool for Decision Support for Managing Patient Falls in a Dynamic Hospital Setting," describes the use of agent-based modeling to address a contemporary issue in patient care. Gokul Bhandari, Ziad Kobti, Anne W. Snowdon, Ashish Nakhwal, Shamual Rahaman, and Carol A. Kolga (University of Windsor) created a simulation for patient falls in a Leamington District Memorial Hospital in Ontario, Canada. They found the optimal nurse shift configuration for reaching patients in the least amount of time. This is a particularly timely topic, as information technology is being seen as a necessity in addressing rising healthcare costs.

In Chapter 9, titled "Context-aware Mobile Medical Emergency Management Decision Support System for Safe Transportation," Frada Burstein (Monash University), Pari Delir Haghighi (Monash University), and Arkady Zaslavsky (Lulea University of Technology) take a different approach to the application of decision support to the heathcare industry. They address a specific, practical problem: emergency medical response for large events. They present a design for new system to manage incident response that uses data from hospitals and information about road and traffic conditions to determine the best route for each patient case. With today's pervasiveness of mobile computing technology, one can see how this system could be deployed in a variety of environments.

One of the goals of our conference was to include teaching aspects of DSS as well as research-oriented topics. In the tenth paper, "General Motors Bailout Problem: A Teaching Case Using the Planners Lab^{TM} Software," two of the "pioneers" of DSS interviewed in Chapter 2 work with two younger researchers to demonstrate how to teach DSS concepts using state-of-the-art decision support software. Jim Courtney (Louisiana Tech University), Krisitin Brewer (Louisiana Tech University), Randy Kuhn (University of Louisville), and Gerald R. Wagner (Bellevue University) combine to illustrate how a model of a complicated business situation can be built using software that supports "rehearsing the future." This case study can be easily adapted for a class covering DSS concepts. The software is also publically available.

This volume concludes with "Assessing Today: Determining the Decision Value of Decision Support Systems" by Gloria Phillips-Wren (Loyola University Maryland), Manuel Mora (University of Aguascalientes), and Guisseppi Forgionne (University of Maryland Baltimore County). These researchers are well-known for taking a systems approach to analyses. They continue that tradition by extending previous studies and linking the type of support provided to the decision maker with the specific DSS design characteristics needed to deliver those services. They implement their framework using an analytic hierarchy process and demonstrate the ability of their design to support further DSS research.

These papers represent a snapshot of the Decision Support Systems field. It can be informative and enlightening to occasionally pause and consider how a field is evolving and in what direction it is headed. One thing that is striking about the papers in this volume is how they reflect many of the contemporary forces shaping our world: mobile technology and ubiquitous computing, globalization, health care, ethics, and the recent financial crisis. We find today that DSS has become so ubiquitous that it often appears under a different name or embedded in some other focus area. Many of the subjects of the articles in this volume, such as data warehousing, business intelligence, knowledge management, and agent-based modeling, continue to develop approaches and ideas that have their foundations in earlier DSS studies. Without doubt, support for decision processes will continue to be important, if not critical, as decision making environments become more complex, dynamic, and ambiguous. We hope you find these papers informative and inspiring, and we look forward to seeing what emerges in the decision support arena over the next couple of decades.

Philadelphia, PA David Schuff
Tallahassee, FL David Paradice
Caulfield East, VIC Frada Burstein
Cedar Falls, IA Daniel J. Power
Stillwater, OK Ramesh Sharda

Contents

Contributors

Gokul Bhandari Odette School of Business, University of Windsor, Windsor, ON, Canada, N9B3P4, gokul@uwindsor.ca

Kristen Brewer Louisiana Tech University, Ruston, LA, USA, klb046@latech.edu

Frada Burstein Centre for Organisational and Social Informatics, Monash University, Caulfield East, VIC 3145, Australia, frada.burstein@infotech.monash.edu.au

Jim Courtney Louisiana Tech University, Ruston, LA, USA, courtney@latech.edu

John R. Drake Eastern Michigan University, Ypsilanti, MI 48197, USA, john.drake@emich.edu

Sean Eom Department of Accounting and MIS, Southeast Missouri State University, Cape Girardeau, MO 63701, USA, sbeom@semo.edu

Guisseppi Forgionne University of Maryland, Baltimore, MD, USA, forgionn@umbc.edu

Ronald Freeze Emporia State University, Emporia, KS, USA, rfreeze@emporia.edu

Paul Gray Claremont Graduate University, Claremont, CA, USA, paul.gray@cgu.edu

Pari Delir Haghighi Centre for Organisational and Social Informatics, Monash University, Caulfield, VIC, Australia, pari.delirhaghighi@infotech.monash.edu.au

Dianne J. Hall Auburn University, Auburn, AL 36849, USA, dhall@auburn.edu

Jeremy Hodges Embry-Riddle Aeronautical University, Daytona Beach, FL, USA, jeremy.hodges@erau.edu

Bob Johansen Institute for the Future, Palo Alto, CA, USA, bjohansen@itft.org

Ziad Kobti Department of Computer Science, University of Windsor, Windsor, ON, Canada N9B3P4, kobti@uwindsor.ca

Carol A. Kolga Kingston General Hospital, Kingston, ON, Canada, ckolga@kos.net

Randy Kuhn University of Louisville, Louisville, KY, USA, jrkuhn01@louisville.edu

Teresa Lang Columbus State University, Columbus, GA 31907, USA, lang_teresa@colstate.edu

Meira Levy Department of Industrial Engineering and Management, Deutsche Telekom Laboratories, Ben-Gurion University of the Negev, Beer-Sheva, Israel, lmeira@bgu.ac.il

Manuel Mora University of Aguascalientes, Aguascalientes, Mexico, mmora@securenym.net

Ashish Nakhwal Department of Computer Science, University of Windsor, Windsor, ON, Canada N9B3P4, nakhwal@uwindsor.ca

Jay Nunamaker University of Arizona, Tucson, AZ, USA, jnunamaker@cmi.arizona.edu

Gloria Phillips-Wren Loyola University Maryland, Baltimore, MD, USA, gwren@loyola.edu

Daniel J. Power Department of Management, University of Northern Iowa, Cedar Falls, IA 50614-0125, USA, daniel.power@uni.edu

James B. Pick University of Redlands, Redlands, CA 92373, USA, james_pick@redlands.edu

Nava Pliskin Department of Industrial Engineering and Management, Ben-Gurion University of the Negev, Beer-Sheva, Israel, pliskinn@bgu.ac.il

Shamual Rahaman Department of Computer Science, University of Windsor, Windsor, ON, Canada, N9B3P4, rahaman@uwindsor.ca

Gilad Ravid Department of Industrial Engineering and Management, Ben-Gurion University of the Negev, Beer-Sheva, Israel, rgilad@bgu.ac.il

Jeff Rodman Polycom, Inc., Pleasanton, CA, USA, jeff.rodman@polycom.com

Ramesh Sharda Department of Management Science and Information Systems, Oklahoma State University, William S. Spears School of Business, Stillwater, OK 74078, USA, ramesh.sharda@okstate.edu

Anne W. Snowdon Odette School of Business, University of Windsor, Windsor, ON, Canada N9B3P4, snowdon@uwindsor.ca

Gerald R. Wagner Bellevue University, Bellevue, NE, USA; University of Nebraska, Lincoln, NB, USA, grwagner@mail.unomaha.edu

Arkady Zaslavsky Lulea University of Technology, Lulea, Sweden, arkady.zaslavsky@ltu.se

About the Authors

Gokul Bhandari is an Assistant Professor of MIS at the Odette School of Business, University of Windsor, Ontario, Canada. His primary research interests are in the area of health informatics and decision support systems. He received his Ph.D. in Management Science/Information Systems from McMaster University, Canada.

Kristen Brewer is a Doctoral student in Computer Information Systems at Louisiana Tech University in Ruston, LA. She received her M.B.A. from Eastern Kentucky University in Richmond, KY, and also holds a B.B.A. in Management from the University of Kentucky in Lexington, KY.

Kristen has presented research and been included in the refereed proceedings of many professional conferences, including Americas Conference on Information Systems (AMCIS), Decision Sciences Institute (DSI), INFORMS, and the International Academy of Business and Public Administration Disciplines (IABPAD). In addition, her research has been published in refereed journals, including the July-August 2010 issue of the *Journal of Education for Business*

Her research interests include knowledge management, inquiring systems and organizations, information assurance and security, ethical decision-making, and empowerment applications to information systems.

Frada Burstein is a Professor at Faculty of Information Technology, Monash University, Melbourne, Australia. At Monash University, Professor Burstein initiated and continues to lead Knowledge Management Research Program, which comprises a virtual Knowledge Management Laboratory. She has been a Chief Investigator for a number of research projects supported by grants and scholarships from the Australian Research Council and industry, including two projects in emergency management decision support. Her current research interests include knowledge management technologies, intelligent decision support, mobile and real-time decision support, and health informatics. Her work appears in journals such as Decision Support Systems, Journal of Organizational Computing and Electronic Commerce, Journal of the American Society for Information Science and Technology, Information Technology & People, European Journal of Operations Research, and Knowledge Management Research and Practice. Professor Burstein is an Area Editor for Decision Support Systems Journal and Co-Editor for Journal of Decision Systems and VINE: The journal of information and knowledge management systems. Professor Burstein has been a guest editor of a few special issues of journals and collections of research papers. The most recent and substantial work was a set of two volumes of Handbook of Decision Support Systems, published by Springer.

James Courtney, Jr. is Professor of Computer Information Systems and holder of the Humana Foundation – McCallister Eminent Scholar Chair in the Management & Information Systems Department at Louisiana Tech University. He formerly was Professor of Information Systems at the University of Central Florida and Tenneco Professor of Business Administration in the Information and Operations Management Department at Texas A&M University. He received his Ph.D. in Business Administration (Management Science) from the University of Texas at Austin in 1974. His academic experience also includes faculty positions at Georgia Tech, Texas Tech, Lincoln University in New Zealand and the State University of New York at Buffalo.

Jim has published over 45 refereed articles in several different journals, including *Management Science*, *MIS Quarterly*, *Communications of the ACM*, *IEEE Transactions on Systems, Man and Cybernetics*, *Decision Sciences*, *Decision Support Systems,* the *Journal of Management Information Systems*, *Database,* and the *Journal of Applied Systems Analysis.* He has also published over 60 papers in refereed conference proceedings and book chapters.

His present research interests are knowledge-based decision support systems, healthcare information systems, information assurance, ethical decision making, knowledge management, inquiring (learning) organizations and sustainable economic systems.

John R. Drake is an Assistant Professor of Computer Information Systems at Eastern Michigan University. He received his doctorate in MIS at Auburn University. His research has appeared in the *International Journal of Integrated Supply Management* and *Journal of Information Technology Theory and Application,* and various national and international conferences. His current research interests include online auctions, human computer interaction, and ethics. Prior to academy, John was an IT professional and consultant for 5 years.

Sean Eom is a Professor of Management Information Systems (MIS) and had been appointed as a Copper dome Faculty Fellow in Research at the Harrison College of Business of Southeast Missouri State University during the academic years 1994–1996 and 1998–2000. He received his Ph.D. Degree in Management Science from the University of Nebraska – Lincoln in 1985. His other degrees are from the University of South Carolina at Columbia (M.S. in international business), Seoul National University (M.B.A. in International Management), and Korea University (B.A.). His research areas include decision support systems (DSS), expert systems, and global information systems management. He is the author/editor of nine books including *The Development of Decision Support Systems*

Research: A Bibliometrical Approach, Author cocitation analysis: quantitative methods for mapping the intellectual structure of an academic discipline and Inter-Organizational Information Systems in the Internet Age. He published more than 50 refereed journal articles and 60 articles in encyclopedia, book chapters, and conference proceedings.

Guisseppi Forgionne is Professor of Information Systems at the University of Maryland Baltimore County. He is author of *Management Science* from Wiley Publishing, and has received many awards for his research. His primary research interests are decision making support systems, e-business strategy and policy making, virtual teams, virtual organizations, telecommuting, and decision science.

Ronald Freeze is an Assistant Professor in the Department of Accounting and Information Systems at Emporia State University. His current research interests include Knowledge Management Capability assessment, Expert System acceptance, Knowledge Processes in ERP systems, IS Success, Formative/Reflective construct development and SEM modeling with a specific interest in Latent Growth Models. His publications include *Journal of Management Information Systems, International Journal of Knowledge Management, Journal of Knowledge Management,* and *Journal of Computer Information Systems.* He has published proceedings at ACIS, AMCIS, ICIS and HICSS.

Paul Gray is Professor Emeritus of Information Science at Claremont Graduate University, Claremont, CA.

Dianne J. Hall is an Associate Professor of Management Information Systems at Auburn University. She holds an undergraduate degree in business from the University of Texas, a Master's degree in Business Administration with a minor in Accounting and a minor in Computer Science, and a doctorate in Information and Operations Management, both from Texas A&M University. She is an active researcher; her work appears in academic and practitioner journals such as *Decision Support Systems, Communications of the Association of Computing Machinery, Communications of the Association for Information Systems, International Journal of Logistics Systems and Management, International Journal of Logistics: Research and Applications, Knowledge Management Research and Practice, and the Journal of Information Technology Theory and Application.* Her work has also appeared in several books and she has over 20 years of consulting experience. Her current research interests include applications of information technologies in support of knowledge management, healthcare, supply chain resiliency, and contingency planning, as well as enhanced decision-making processes.

Bob Johansen is Distinguished Fellow and former President of The Institute for the Future, Palo Alto, CA. He is the author of Groupware (Free Press, 1988).

Pari Delir Haghighi is a research fellow at Faculty of Information Technology, Monash University, Australia. She was awarded the Ph.D. degree in Computing in

March 2010 from Monash University. Her Ph.D. study has resulted in eight successful publications. She graduated with Bachelor of Computing (Hons) in 2004 with first class honours. She received the Graduate Certificate in Commercialization Research in December 2009 from Monash University. During her study, she has awarded three scholarships including Monash Graduate Scholarship, Sir John Monash Deans scholar's award for Honours study, and Australian Postgraduate Award (APA). She has served as reviewer for journal articles (Fuzzy Sets and Systems) and book chapters (Pervasive Computing: Innovations in Intelligent Multimedia and Applications. Her current research interests include context-aware computing, decision support systems and emergency management. She is a member of DSSE (Distributed Systems and Software Engineering Centre) and Knowledge Management (KM) Research Program at Monash University.

Jeremy Hodges is an Adjunct Assistant Professor in the Department of Aeronautics at Embry-Riddle Aeronautical University-Worldwide. Concurrently, he is a United States Air Force Reservist serving as Chief of Standardization and Evaluation at the Headquarters, Reserve National Security Space Institute. He received his Ph.D. in Business Administration from Northcentral University in Prescott Valley, Arizona. His current research includes knowledge management capability modeling in educational organizations for quality improvement, and he has previously published and presented original work in the area of knowledge management at AMCIS.

Ziad Kobti is a tenured Assistant Professor in the School of Computer Science and the Director of the Centre for Applied Social Intelligent Systems. He is also an adjunct researcher with Washington State University specializing in multi-agent systems, simulating artificial societies and artificial cultural evolution. He received his Ph.D. in 2004 from Wayne State University and M.Sc. in 1999, and B.Sc.H. 1996 from the University of Windsor.

Carol A. Kolga completed her Master's in Nursing at the University of Ottawa. As a Professor in the Collaborative Nursing Program at St. Clair College, Windsor, Carol was engaged in a variety of research initiatives. Most recently, she has joined the Kingston General Hospital in Kingston, ON as the Director of Professional Practice – Nursing. As a Ph.D. student at the University of Western Ontario in Health and Rehab Science, Carol's focus remains in health promotion and injury prevention within the older adult demographic.

Randy Kuhn, Jr. is an Assistant Professor in the School of Accountancy at the University of Louisville. He earned his Doctorate of Philosophy in Business Administration with a major in Management Information Systems and minor in Accounting from the University of Central Florida. At UCF, Dr. Kuhn taught accounting information systems, enterprise systems, internal auditing, financial accounting concepts and analysis, and principles of financial accounting. His primary research interests are accounting information systems, information systems assurance, auditing, knowledge management, cognitive mapping, and individual/group judgment and decision making. In addition to the Ph.D., Dr. Kuhn earned an M.B.A. from the Katz Graduate School of Business at the University of Pittsburgh and a B.S. in Accounting from the University of Central Florida. Prior to entering academia, he spent 10 years of in public accounting and practice with Grant Thornton LLP, KPMG LLP, Deloitte & Touche LLP, Siemens Westinghouse Power Corp., and NASA Kennedy Space Center.

Teresa Lang, Ph.D., CPA, CISA is an Associate Professor of Accounting at Columbus State University. She earned her doctorate at Auburn University while working as a full-time instructor. She is a licensed CPA with 15 years experience with "Big", medium, and local accounting firm firms. Her research has appeared in several academic journals such as *Journal of Computer Information Systems*, *Omega*, and *Academic Exchange Quarterly.* Conference presentations include AAA, AMCIS, ICIS, and AIS. Her current research interests include technology in education, privacy and control issues related to data management, IT auditing, and ethics.

Meira Levy is a senior lecturer at the Department of Industrial Engineering and Management, Shenkar College, Israel, having completed a Postdoctoral Fellowship at the Department of Industrial Engineering and Management, and at Deutsche Telekom Laboratories, Ben-Gurion University of the Negev, Israel. She received her Ph.D., M.Sc. and B.Sc. degrees from the Technion, the Israel Institute of Technology. She has extensive experience in the software engineering industry in technical and management positions. Her research interests include: Distance learning; Knowledge engineering and management, both from human and technological perspectives, including: KM audit and requirements analysis methodologies, modeling and design of knowledge systems, embedding KM frameworks within business processes, identifying KM culture barriers and Knowledge representation. Her research papers have been published in conference proceedings and in the journals *Decision Support Systems, Journal of Knowledge Management,* and *Journal of Information Systems Education.*

Manuel Mora is an Associate Professor of Information Systems in the Autonomous University of Aguascalientes (UAA), México, since 1994. Dr. Mora holds a B.S. in Computer Systems Engineering (1984) and a M.Sc. in Artificial Intelligence (1989) from Monterrey Tech (ITESM), and an Eng.D. in Systems Engineering (2003) from the National Autonomous University of Mexico (UNAM). He has published around 45 research papers in international top conferences, books and/or journals. Dr. Mora serves in the editorial review boards of about five international journals focused on DSS or Systems Science, and he is a Senior Member of the ACM (from 2007). His main long-term research interest is the development of a common management and engineering body of knowledge for software engineering, systems engineering and information systems underpinned in the Systems Approach.

Jay Nunamaker is Regents Professor at the University of Arizona and director of its Center for Management Information, Tucson, AZ.

Ashish Nakhwal and **Shamual Rahaman** are graduate students in the School of Computer Science, University of Windsor.

David Paradice is Sprint Professor of MIS and Associate Dean. He has published over 50 articles and book chapters on the use of information systems in support of managerial problem formulation, and has served on over 50 doctoral dissertation committees. He is active in the Association of Information Systems and the United Nations sponsored International Federation on Information Processing. Prior to joining Florida State, Dr. Paradice was Director of the Center for MIS and a university teaching award winner at Texas A&M University. He has served on several corporate advisory boards, and has worked as a programmer and consultant.

Gloria Phillips-Wren is Associate Professor and Chair of Information Systems and Operations Management in the Sellinger School of Business and Management at Loyola University Maryland. She is Founder and Co-Editor-in-Chief of *Intelligent Decision Technologies Journal (IDT),* Chair of the KES Focus Group in Intelligent Decision Technologies, and on the Executive Board of the Special Interest Group in Decision Support Systems (SIGDSS) organized under the Association of Information Systems. She is a member of the Editorial Board of the Journal of Decision Systems and active in the DSS area of IFIP. She holds a Ph.D. and M.S. from the University of Maryland Baltimore County, and a MBA from Loyola University Maryland. Phillips-Wren has published numerous papers on data analysis, simulation, intelligent decision support, and their applications. Her most recent book (co-edited) is entitled *Intelligent Decision Making: An AI-Based Approach.* Her research interests are decision support systems, intelligent systems, data mining, and global and strategic issues in information technology applied to healthcare, management, crisis response, and collaboration.

James B. Pick is Professor in School of Business at University of Redlands. He is past chair of the Department of Management and Business and past assembly chair of the School of Business. He is the author of 115 journal articles, book chapters, and refereed proceedings in the research areas of management information systems, geographic information systems, population, and urban studies, and author or co-author of eleven books, including *Geo-Business: GIS in the Digital Organization* (2008) and *Exploring the Urban Community: A GIS Approach* (2006). He has been funded by the US Small Business Administration, Ford Foundation and other agencies, and serves on five journal editorial boards. He holds a B.A. from Northwestern University, M.S.Ed. from Northern Illinois University, and Ph.D. from University of California Irvine.

Nava Pliskin is in charge of the Information Systems programs at the Department of Industrial Engineering and Management, Ben-Gurion University of the Negev, Israel. Previously she was a Thomas Henry Carroll Ford Foundation Visiting Associate Professor at the Harvard Business School. Her Ph.D. and S.M. degrees are from Harvard University. More than 140 of her research papers, focused on longitudinal analysis of IS impacts at the global, national, organizational, and individual levels, have been published in conference proceedings (most recently ICIS2008 and ICIS2009) and in such journals as *IEEE Transactions on Engineering Management, ACM Transactions on Information Systems, The Information Society, Communications of the ACM,* and *Decision Support Systems.*

Daniel J. Power is a pioneer developer of computerized decision aiding and support systems. During 1975–1977, he developed a computerized system called DECAID, DECision AID. In 1981–83, he reprogrammed and expanded the system for the Apple II PC. In 1986–1987, he designed a set of decision aiding tools for the Management Decision Assistant package from Southwestern Publishing. He is a Professor of Information Systems and Management at the College of Business Administration at the University of Northern Iowa, Cedar Falls, Iowa and the editor of DSSResources.COM, the Web-based knowledge repository about computerized systems that support decision making and the editor of DSS News, a bi-weekly e-newsletter. Also, Dan is the Decision Support Expert at the Business Intelligence Network.

Gilad Ravid is a senior lecturer at the Department of Industrial Engineering and Management, Ben-Gurion University of the Negev, Israel. He was a Postdoctoral Fellow at USC Annenberg Center for Communication. He has published in the areas of distance education, supply chain management, simulations, group online communication, grassroots systems and social networks. Dr. Ravid has a Ph.D. from the University of Haifa, an MBA specialization in Management Information Systems and Operations Research from the Hebrew University of Jerusalem and received his B.Sc. in Agricultural Engineering at Technion, the Israel Institute of Technology. His research papers have been published in conferences proceedings and in such journals as *Information systems research (ISR), Information Systems Journal (ISJ),* and *Journal of Computer Mediated Communication (JCMC).*

David Schuff is an Associate Professor of Management Information Systems in the Fox School of Business at Temple University. He holds a B.A. in Economics from the University of Pittsburgh, an M.B.A. from Villanova University, an M.S. in Information Management from Arizona State University, and a Ph.D. in Business Administration from Arizona State University. His research interests include the application of information visualization to decision support systems, data warehousing, and the assessment of total cost of ownership. His work has been published in *MIS Quarterly, Decision Support Systems, Information & Management, Communications of the ACM,* and *Information Systems Journal.*

Ramesh Sharda is Director of the Institute for Research in Information Systems (IRIS), ConocoPhillips Chair of Management of Technology, and a Regents Professor of Management Science and Information Systems in the College of Business Administration at Oklahoma State University. He received his B. Eng. degree from University of Udaipur, M.S. from The Ohio State University and an MBA and Ph.D. from the University of Wisconsin-Madison. His research has been published in major journals in management science and information systems including *Management Science, Information Systems Research, Decision Support Systems, Interfaces, INFORMS Journal on Computing, Computers and Operations Research,* and many others. He served as the Founding Editor of the *Interactive Transactions of OR/MS* and serves on the editorial boards of other journals such as the *INFORMS Journal on Computing, Information Systems Frontiers, Journal of End User Computing,* and *OR/MS Today.* One of his major activities in the last few years was to start the MS in Telecommunications Management Program at Oklahoma State. Now he is establishing a major interdisciplinary Institute for Research in Information Systems (IRIS) at OSU. His research interests are in decision support systems, information systems support for collaborative applications, and technologies for managing information overload. Defense Logistics Agency, NSF, Marketing Science Institute, and other organizations have funded his research. Ramesh is also a cofounder of a company that produces virtual trade fairs, iTradeFair.com.

Jeff Rodman is Chief Technical Officer and co-founder of Polycom Inc., Pleasanton, CA).

Anne W. Snowdon is currently a Professor at the Odette School of Business, University of Windsor. Her expertise includes Health System Leadership and innovation and Injury Prevention. She is also the Theme Coordinator for Health and Safety Research for the AUTO21 Network of Centres of Excellence, a national network of Canadian researchers that focus on automotive research.

Gerald R. Wagner is Distinguished Research Fellow and Director of the International Academy for Advanced Decision Support (IAADS) for the Peter Kiewit Institute, University of Nebraska, Lincoln.

Arkady Zaslavsky is holding a Personal Chair (Chaired Professor) at Lulea University of Technology, Sweden. He worked at Monash University, Australia before joining LTU. He received M.Sc. in Applied Mathematics majoring in Computer Science from Tbilisi State University (Georgia, USSR) in 1976 and Ph.D. in Computer Science from the Moscow Institute for Control Sciences (IPU-IAT), USSR Academy of Sciences in 1987. Professor Zaslavsky has published more than 240 research publications throughout his professional career. He organised and chaired many workshops and conferences in mobile computing area. He is a “Distributed databases” area editor for IEEE Computing-Online. His research interests include mobile and pervasive computing; distributed and mobile agents and objects; wireless networks; distributed computing and database systems; distributed object technology and mobile commerce. Professor Zaslavsky has been awarded and involved in many research grants and projects including “M3: Enterprise Architecture for Mobile Computation”, “Context-rich mobile agent technology to support information needs of financial institutions”, “Adaptive Distributed Information Services”, “Mobile City” and others. He is a member of ACM, IEEE Computer and Communications Societies.

Chapter 1
GDSS Past, Present, and Future

Paul Gray[1], Bob Johansen[2], Jay Nunamaker[3], Jeff Rodman[4], and Gerald R. Wagner[5]

[1] Claremont Graduate University, Claremont, CA, USA, paul.gray@cgu.edu
[2] Institute for the Future, Palo Alto, CA, USA, bjohansen@itft.org
[3] University of Arizona, Tucson, AZ, USA, jnunamaker@cmi.arizona.edu
[4] Polycom, Inc., Pleasanton, CA, USA, jeff.rodman@polycom.com
[5] University of Nebraska, Lincoln, NB, USA, grwagner@mail.unomaha.edu

1.1 Introduction

This paper is based on the panel that began ICDSS 2009 in San Francisco. The five panelists, each of whom has a long association with Group Decision Support Systems (GDSS), were asked to use their experience to discuss where GDSS came from (1960s and earlier), where it is now (2009), and where it is going (2039 and beyond). That is, they were to:

- Reflect on when GDSS started,
- Assess where GDSS is currently, and
- Envision tomorrow to explore what the future holds.

The three elements (past, present, and future) were the theme of the meeting.

The following sections summarize the individual contributions to the panel:

Section 1.2	An Overview of GDSS by Paul Gray
Section 1.3	The Role of Leaders in GDSS by Bob Johansen
Section 1.4	Global Teams by Jay Nunamaker
Section 1.5	The Entrepreneurial View by Gerald R. Wagner
Section 1.6	Telepresence by Jeff Rodman

Each section reflects the view of its author. Taken together, they present a broad picture of one important area of Decision Support Systems.

1.2 Overview of GDSS by Paul Gray

This section is based on my personal history with GDSS, rather than an academic catalog of the field It should, however, give you, the reader, an understanding of how the field unfolded.

D. Schuff et al. (eds.), *Decision Support*, Annals of Information Systems 14,
DOI 10.1007/978-1-4419-6181-5_1, © Springer Science+Business Media, LLC 2011

1.2.1 The Forerunner

I do not claim that I was the first to think about the idea of what became today's GDSS. It probably floated around in many heads before the technology came along to make it possible. The idea first occurred to me in early 1952 when I was fresh out of college and a year of graduate school. I was working on air defense problems at the University of Michigan's Willow Run Research Center on the general problem of defense against submarine-launched V-2 class missiles, then considered a significant threat against the United States.

The problem arose in the following way. The Center's aeronautical engineers had proven that it was possible to build defensive missiles that could intercept V-2's in flight. However, the real problems turned out to be determining whether missiles were launched, where they were coming from, and where they were headed. That problem was, in a sense, similar to the problem of defending Great Britain against bomber attacks during and after the Blitz. It was a classic problem in command, control, and communications on a much shorter time scale than ever before.

The group in which I worked was assigned the task of researching the command and control problem. Given the analogy with British air defense, we looked at the experience in the United Kingdom. We found that the British Air Defense Command used command and control centers where radar data on friendly fighters and hostile bombers were sent for analysis and decision. These centers contained "plotting rooms" each containing a large table covered by a map showing the location of radars and fighter bases, and tokens representing the location of aircraft[1] The operators were members of the British Women's Army Air Force (known as WAAF's) who used croupier's sticks[2] to move the current location of aircraft as a battle progressed. Commanders used these manual displays to make decisions about which aircraft to commit to which hostile bombers. The process was manual with radar stations sending voice information to the command centers.

Our group, headed by a psychologist named Robert DeVore, was working on a simple electro-mechanical display to speed up the process so it was compatible with the rate at which events now took place. The display was mounted vertically at the front of a room that showed the location of fixed objects (cities, radars) and used lights to indicate the location of stationary and mobile forces. The idea was that commanders could use such displays to make decisions much more quickly. It struck me that display boards, with really good technology,[3] perhaps coming from a computer, would make a good addition to a meeting room.

---

[1]For a picture of such a room go to:http://books.google.com/books?id=Q1N-rzBRshsC&lpg=PP1&dq=WAAF%20%20ESCOTT&pg=PP1#v=onepage&q&f=false

[2]A croupier is the person at a gambling table, such as for 21 or craps, who runs the game. He or she uses a hoe-shaped wooden stick to distribute (or rake in) chips to the players, depending on whether they won or lost.

[3]Computers in 1952 were still in the vacuum tube era. It would be 5 years before the first commercial transistor-based computer (the IBM 608) was shipped.

1.2.2 The Churchill War Room

Winston Churchill's War Room is an example of an early, completely manual GDSS. This set of rooms is located underground, near 10 Downing Street,[4] where it served as an air raid shelter and as a decision room. Today it is museum, known as the Winston Churchill Museum and War Rooms which charges a relatively high entrance fee to tourists. The cabinet ministers who went to this complex of rooms when it was a working facility were doing more than hiding from bombs. Their job was to make decisions about how to fight the war.

When you go into the decision room the first thing you see are the maps on the wall, representing the world in Mercator projection, with the enormous territory that was then part of the British Empire[5] depicted in red. As shown in Fig. 1.1, the principal item in the room was simply a rectangular table with pads in front of the seated individual. Ministers would bring their red boxes that contained their working papers with them. Side rooms (not shown) contained communications centers where data from the outside entered and was disseminated to the attendees, areas for support staff who worked on specific problems, and sleeping quarters. The 3-acre site provided working space for 528 people.

Fig. 1.1 The Churchill war room (The picture is copied from the brochure handed to visitors in the early 1990s)

[4]Today its street entrance is across the street from St James Park. It is located under the Treasury Building.

[5]During World War II, the United Kingdom included Canada, India and Pakistan, Australia, South Africa, Ireland, Singapore, and much more.

1.2.3 *Engelbart's Decision Room at SRI (ca. 1967)*

The first implemented electronic decision room I saw was created at Stanford Research Institute (now SRI International) in Menlo Park, California where I worked during the 1960s. I was going from the third floor to my office on the fourth floor of SRI's main building when the legendary Doug Engelbart waved me down and invited me to come into his laboratory (Fig. 1.2) to see his latest invention.

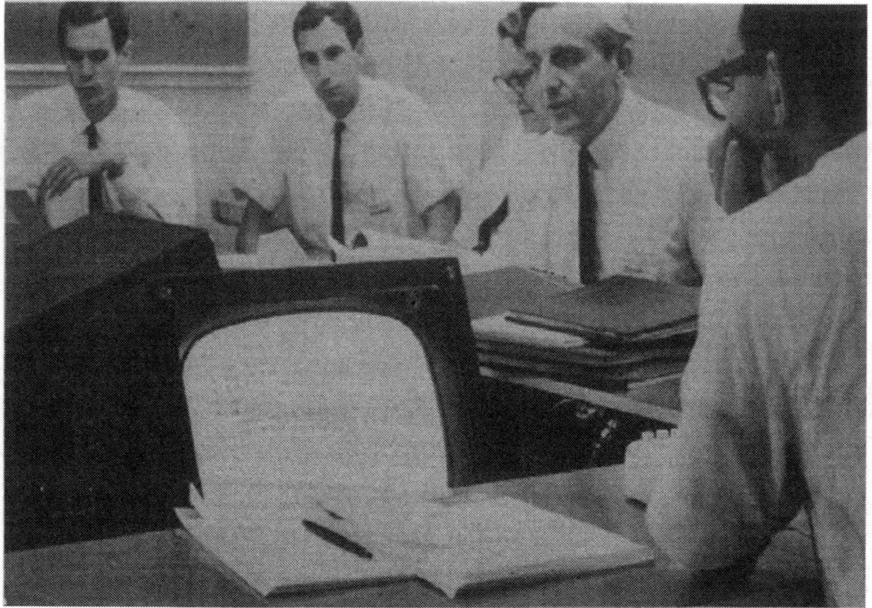

Fig. 1.2 Doug Englebart's decision room

As can be seen from the picture, the room provided displays for a group of people who sat at computer-driven display screens. You could retrieve pictures and text from the central computer so that everyone would see them on their screen. Engelbart told me about the room and displayed his newest invention: the mouse, a wooden box with a wire running out of it that vaguely resembled a mouse and its tail. The idea was that as you moved the wooden box with your hand, a lighted dot on the screen (the cursor) would move in the same direction as your hand. With the mouse you could point to a specific object or word on the screen and participants could discuss that part of the image. I hate to say it, but I privately wondered at the time why anyone would ever want to use such a device. Little did I know.

1.2.4 University of Southern California (USC)

Steven Alter came to USC in 1974, having completed a monumental thesis on decision support.[6] I learned about DSS from him and became a convert. I revived the idea of an electronic war room for managers and suggested to colleagues at the Center for Futures Research in the Business School that we build what we now call a GDSS as a way to support decisions. Unfortunately, there were no takers for the idea because there were no funders, no space, and no equipment available to implement it.

1.2.5 Southern Methodist University (SMU)

I moved to SMU in Dallas in August 1979 to Chair a department that taught information systems and management science in the Business School. The next spring, my boss, Dean Alan Coleman, came into my office one afternoon to tell me about a lunch he had earlier that day with people from Atlantic Richfield (ARCO), a large oil company. They regularly gave half-million dollar grants to engineering schools in cities where they had headquarters, and one of their headquarters was in Dallas. He believed that, even though we were a business school, we could receive a part of a grant to the university. He asked: "Do you have any ideas?" Now, when your boss asks you whether you have any ideas, you don't say no. So I proposed the GDSS concept. ARCO awarded $250,000 of its grant to the University to implement our proposal. We opened my first GDSS, the SMU Decision Room,[7] in 1981.

In brief, we built two rooms, a large room in the SMU Business School and the other a smaller satellite in the Engineering School across the street, connected with one another by a video cable. In this way, the groups in each room could see and hear one another and share computer-based information. The large room offered eight 21-in. screen Xerox Star work stations on a network, connected to a Prime minicomputer and projection equipment for a public screen. The small room consisted of 6 Cromemco PCs on a network.[8] A one-way glass observation area looking into the large room permitted experimenters to observe what was going on.

1.2.6 Claremont Graduate University

I moved to Claremont Graduate University (CGU) in 1983. In 1986, the University received a 2 million dollar grant from IBM Corporation which included funds and

---

[6]The thesis was published in edited form as a book: Alter, S. (1975). *Decision Support Systems*. Reading, MA: Addison Wesley.

[7]Gray, P. et al. (June 1981). *The SMU Decision Room Project*. Proceedings of DSS '81.

[8]The SMU rooms were set up before the IBM PC came on the market and used computers that were state of the art at the time. The Star computers were a gift of the Xerox Corporation.

equipment for the CGU Decision Room. It became operational in late 1987. This facility was similar in design to the one at SMU. It consisted of two adjacent rooms with video and audio connections between them as well as a one-way glass observation area and a public screen. The University of Arizona GroupSystems software, developed by Jay Nunamaker and his coworkers was the prime communications tool. In addition to the IBM Model 60 and 70 PC's in the main room, a grant from HP provided touch screen HP computers in the second room. Figure 1.3 shows the main room.

Fig. 1.3 The main room of the CGU decision room

1.2.7 Other Rooms

The 1980s saw the nearly simultaneous creation of GDSS rooms around the world. The following is a list of the GDSS research facilities I visited in the U.S., Great Britain and Japan.

- Execucom's Planning Laboratory led by G. R. Wagner (Austin, TX)[9]
- University of Arizona, led by Jay Nunamaker (Tucson, AZ). Three rooms were built. The second, using gallery seating is shown in Fig. 1.4.
- University of Minnesota, led by Gary Dickson and Gerardine DeSanctis (Minneapolis, MN)

[9]See Section 1.5 for a description of the Planning Laboratory.

Fig. 1.4 The second University of Arizona GDSS facility

- University of Georgia led by Bob Bostrum, Athens, GA
- Colab at XEROX Parc, built around the Xerox Star, Palo Alto, CA
- London School of Economics led by David Phillips, London, UK

Commercial implementations included:

- IBM
- Metapraxis (London, UK)
- Nippon Electric (Tokyo, Japan)

1.3 The Role of Leaders in GDSS by Bob Johansen

When I wrote *Groupware: Computer Support for Business Teams*[10] more than 20 years ago, GDSS was a relatively new technology. The focus of Groupware was

[10]Johansen, R. (1988). New York, NY: The Free Press.

on how this combination of software, hardware, and human leadership skills could improve meetings, give teamwork a boost, and cut distance as a factor by altering the travel/telecommunications tradeoffs. The book contained seventeen groupware scenarios, a few of which were already being implemented then, although mostly in research environments. A number of the scenarios are described by the other members of this panel, who brought the concept of groupware to live.

My work was done as part of ongoing research at Institute for the Future, an independent nonprofit think tank in Palo Alto, CA at which I have been affiliated for more than a quarter of a century. As is the nature of the work at the Institute, my efforts moved on to other emerging technologies and forecasts. Yet, I was acutely aware that the GDSS field would be much affected by how business leadership accepted, adapted, and extended the early technology of groupwork. In this brief talk, I share some of my insights about what used to be called groupware and leadership, which is part of the work I have been doing in recent years.[11]

As shown in Fig. 1.5, all leaders can benefit from a creative mix of:

- Foresight
- Insight
- Action

Foresight requires sensing provocative futures that can change what has been done routinely in the past. Foresight – even if you don't agree with it – can provoke insight and insight inspires strategy.

The diagram shown in Fig. 1.5 is elaborated in Fig. 1.6:

- Foresight involves preparing the mind through *understanding* of the futures context and the external future forces that will be important.
- Insight requires *clarity* of thinking so that a viable strategy can be imagined and then created.
- The action to implement the strategy usually requires getting there early. Action must, in an uncertain world, be action with agility.
- Whatever the outcome, hindsight (for example, an "after action review") is required to evaluate its success and prepare the mind for the next round of foresight.

In the future, leaders will need skills and competencies like this in order to thrive. The more advanced future leadership skills like smart mob organizing and commons creating will be enabled by the next generation of group decision support systems.

In the future, the leadership skills that will be need to implement Fig. 1.6 are:

---

[11] Johansen, B. (2009). *Leaders Make the Future: Ten New Leadership Skills for an Uncertain World*. San Francisco, CA: Berrett-Koehler Publishers. See also Johansen, B. (2007). *Get There Early: Sensing the Future to Compete in the Present*. San Francisco, CA: Berrett-Koehler Publishers.

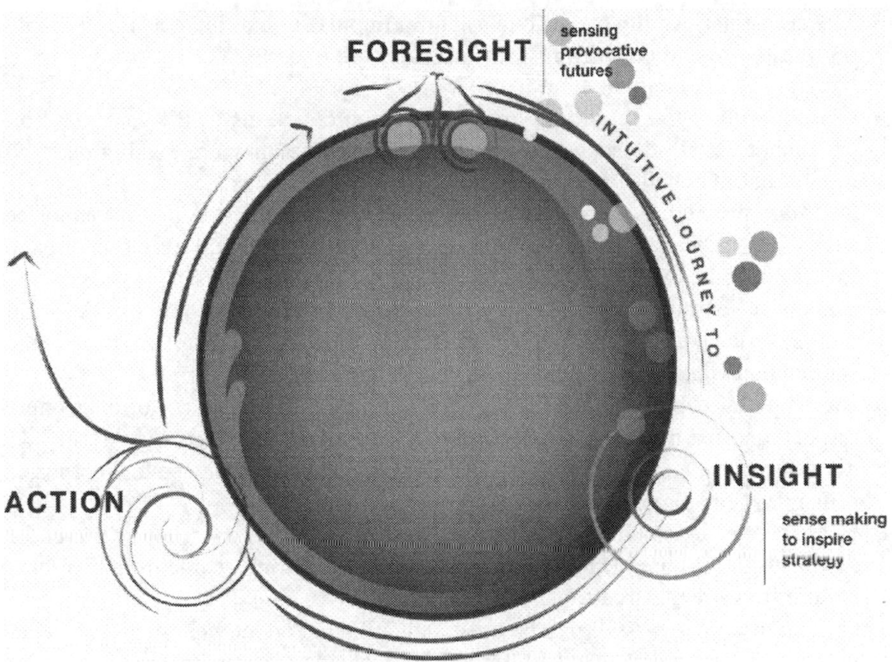

Fig. 1.5 The three elements of leadership

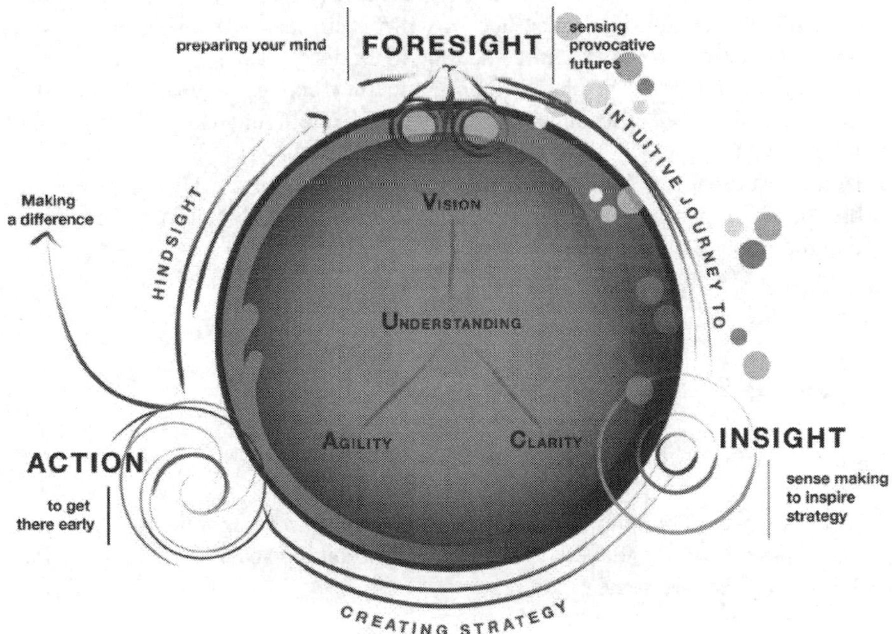

Fig. 1.6 A more detailed view of the elements of leadership

- Maker instinct: Ability to turn one's natural impulse to build into a skill for making the future and connecting with others in the making. The maker instinct is basic to leadership in the future
- Clarity: Ability to see through messes and contradictions to a future that others cannot yet see. Leaders are very clear about what they are making but very flexible about how they get it made.
- Dilemma flipping: Ability to turn dilemmas-which, unlike problems cannot be solved–into advantages and opportunities. (GDSS can help develop scenarios to explore how the challenges might be flipped into opportunities.)
- Immersive learning ability: Ability to dive into different-for-you physical and online worlds to learn from them in a first person way. (A good GDSS experience is an immersion experience, to create deeper learning.)
- Bio-empathy: Ability to see things from nature's point of view: to understand, respect, and learn from nature's patterns. Nature has its own clarity if only we humans can understand and engage with it. (GDSS can be designed to incorporate principles of nature and to help augment experiences in nature.)
- Constructive depolarizing: Ability to calm tense situations where differences dominate and communications has broken down-and bring people from divergent cultures toward constructive engagement.
- Quiet transparency: Ability to be open and authentic about what matters to you-without advertising yourself. (GDSS helps provide transparency and effective ways to communicate that transparency.)
- Rapid prototyping: Ability to create quick early versions of new innovations, with the expectation that later success will require early failure. (GDSS is all about rapid prototyping in a group setting, to explore options.)
- Smart mob organizing[12]: Ability to bring together, engage with, and nurture purposeful business social-change networks through intelligent use of electronic and other media.
- Commons creating: Ability to stimulate, grow, and nurture shared assets that can benefit other players-and allow competition at a higher level. (Creating a commons is the ultimate goal for many GDSS efforts.)

1.4 Global Teams by Jay Nunamaker

1.4.1 Collaboration

GDSS is about collaboration. That is, groups of people working together on solving problems. In my view, collaboration is more important than ever as we look forward to the future. Here are some of the reasons:

[12]See: Rheingold, H. (2002). *Smart Mobs*. New York, NY: Basic Books and Surowiecki, J. (2005). *The Wisdom of Crowds*. New York, NY: Anchor Books.

1. *Outsourcing and Strategic Alliances*. The trend in information systems is toward outsourcing and strategic alliances. These efforts require close collaborations between the two contracting parties. A firm can't simply award a contract to another, be they in the same country or in another country, and expect that the work will be done correctly and on time. It is simply not possible (nor desirable) to write the work statement to cover all contingencies. Even with a tightly written contract, situations and circumstances change. Furthermore, within a firm, many people are involved with their outside counterparts. The group in the firm collaborates to make sure that they speak with a single voice to their contractual partners.
2. *Internet Technology*. The Internet is ubiquitous in how people work. People rely on inputs from and provide outputs to people outside the firm.
3. *Competitive Environment*. The competitive environment is changing rapidly. As firms grow larger and span more products and industries, firms compete in some areas and collaborate in others.
4. *Cycle Times*. The pace of change is increasing as a result of shorter projects and shorter cycle times for new products that are made possible in part by shorter supply chains, faster communications, and increased use of IT. In this environment, firms need to collaborate in their efforts just to remain competitive.
5. *Decisions*. The increasing competitiveness and the shorter cycle times require the quality of decisions to improve and to be made more quickly.
6. *Travel Restrictions*. Where once funds and time were available for people to travel for meetings and conferences, the effects of recession-caused budget restrictions, the faster pace, and the increasing distances to outsourcers, make it necessary to use technology for collaboration.
7. *Terrorism*. The threat of global terrorism restricts travel and makes it imperative for people to be able to work together even though separated by distance.

As the foregoing items indicate, collaboration is becoming more necessary, teams are becoming virtual, and they are now global.

1.4.2 Challenges Facing Global Virtual Teams

By virtual teams we mean teams whose members are not co-located within a firm and whose membership is global, spanning many firms. Such teams are complex to assemble and to manage in such a way that its members work well together. The challenges that they face include:

Time Zones. A global team is scattered over many time zones. Its members are not just located 3 h away between, say, New York and Los Angeles but span distances such as Chicago to Beijing or Los Angeles to South Africa. Time zones add complexity to the ability of team members to communicate and to work with one another.

Convergence to Explicitness. With linguistic differences from multiple languages and cultures, it becomes difficult for teams to converge to explicit results. People in Brazil, China, France, the U.S. start with different assumptions and different backgrounds. The result is different assumptions about what is the right way to go, which, in turn, lead to different outputs for the same problem.

Convergence to Consensus. The lack of convergence to explicitness makes reaching consensus among team members and between teams and general management more difficult.

Team Goals. When multiple firms and multiple cultures are involved, it takes time to define team goals. Even after goals are defined, the background differences among team members result in slowing progress toward team goals.

Sense Making and Understanding. At the individual level, getting team members to make sense from and understand what they observe is challenging. Yet team members need to be on the "same page" if they are to collaborate effectively.

Coordination. At the managerial level, virtual teams scattered over the globe are much more difficult to manage than when there is, say, line-of-sight supervision. Face-to-face coordination occurs at longer intervals with many members of the team rarely or never seeing one another. Managers rely more on reports and short burst of video meetings. GDSS conferences can help ameliorate coordination difficulties.

Focus and Goals. Effective teams require shared focus on what they do and shared goals on what they are trying to achieve. In a global team environment, sharing focus and goals is hard to establish and to maintain over time.

1.4.3 Trade-Offs

Table 1.1 shows the trade-offs made by global and virtual teams between face-to-face and virtual work arrangements. Note that face-to-face meetings provide more of the properties that you would like to have in a meeting. Many of the difficulties discussed in the previous section occur when meetings are virtual, because people are separated in time and space.

Table 1.1 Trade-offs in global/virtual teamwork

Face to face meeting	Virtual meeting
Higher participation	Lower participation
High sense of community	Low sense of community
High commitment	Low commitment
Many verbal signals	Limited non-verbal signals
Many informal conversations	Few informal conversations

Table 1.2 Behavioral limitations in a virtual meeting

No gesturing	No handshake
No fist pounding or pointing	No pat on the back
No eye contact	No power seat
No body language	

The tradeoffs shown in Table 1.1 are the result of behavioral limitations facing virtual teams. The behavioral limitations in a virtual meeting are shown in Table 1.2.

1.4.4 Effective Collaboration

The previous discussion focused on the challenges involved in creating effective global/virtual teamwork. Despite these problems, the effectiveness of global/ virtual teamwork can be increased significantly. The following is a list of 10 principles to help achieve effectiveness.

1. Use shared workspace to focus attention
2. Raise the salience and value of team goals
3. Heighten identity through virtual and face-to-face interaction
4. Establish standards and the meaning of terminology
5. Use anonymity when necessary
6. Articulate and communicate directions and expectations
7. Be flexible with the structure imposed to complete a task
8. Enable self-facilitating teams
9. Embed collaboration technology into members' existing work processes
10. Use just enough technology to complete a task

1.4.5 Conclusions

In this section we focused on the challenges and problems associated with virtual teams spread across the globe. This way of working can only be expected to increase as developing economies emerge with the skilled workforces needed to compete.

Group decision support systems, started 30+ years ago[13] with the assumption that people would meet to coordinate and collaborate in single rooms provided with the latest in technology and coordination methodology. The technologies created since then moved the capabilities of these original rooms to multiple systems interconnected by communications and information technology. They help us overcome the seemingly inherent difficulties to make global and virtual teams as seamless as

[13]See Section 1.1 for a discussion of the initial systems.

teams of old. As shown in Section 1.6, tomorrow's technology offers increasing collaboration capabilities. These technologies need to be coupled with advances in how humans accomplish their work to create effective solutions.

1.5 The Entrepreneurial View by Gerald R. Wagner

I have been involved with DSS and GDSS for 30 years as an academician and as an entrepreneur. As a Professor and head of Operations Research at the College of Engineering at the University of Texas at Austin, I worked together with a team of graduate students to create what later became one of the first DSS software products. Seeing its commercial possibilities, I resigned from UT in 1978 and founded Execucom Systems Corporation in Austin, Texas.

The product that evolved was called the Interactive Financial Planning System (IFPS). Paul Gray (Fig. 1.7) and Royer Hayen each wrote books for teaching IFPS.

IFPS dominated its market space commercially and academically. It was given to Universities for use in classes. The products basis was its English like modeling language for describing model assumptions in plain English or other natural language. It had built in What If and Goal Seeking capabilities which, at that time, were new terms.

The equations (assumptions) were understandable by senior management as well as the technical model builder. Uncertainties for risk analysis were built in by using keywords such as TRIRAND to describe a variable as following a triangular distribution.

Figure 1.8 shows a simple IFPS model.

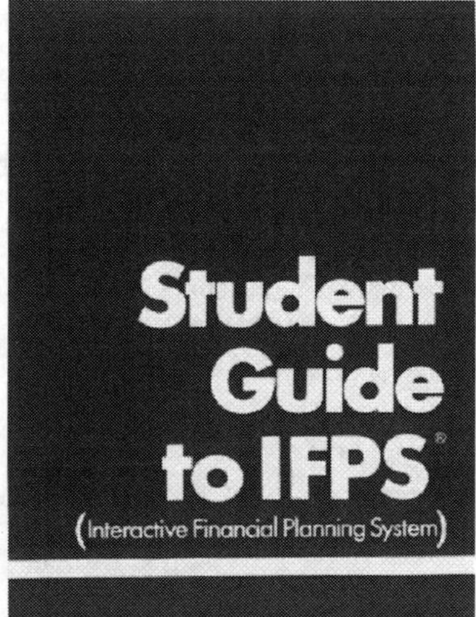

Fig. 1.7 Student guide to IFPS by Paul Gray (Gray, P. (1983). *Student Guide to IFPS: Interactive Financial Planning System.* McGraw-Hill, New York, NY)

```
Period 2009 – 2015
Sales Price = 60000
Number of Sales =85, Previous*TRIRAND (0.99, 1.04,1.12)
Revenue = Sales Price*Number of Sales
```

Fig. 1.8 An example model in IFPS

In about 1979 I became interested in "War Rooms" that were beginning to pop up. So I did what later would have been known as a "skunk works" project that was low key and avoided attention. I hired a part time student programmer who later went on to start his own company and become a multi millionaire (not in DSS or GDSS). This low key project evolved into what later became known as the Planning Laboratory.

1.5.1 The Planning Laboratory

I was intrigued with the Planning Laboratory idea because of the potential for improving executive communications and as a process for identifying and quantifying assumptions for use in IFPS models. The facility was called the Planning Laboratory but, with the help of outside consultants, we ended up calling the software MindSight.

This skunk works project grew. We built a custom oval shaped table with embedded dumb terminals connected to a mini computer. Even though early and primitive its functionality was very similar to that which appeared in GDSS's years later.

We quickly became aware that the place had a lot of WOW factor and visitors were intrigued. As they entered the room we played Star Wars music to fit the ambience. We demonstrated how to use the software to generate ideas for variables (left hand sides of equations) and how to generate assumptions (right hand side of assumptions).

The Planning Laboratory and its MindSight software was not intended as a standalone product but rather was used as a tool to market and sell IFPS and build IFPS models.

1.5.2 Next Version

In about 1981 we moved into a new building and created a much larger and more elaborate Planning Laboratory. Figure 1.9 is a picture of the facility which included a custom U- shaped table, touch screen terminals, projector, and embedded dumb terminals. Note the Public screen using a Sony projector and the two one-way windows that allow observation of the activities in the room from an observation area. But, its primary use continued as a marketing tool for IFPS. The company did however actively use the space for its own financial planning and forecasting. As a 250 person software company Execucom was a big company for its time and it was growing rapidly.

Fig. 1.9 Execucom planning laboratory 1981

Then the investors and a few employees with shares of stock got antsy and wanted to cash out. The company ended up being acquired by Contel (later GTE) in 1984. Contel thought they wanted to be in the "hot" DSS market. As could be expected, they soon learned that they should not be in that market and sold the company. It was resold a number of times and ended up being acquired by a firm that had been a competitor. Thus the end of MindSight, the Planning Laboratory, and IFPS.

After Execucom was acquired I moved to a small historic community called Bastrop outside Austin. There I became overly involved in many entrepreneurial ventures ranging from architectural preservation to PC Clone manufacturing. But, my love for GDSS had not gone away.

1.5.3 Vision Quest, Web IQ

In 1988 I moved back to Austin and obtained venture capital to invest in Collaborative Technologies Corporation and its product Vision Quest. It was a true stand-alone GDSS product typical of what was by then and continued to be the commercial market space. The product was actually doing quite well but I had conflicts with the investors. The end of the story is that I resigned, the company was sold, and now the company and product no longer exists.

But the bug continued. So I did it again in 1998 with a company and product named Web IQ. This internet product was known for its ease of use. In fact the one thread that runs through all the software I've developed is ease of use. Web IQ was also doing quite well when the investor issue occurred again (different investors though) and again I resigned. The Internet Protocol (IP) was acquired and still does exist with a consulting company in Washington DC.

Just a note here. For IFPS, Vision Quest, and Web IQ the academic community strongly embraced all of them. I started what might have been the first university support program whereby academic institutions got the software for free. Today such policies are common.

Something that is clear in retrospect was the insignificant market for GDSS. It was wonderful stuff intellectually and philosophically but the general product category never had much of a market.

1.5.4 Reincarnation of IFPS

Often throughout the years after IFPS was sold I had old customers contacting me wondering how they could get their hands on the software. They loved IFPS but it was no longer on the market.

When I came to the University of Nebraska in 2001 I decided to think about a new kind of IFPS with state of the art data visualization but with a nearly identical modeling language. The modeling language was the single key factor in the success of IFPS. So out of this concept evolved what is now known as the Planners Lab™. The Planners Lab has not been commercially successful. It has only had modest marketing attempts but it could not overcome the fact that Excel is embedded everywhere. Regardless of Excel's faults and inadequacies it is impossible to dislodge it. Also a factor is that the term and field of DSS has essentially disappeared. It is rare to find anyone in business that has any idea of what DSS means as it was defined in the early days, i.e., modeling to support decision making. Even the term modeling has nearly disappeared from business vocabulary.

The Planners Lab does continue and several international Universities use it for teaching. A major Planners Lab chapter in the upcoming book from Efriam Turban and Ramesh Sharda will probably escalate the numbers. Figure 1.10 is a typical screenshot.

1.5.5 Concluding Thoughts

This section recounts the ventures of a DSS and GDSS entrepreneur. In my case, it involved starting and running a number of companies that were, basically, involved in software innovation for decision support. In the 30+ year course of these ventures both software and hardware systems were built and marketed, often funded by venture capital. As is always the case, some ventures were profitable while others resulted in losses.

In this 30 year period DSS evolved as a discipline and was hot for several years. Now it has waned as a discipline and all but disappeared. I've learned that decisions to spend time, energy, talent, and money on new product development should be backed up with more market research and market need rather than by emotions and love for a technology. Also, pick your investors carefully. Don't just jump at whoever is willing to support you. Make sure you are aligned. Nonetheless, it has

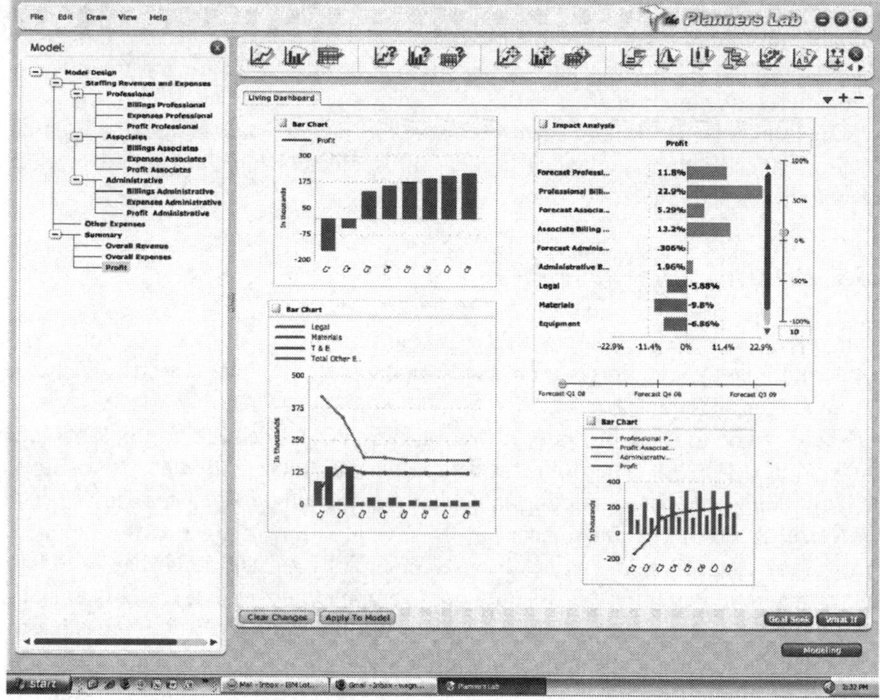

Fig. 1.10 Sample planners lab output

been a fun ride and I keep looking forward for what might be next for innovative software.

1.6 Telepresence by Jeff Rodman

1.6.1 Definition

The term “telepresence” describes a set of technologies that enable people to feel or appear as if they were present in a location in which they are not physically. Telepresence systems span a continuum, from desktops, to conference rooms, to fully “immersive” telepresence systems.

In short, telepresence provides the experience of being present at a physically remote location. In many cases, especially that of the fully immersive rooms, telepresence is “just like being there.”

A number of technologies are brought together to create this experience - these include high definition voice and HD video, established data communications networks such as IP and ISDN, and a variety of interactive elements such as shared content, and identical room set-ups. Currently in use by hundreds of companies, telepresence is enabled by open standards and is a pivotal element in the future of collaboration systems in all applications. As such, telepresence continues to grow in uses from analysis and decision-making, to distance education, telemedicine, legal, and applications that can benefit from enhanced agility and better communication among a distributed team. In this section we describe the trends in telepresence, in the context of commercial equipment and research systems offered through Polycom Inc. as a way to bring telepresence to the mainstream.

1.6.2 What Is in This Section

We look at:

- the drivers of telepresence and of group decision support and problem solving processes,
- barriers to mainstream adoption today,
- what has changed, and
- what is coming

We know that worldwide international growth in telecommunication has been averaging 40% year to year. International growth in 2008 alone is estimated to be 14 terabytes per second.

1.6.3 Telepresence Drivers, 2010–2030

The drivers for telepresence over the next 20 years include:

- Globalization
- Business Efficiency
- Network Expansion
- Outsourcing
- Social Pressures
- Environmental Impact

We discuss each of these in turn:

Globalization. As firms continue to globalize, their staff and consultants are increasingly scattered around the globe. Bringing the right people together in a single place at the same time, whether it be for decision-making, educational purposes, or other reasons, has become increasingly difficult and unaffordable. Some of the needed people inevitably cannot travel at the required time, and when they do travel, productivity is greatly impacted. The participation of people in widespread time zones also raises the likelihood that a meeting will be needed at what might be thought of as "home" time, thereby making home telepresence, or telecommuting, nearly essential for a lot of jobs.

Outsourcing. Outsourcing, particularly outsourcing overseas, creates the same problems as globalization but often on a larger scale. In outsourcing, people at the outsourcer and at the home firm need to communicate almost instantly when problems or opportunities arise. Travel to remote sites is neither practical nor affordable in many cases.

Business Efficiency. Collaboration among and between organizations requires communication on relatively short notice. When conferences need to be set up days or weeks in advance, the efficiency of the business is reduced and productivity nosedives.

Social Pressures. Information exchange and decision-making have a strong element of social interaction among the people involved. Although many interactions can be handled by email and by phone, others cannot. Presence is required. When face-to-face meetings cannot be arranged, telepresence is a viable substitute for working with other people, learning, exchanging information, and for handling most situations. Furthermore, because the technology allows multiple people to participate from each location, the extent of the social interaction is broader and more inclusive – some locations can have groups of people, others can be a single person at a desk or remote device.

Network Expansion. Everyone likes to deal with people they know. At the simplest level, people want an image of a face and an understanding of body language. If they have not previously met a person before, they are less likely to trust that person. Telepresence makes it possible to add new people into an individual's network remotely, while retaining a high degree of this personal connection. Participants can build rapport with one another that isn't achievable through phone and email conversations. Furthermore, when the technology allows multiple people to interact at the same time, conversations become more spirited, participants become more engaged, and the existence of the intervening technology, in a well-designed system, no longer impedes this free exchange.

Environmental Impact. Transporting people to common locations is has a negative impact, not only in terms of resources, but also in terms of carbon footprint. The ability to participate in meetings from their normal locations through the use of telepresence eliminates this element of environmental loading.

1.6.4 The Telepresence Vision

Figure 1.11[14] shows an early vision of telepresence, where the audio was a bullhorn-type microphone and a wax cylinder for recording. By the 1960s, even the Jetsons[15] had visual telepresence and in the 1968 film "2001" we witnessed a father talking to his daughter from a ship far out in space, an application mirrored shortly thereafter when we watched Neil Armstrong step onto the moon, via a live video link, on July 20 1969.

[14]Source: A French postcard by Villemard (1910). Paris, BNF, Estampes., http://commons.wikimedia.org/wiki/Videophones, Last consulted December 8, 2009.

[15]The Jetsons was a popular cartoon show on prime time television in the 1960s.

Fig. 1.11 The 1910 telepresence vision

Clearly, telepresence was coming from imagination to practice. Figure 1.12 shows the first exhibit of commercial video conferencing, which was presented by AT&T at the 1964 World's Fair. The system was based on three communications lines: two lines of simplex 1 MHz video specially equalized plus one audio channel. This system was marketed for a short time but the technology proved too demanding for the time. However, by the 1970s video conferencing was being offered commercially by AT&T.

The evolution of video conference and telepresence to this point converges perfectly with the vision of group decision support systems (GDSS); since the early 1980s the dominant view of communications-driven GDSS has included groupware, bulletin boards (or other static communications), and audio and video conferencing.

Today's vision of communication-driven GDSS includes:

- Unified communications
- Applications
- Data access
- Social Networking
- Scheduling
- HD Interactive Computing
- Presence

Collaboration tools are moving rapidly in this direction, a trend demonstrated by smartphones like the iPhone and its applications, presence, and social tools. Both audio and video conferencing are moving to IP from their respective networks. This

Fig. 1.12 Video conferencing as demonstrated at the 1964 world's fair

trend enables the unification of these tools and is expected to encourage the rapid evolution of more.

The key to this evolution is the transition to a unified IP network. With this shift, the network becomes transparent because all media can flow with equal facility, and the principal impediment to Unified Communications disappears.

> voice and video delivered using the Internet protocol have greatly expanded the possibilities for synchronous communications-driven DSS – D. J. Power[16]

1.6.5 Technical Enablers

The goal was understood for a long time. What changed is that the technology, the network, and the economics all developed to make the vision possible. The cornucopia of technical innovations includes:

- Digital compression
- Digital networks
- Open standards
- Versatile platforms
- Consumer demand

---

[16]Source: Power, D. J. A Brief History of Decision Support Systems. http://DSSResources.COM/history/dsshistory.html, version 4.0, March 10, 2007 (last consulted August 10, 2009).

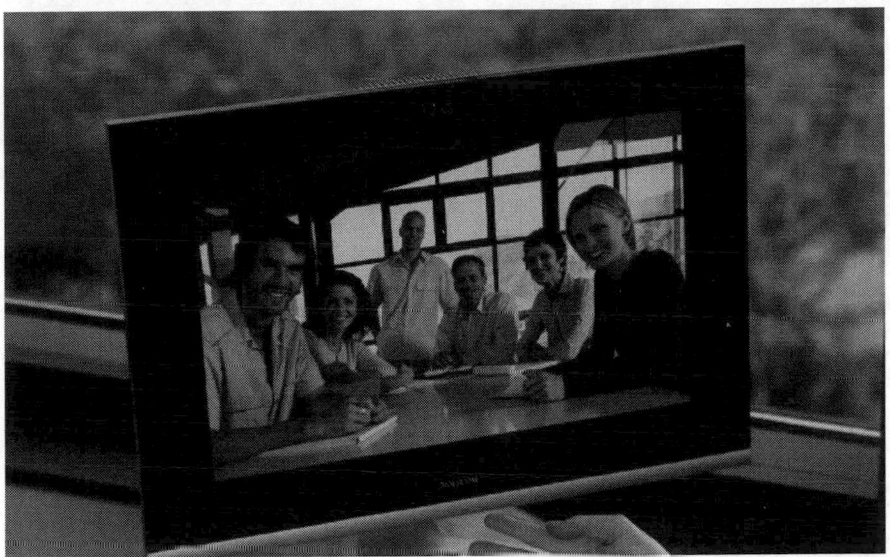

Fig. 1.13 Desktop telepresence from polycom

Fig. 1.14 The polycom fully immersive HD telepresence suite

Figures 1.13 and 1.14 show two commercial examples of telepresence systems, with two-way high-definition video and audio, from mid-2009.

The commercially available system in Fig. 1.14 shows two rooms where people can see and interact with each other in real time. Note that the people on the right are seeing their counterparts on a video screen. In the best immersive systems of this sort, the entire environment is managed to ensure that illumination, geometries, acoustics, and placement of microphones, speakers, cameras and displays all work together to provide the experience of "being there."

1.6.6 Summary

The future of telepresence can be summarized as:

- Moving from sporadic to continuous application
- Unlimited sensory connection
- Smoothly integrated services such as translation and research
- Open standards for platform independence
- Location of participants becoming irrelevant
- Wide accessibility

We are well on the way to being there.

Chapter 2
Reflections on the Past and Future of Decision Support Systems: Perspective of Eleven Pioneers

Daniel J. Power[1], Frada Burstein[2], and Ramesh Sharda[3]

[1] Department of Management, University of Northern Iowa, Cedar Falls, IA 50614-0125, USA, daniel.power@uni.edu
[2] Centre for Organisational and Social Informatics, Monash University, Caulfield East, VIC 3145, Australia, frada.burstein@infotech.monash.edu.au
[3] Department of Management Science and Information Systems, Oklahoma State University, William S. Spears School of Business, Stillwater, OK 74078, USA, ramesh.sharda@okstate.edu

2.1 Introduction

Periodically members of a research discipline need to examine and reflect upon past accomplishments. Too often we focus on the most recent research on a topic and neglect the origins of a research stream. Examining prior accomplishments and developments in the field of Decision Support Systems can help assess the present state of progress in meeting research and practical needs and can help determine unmet expectations and chart future research directions.

Today Decision Support Systems is a broad area of research and practice. According to DSSResources.com, a "Decision Support System (DSS)" is an interactive computer-based system or subsystem intended to help decision makers use communications technologies, data, documents, knowledge and/or models to identify and solve problems, complete decision process tasks, and make decisions. Decision Support System is a general term for any computer application that enhances a person or group's ability to make decisions. Also, Decision Support Systems refers to an academic field of research that involves designing and studying DSS in their context of use. In general, DSS are a class of computerized information systems that support decision-making activities. Five more specific Decision Support System types include: (1) communications-driven DSS, (2) data-driven DSS, (3) document-driven DSS, (4) knowledge-driven DSS, and (5) model-driven DSS (Power, 2002). Historically, DSS were associated with managerial, long-term, strategic decision-making (Alter, 1980). However, the wide availability of computing resources and increased level of sophistication of DSS users encourage further advancements in research and development of new tools which enhance users' effectiveness in making complex decisions as well as getting access to better information about available decision alternatives.

D. Schuff et al. (eds.), *Decision Support*, Annals of Information Systems 14,
DOI 10.1007/978-1-4419-6181-5_2, © Springer Science+Business Media, LLC 2011

This chapter provides an overview of the field of DSS, its history and a progress report on an ongoing research project to explore the perceptions of selected DSS researchers, who made significant contribution to this field. This chapter comprises analysis of the reflections on the pioneering efforts of these academics and technology entrepreneurs to meet decision support needs using information technologies.

The next section discusses the major milestones, accomplishments and the timeline of DSS research. The third section describes the research project to gather reflections of decision support pioneers and map a trajectory of development of a DSS field using these reflections as a lens. The fourth section reviews the observations of eleven DSS pioneers from their experiences with computerized DSS. The reflections of eleven DSS pioneers are reported, including: James F. Courtney, Paul Gray, Clyde W. Holsapple, George P. Huber, William H. Inmon, Frank F. Land, Andrew M. McCosh, Michael S. Scott Morton, Gerald R. Wagner, Hugh J. Watson and Andrew Whinston. This section also examines issues associated with decision support that the pioneers believe to be still unresolved. The final section is our conclusions about 60 years of DSS research and some recommendations for future research directions.

2.2 DSS Research and Development Timeline

Computerized decision support systems have been in use for almost 60 years. One can trace the origins of DSS to 1951 and the Lyons Tea Shops business use of the LEO I (Lyons Electronic Office) digital computer. Decision support software factored in the weather forecast to help determine the goods carried by "fresh produce" delivery vans (Caminer, 1997; Power, 2007). One of LEO I's early tasks was the capture of daily orders that were phoned in every afternoon by the tea shop staff and used to calculate overnight production requirements, assembly instructions, delivery schedules, invoices, costings and management reports. Both David Caminer and Frank Land, London School of Economics, worked on the LEO I project. Caminer became Director of LEO Computers Ltd in 1959. The SAGE (Semi-Automatic Ground Environment) air defense system for North America built for the U.S. military in the late 1950s and completed in 1962 was another first generation decision support application. It was probably the first computerized real-time, data-driven DSS (Power, 2007).

The management decision system built by Michael Scott Morton in 1966 for his Harvard dissertation started efforts to build model-driven decision support applications with second generation computing technology (cf., Scott Morton and Stephens, 1968; Scott Morton, 1971). Scott Morton studied how computers and analytical models could help managers make a recurring key business planning decision. He conducted an experiment in which managers actually used a Management Decision System (MDS). Marketing and production managers used the MDS to coordinate production planning for laundry equipment. The MDS ran on an IDI 21 in. CRT with a light pen connected using a 2,400 bps modem to a pair of Univac 494 systems. The term decision support system was first used in Gorry and Scott Morton's (1971) Sloan Management Review article. They argued that Management Information Systems primarily focused on structured decisions and suggested that information systems for supporting semi-structured and unstructured decisions should be termed "Decision Support Systems". Scott Morton and McCosh (1968) described a number of DSS related projects which they collaborated on. By 1970 a number of computing journals started publishing papers on systems supporting better decisions (Sprague and Watson, 1979; Rinehart, 2006).

In general, a model-driven DSS emphasizes access to and manipulation of financial, optimization or simulation models. The core of these is quite often based on simple quantitative models and they provide the most elementary level of functionality. Model-driven DSS use limited data and parameters provided by decision makers to aid them in analyzing a problem situation (Power, 2002). Early versions of model-driven DSS were called "model-oriented DSS" by Alter (1980), computationally-oriented DSS by Bonczek et al. (1981) and later spreadsheet-oriented and solver-oriented DSS by Holsapple and Whinston (1996). The first commercial tool for building model-driven DSS using financial and quantitative models was called IFPS, an acronym for interactive financial planning system (Gray, 1983). It was developed in the late 1970s by Gerald R. Wagner and his students at the University of Texas. Wagner's company, EXECUCOM Systems, marketed IFPS until the mid 1990s. Paul Gray's Guide to IFPS (1983) promoted the use of the system in business schools.

Data-driven DSS emphasizes access to and manipulation of a time-series of internal company data and sometimes external and real-time data. Simple file systems accessed by query and retrieval tools provide the most elementary level of functionality. Data warehouse systems that allow the manipulation of data by computerized tools tailored to a specific task and setting or by more general tools and operators provide additional functionality. Data-driven DSS with On-line Analytical Processing (cf., Codd et al., 1993) provide the highest level of functionality and decision support that is linked to analysis of large collections of historical data. Executive Information Systems are examples of data-driven DSS (Power, 2002). Initial examples of these systems were called data-oriented DSS and analysis information systems (Alter, 1980) and retrieval-only systems by Bonczek et al. (1981).

One of the first data-driven DSS was built using an APL-based software package called AAIMS, An Analytical Information Management System. It was developed from 1970 to 1974 by Richard Klaas and Charles Weiss at American Airlines (cf. Alter, 1980). In 1979 John Rockart's research stimulated the development of executive information systems (EIS) and executive support systems (ESS). In the late 1970s, Courtney and Jensen developed and used SLIM, System Laboratory for Information Management data management system for teaching DSS. These systems evolved from single user model-driven decision support systems and from the development of relational database products. The first EIS used pre-defined information screens maintained by analysts for senior executives. In the Fall of 1978, Lockheed-Georgia began development of an EIS called Management Information and Decision Support, called MID (cf., Houdeshel and Watson, 1987). For many years Hugh Watson was an active proponent of EIS (cf., Watson et al., 1997).

Using computer-based communication for decision support had its origins in the early 1960s. Douglas Engelbart's, 1962 paper "Augmenting Human Intellect: A Conceptual Framework" is the anchor for much of the later work related to communications-driven DSS. In 1969, he demonstrated the first hypermedia/groupware system NLS (oNLine System) at the Fall Joint Computer Conference in San Francisco (Engelbart, 1962). Engelbart invented both the computer mouse and groupware. Murray Turoff's (1970) article introduced the concept of Computerized Conferencing. He developed and implemented the first Computer Mediated Communications System (EMISARI) tailored to facilitate group communications.

In the early 1980s, academic researchers developed a new category of software to support group decision-making called Group Decision Support Systems abbreviated GDSS (cf., Gray, 1981; 2008; Huber, 1982; Turoff and Hiltz, 1982). Mindsight from Execucom Systems, GroupSystems developed at the University of Arizona and the SAMM system developed by University of Minnesota researchers (DeSanctis and Gallupe, 1987) were early Group DSS.

The precursor for document-driven DSS is Vannevar Bush's (1945) article titled "As We May Think". Bush wrote "Consider a future device for individual use, which is a sort of mechanized private file and library. It needs a name, and to coin one at random, 'memex' will do". Bush's memex is a much broader vision than that of today's document-driven DSS. Text and document management emerged in the 1970s and 1980s as an important, widely used computerized means for representing and processing pieces of text (Holsapple and Whinston, 1996). A pioneering scholarly article for this category of DSS was written by Swanson and Culnan (1978). They reviewed document-based systems for management planning and control. Until the mid-1990s little progress was made in helping managers find documents to support their decision making.

In the early, 1990s, Bill Inmon and Ralph Kimball actively promoted decision support systems built using relational database technologies. For many Information Systems practitioners, DSS built using Oracle or DB2 were the first decision support systems they read about in the popular computing literature. Ralph Kimball was known as "The Doctor of DSS" and Bill Inmon was the "father of the data warehouse" (Inmon, 1990; Kimball, 1994).

Finally, Bonczek et al. (1981) book created interest in using technologies for creating knowledge-driven DSS. In 1983, Dustin Huntington established a company called EXSYS (www.exsys.com). That company and product made it practical to use PC based tools to develop expert systems and knowledge-driven DSS. These systems were called suggestion DSS by Alter (1980).

The roots of modern decision support research extend to practical applications, theoretical contributions and empirical studies. Early DSS projects emphasized important tasks like production planning and forecasting, monitoring current operations, and monitoring hostile activities to increase national security. The DSSResources.COM resource created and maintained by Dan Power contains a comprehensive entry about the history of DSS (see Power, 2007).

In 2007, DSSResources.com started a feature called "Reflections of Decision Support Pioneers" and posted an initial reflections interview with Paul Gray. The aim of this effort was to document the reflections of the people, who were visionary enough to predict the value of using new technologies in helping people to make better decisions and who started development of the theories and methods in this respect, which laid the ground for the discipline of decision support systems. In the next section we describe the history of the project, its instrument and provide analysis of some data it collected to help identify the future directions for decision support research and practice.

2.3 Reflections on Decision Support Pioneers – Research Project

The initial Decision Support Pioneers page with photos and short biographical sketches was posted at DSSResources.com on September 29, 2006. The URL is http://dssresources.com/history/pioneers/pioneerslist.html. DSS pioneers are being defined and approached based on major intellectual contributions to our understanding of how, what, why, and when computing, information technologies and software are and should be used to aid, assist, support and even replace people in decision making activities, processes, and tasks.

Who are pioneers? Pioneers are those who are brave enough to move forward to the unknown. Pioneers break new intellectual ground and open new areas for research. In this context, it was assumed that DSS pioneers may have written or co-authored a seminal theoretical book or article. Alternatively, the person led a ground-breaking technology implementation. In some cases, a pioneer completed a research study that started an important stream of research. In general, those people on the list made an ongoing and sustained contribution that significantly advanced the field of computerized decision support. A common characteristic of all of the pioneers is that they dealt with new ideas. The review of the history of DSS presented in the previous section referred to many of the researchers and practitioners who justifiably belong to this category based on their contribution to the DSS filed.

People were selected as pioneers based on: (1) perception of experts about who proposed influential new ideas, (2) nominations, (3) literature review, and (4) citations analysis. Based on these criteria 37 individuals are currently included on the DSSResources.com DSS Pioneers page. A number of the pioneers of DSS research and practice have died and many have reached advanced age. We recognize the many contributions of Robert H. Bonczek (April 17, 1951–June 7, 1985), David T. Caminer (June 26, 1915–June 19, 2008), Edgar F. Codd (August 23, 1923–April 18, 2003), George B. Dantzig (November 8, 1914–May 13, 2005), Gerardine Desanctis (January 5, 1954–August 16, 2005), Oleg I. Larichev (September 20, 1934–January 19, 2003) and Herbert A. Simon (June 15, 1916–February 9, 2001).

The goal of the Decision Support Pioneers page is to recognize those individuals who made major contributions to the study and practice of using computers to support decision making. These influential people developed this applied research area and demonstrated how information technology could be used to support decision making. Identifying these individuals and capturing their perspective helps place the study and practice of building DSS in a historical context.

The DSS pioneers have been asked a common set of questions. The idea is to have everyone associated with innovation in decision support research and technologies respond to the same six questions. The questions include:

- *Q1:* How did you get interested in computerized decision support?
- *Q2:* What do you consider your major contribution to helping support decision makers using computers? Why?
- *Q3:* What were your motivations for working in this area?
- *Q4:* Who were your important collaborators and what was their contribution?
- *Q5:* What are your major conclusions from your experiences with computerized decision support?
- *Q6:* What are the issues associated with decision support that we still need to address?

The pioneers included in this chapter are a highly representative sample of senior DSS scholars from a longer list. In this chapter we report on analysis of the reflections of pioneers focusing mainly on the last two questions. The reflections capture the past and help guide the future of computerized decision support.

2.4 Reflections of DSS Pioneers

This section includes the reflections on the last two questions of James F. Courtney, Paul Gray, Clyde W. Holsapple, George P. Huber, William H. Inmon, Frank F. Land, Andrew M. McCosh, Michael S. Scott Morton, Gerald R. Wagner, Hugh J. Watson and Andrew Whinston. These eleven pioneers had answered our questions prior to June 2010. The two questions addressed in this chapter are useful for the purpose of the chapter of reflecting on the past of DSS history and identifying future directions, thus the questions selected were: "What are major conclusions from experiences with computerized DSS?" and "What are the issues associated with decision support that we still need to address?" The complete transcripts of the interviews are available on the World Wide Web at http://dssresources.com/reflections/index.html.

2.4.1 Major Conclusions from Experiences with Computerized DSS

In the late 1960s, Michael Scott Morton and Andrew McCosh initiated business and management research on Decision Support Systems. They and their colleagues at Harvard and MIT initiated a long stream of research related to model-driven decision support. Both received their DBAs at Harvard. Scott Morton's dissertation completed in 1967 was the first systematic study of a computerized management decision system.

Scott Morton identified two major conclusions from his experience. "First is how slow we humans are to change our routines and organizations, despite evidence there are better ways of doing things. Secondly, I am increasingly struck by the relatively ineffective link between business schools/business research and the realization of better ways of doing things in the 'real' world we all live and work in. It takes a very long time for good ideas (in all fields, not just computers and management) to be adopted and to have an impact on our performance." Scott Morton explained "the American automobile industry is a case in point.... DSS is similar, the ideas and concepts were developing in the early 1970s, and the technology became widely available at reasonable cost in the 1980s and in 2008 they are rarely used effectively. When they are, there are huge beneficial impacts; indeed some firms could not exist without them."

McCosh concluded "the most important feature of a DSS is to make sure it is flexible and understood by the company executive who has to use it. If the designer tries to make the whole thing operational in one go, he will almost certainly lose his audience. The exec will get lost. He needs to have a huge role in the design and layouts. If you do not ensure he has big role in development, the model will probably be binned in a few years." Both McCosh and Scott Morton remain optimistic about the need for and effectiveness of DSS.

Frank Land worked with David Caminer at Lyons & Co. on a DSS application for the Leo I computer in the 1950s and went on to teach Information Systems and DSS at London School of Economics. He concluded "The best DSS are those which provide clear explanations of the rationale behind the alternatives offered up for consideration and permit the decision makers to explore the decision space and to bring to the surface underlying assumptions and hidden conflicts. But to make the process work it needs a facilitator with an understanding of group behavior as well as of the way the DSS is constructed."

He noted DSS "at their best, when designed jointly with the decision makers, they can be highly successful." But he had some cautions for DSS builders, "A DSS which is simply parachuted into the decision situation has little chance of being adopted. Ideally the DSS is the outcome of collaboration between the decision makers and systems designers. The way the DSS is deployed is highly dependent on the working style of individual or group decision makers."

Hugh Watson and Ralph Sprague extended the theoretical boundaries of DSS in the 1970s and 1980s. Watson especially examined Executive Information Systems and data-driven DSS. Watson noted in his response to the interview question

"A couple of conclusions come to mind. First, almost everything that is touted as 'new' has significant antecedents. For example, dashboards and scorecards are currently the rage. But if you are familiar the history of decision support, you know that the idea of using performance metrics to monitor what is taking place and to motivate workers is an old idea that dates back to critical success factors in the 1970s and executive information systems in the 1980s. The technology may be new and vendors may hype the ideas as new, but the basic concepts have typically been around for quite a while."

Watson continued, "The greatest days for decision support are still ahead. To date, decision support has not been an integral part of the running of most companies. Most decision support has involved analysts analyzing data and passing the findings on to others. We are starting to see decision support become more pervasive and integrated into business processes and how companies are run. Examples of this include event triggers and alerts that inform organizational personnel through a variety of digital channels about recent developments, business activity monitoring that monitors current operations, and rules engines that automate or support operational decision making. Many of the most exciting developments are due to the availability of real-time data through real-time data warehousing, enterprise application integration (EAI), and enterprise information integration (EII). It isn't a coincidence that leading software vendors such as Microsoft, Oracle, and SAP have recently made significant investments in decision support."

Bill Inmon was also a major proponent of data-driven DSS. Inmon is generally recognized as the "father of the data warehouse" and co-creator of the "Corporate Information Factory. His work on concepts related to data warehouses began with a 1983 Computerworld article, "What Price Relational?" He stated bluntly "Computerized DSS is in its infancy. There are so many possibilities that our grandchildren will look back on us and wonder about how naïve and unsophisticated we were."

Clyde Holsapple and Andrew Whinston have made many contributions to the DSS literature and field. Whinston has edited the major journal in the field for many years and he continues his search for major conclusions and promotes research in the discipline. Holsapple is a prolific author and researcher. He noted "From a practical standpoint, decision support systems have become so widespread in use as to be almost invisible – supporting decisions of consumers, managers, groups, enterprises, and inter-organizational systems such as supply chains." He observed, "many vendors have been quite successful in developing and marketing DSS software and services – with recent major consolidation in this sector indicating DSS importance to strategies of such firms as IBM, Oracle, and SAP." He concluded "From a scholarly standpoint, we see that the DSS field has become a major expansion of the IS discipline, going well beyond its important predecessors of data processing and management information systems, becoming heavily interrelated with newer IS expansions such as organizational computing, electronic commerce, and pervasive computing. Advances in the DSS area have had major impacts on the productivity, agility, innovativeness, and reputation of decision processes and their outcomes. Continuing advances will extend impacts in these directions."

Jim Courtney worked with both data-driven and group DSS. He concluded, "First, everything is connected with everything else, at least in-so-far-as important problems are concerned. Global warming is a clear example of that. You need to try to uncover hidden assumptions and different perspectives that various parties have in making important decisions. You need to define problems as broadly as feasible and include stakeholders affected by the problem in the decision-making process. You must be especially careful in formulating problems, as getting the problem right is critical to solving it. A good solution to the wrong problem may actually make it worse."

"My answers" states Paul Gray, a leader in both GDSS and data-driven DSS research, "reflect where I think we are today."

1. Group decision support systems, under that name, is an idea which has come and, sad to say, has gone. Although there are still vendors such as Groupsystems in Colorado and they have a users group, the concept has not had legs under the GDSS name. That doesn't mean that the many methods, studies, and experiments did not have an effect. They did. What we now have is many uses and extensions, including for example, distributed GDSS.
2. New fields (such as business intelligence, competitive intelligence, knowledge management) came on the scene and are beholden to the findings of the over 40 years of history of the field. Technological inventions, such as the data warehouse and the data mart, also contributed.
3. Many original concepts, however, have been superseded. We started out in management science and computer science and the techniques of these fields were pervasive in its beginnings. We have moved past the elitist view that managers would be able to use Iverson notation (i.e., APL) and the populist view that all managers could do is look at chart books to a much more nuanced and user friendly vision.
4. Some early frameworks (e.g., Alter's taxonomy, Power's, Sprague and Carlson's) have proved durable and highly useful.
5. Although data-driven DSS is still the dominant paradigm, we are starting to see analytics coming back to the forefront as witnessed by Tom Davenport and Jeanne Harris's book *Competing on Analytics* published in March 2007 by Harvard Business School Press.

Group DSS theorist George Huber stated "My experiences with computerized decision support didn't cause me to reach any major conclusions, except to concur with the common belief that DSS greatly increased decision quality and timeliness."

Finally, entrepreneur and academic Gerald Wagner, affirmed "DSS, as I prefer to believe it should be defined, had a short life. It lasted until about 1984 when Executive Information Systems came along. EIS had an emphasis on historical data vs. assumptions about the future. Since then we have been pre-occupied with looking backwards rather than forward. I believe the value of DSS is to 'rehearse the future' using Peter Keen's words. The value is not in endless volumes of historical data. Now Business Intelligence is dominant and it is also not about rehearsing the future, i.e., it is about looking backward to what has already happened." Wagner continues his efforts to develop financial planning decision support tools to help managers envision the future.

These pioneers have had extensive experience with DSS research, development, implementation, evaluation and commercialization. Their divergent views on their experiences reflect these diverse backgrounds. Whereas Whinston is still searching for final conclusions, many others had strong views on issues related to DSS. Some consider technologies such as model-driven DSS and GDSS to be now past their prime. Many of the pioneers recognize the role of DSS related executive information systems and the popular term business intelligence. They all appear to be still enthusiastic about the prospects and potential of computerized decision support systems.

2.4.2 Continuing Issues Associated with Decision Support

Courtney stated "I think we need to broaden our view of decision making. Mitroff and Linstone would consider our view the technical one, I believe. We need to also be concerned with other individual perspectives, organizational perspectives, ethical issues and even aesthetics in our work. We need to be cognizant of social and cultural issues to the extent that we can to try to avoid some of the mistakes of the past. I believe we really need to think holistically in an age when our technology is having such a vast impact on the planet and all its creatures. I am discouraged that so much IS research is reductionist and that is what the leading journals tend to emphasize. There is also a great deal of emphasis on theory development, but the theories that we have seem quite shallow and don't explain very much."

Six issues were identified as most important by Paul Gray:

1. Increasing the level and breadth of innovation
2. Knowledge transfer from academia to practice, both at the firm and at the vendor level
3. Knowledge transfer to academia from practice (I think we keep up with the vendors)
4. Improving the technical and social science capabilities of academics so that they can explore areas that they now do not touch
5. Getting students interested in DSS. The number of courses being offered at graduate and undergraduate levels seems stagnant
6. Multidisciplinarity. DSS is a multidisciplinary field. Multidisciplinarity would be helped by better interaction between DSS people (who are mostly in business schools) with decision analysts and other people in business schools who study decision making, with computer science, and with psychology and other social science fields

Clyde Holsapple emphasized "One of the issues for which there is a particular opportunity to have a major impact is to better understand the relationship between DSS features and usage on the one hand and decision-maker competitiveness and performance on the other. From a completely different perspective, there is the issue of how research on decision support systems is regarded within the IS field. All too often, it is treated as a side show, rather than a key component at the heart of IS research. All too often, IS researchers who apparently are not very familiar with the DSS area miss opportunities to enhance their research by recognizing its potential for connections to DSSs." Holsapple argued there is a need for other IS researchers "to greatly improve the depth of their familiarity with the DSS research literature – for enriching their own research and for improving their capabilities as reviewers of DSS-related manuscripts."

Finally, Holsapple concluded "one last issue important for continuing development of the DSS field concerns the attitudes of those who perform and evaluate research. So far, the field has tended to benefit from an inclusive attitude that welcomes innovation, recognizes the applicability of diverse methodologies, and is open to provocative/stimulating work.... It is important for DSS researchers not to fall into such a predicament, but to press onward with a pioneering attitude that makes forays into the intellectual wilderness – in efforts to see, understand, and map out new DSS possibilities – rather than incrementally treading along well-worn paths of conformance."

Inmon said there is a long list. "But some of the items include:

- the politics of DSS
- unstructured data and DSS
- metadata and DSS
- business metadata
- non numerical visualization"

"Note the importance of keeping the logic in line with changing conditions in a turbulent world" asserts Frank Land. "Too often decision makers, not fully understanding the underlying logic, rely on a model embedded in the DSS which has ceased to reflect the changed world. Designers, on the other hand, often do not ensure the mechanisms are provided for the rapid and easy updating of the models underlying the DSS."

He argues "The importance of informal systems and their role in decision making is often neglected by systems designers. However, developments in the use of the internet such as Web 2.0 and the ideas behind the open source movement are permitting the informal to infiltrate computer based systems."

Land states "Perhaps most importantly we need to further improve our understanding of how decisions are made and the role played by non-instrumental issues such 'office' politics, human relations and intelligence."

McCosh thinks "we need to spend more time on decision analysis and decision definition than has been the case in recent work I have seen at conferences."

"The general unresolved issue," according to Scott Morton is "understanding the management of change." Without a better understanding of this it is hard to implement and learn from DSS applications. As an engineer trained in the technology it took me a while to understand that the hard problems lie in the "soft" domains of management and of human behavior, not in the hardware and software.

More particularly, there is the still poorly understood shifting boundary between what computers can do well and what humans can do well. This has major implications for the relevant application set for DSS and therefore their successful use in organizations.

Wagner sees the major issue of DSS as "Getting back to its origins and helping decision makers to see alternative futures. Start teaching modeling and logical thinking again. Professors have lost sight of that. Today they teach Excel which is an electronic calculator and not a modeling tool. We are lacking in innovation in terms of the primary focus of rehearsing the future. Data visualization has great promise but there also we are lacking innovation. We have faster, sexier, and prettier charts but they are the same old line and bar charts. There are complicated 3-D and the like but real people can't understand those. The need is for new metaphors for visualizing business data that are intuitive and easily understood by real people."

A major issue according to Hugh Watson, "is to make decision support easier to use and more accessible to everyone. This issue was recognized back in the 1970s when "easy to use" was a defining characteristic of DSS. ... In general, decision support applications have become easier to use but additional progress is still needed. For example, we have made strides with visual displays of data and data visualization but they pale in comparison to the video games that the future captains of industry play. A graph that shows actual versus budgeted cash flow does not have the same impact as a screen that shows a growing pile of dollars and audio sounds that indicate whether cash flow is meeting expectations. Google has changed our expectations for how we should be able to locate information. We should be able to "Google" any kind of decision-related information and tool. In most organizations, structured and unstructured data exist in separate silos. Users want to be able to easily access both kinds of data seamlessly. For example, a product manager who uses quantitative data and sees that an ad campaign did not generate the anticipated lift might want to see the video clips of the ads that were run. We also need to make it easier for work teams to use decision support tools collaboratively."

Finally, Andrew Whinston succinctly addresses our challenge. "The world is changing so rapidly that it is hard to predict what should be the next focus. It is driven by constant advances in technology and what people are able to get access to."

Table 2.1 provides a summary of thematic analysis of the pioneers' comments along seven dimensions. Not all pioneers addressed each of the dimensions, but the summary highlights key themes. Comments from the pioneers offer several ideas for continuing research needed related to DSS. They note the need for taking a holistic view, considering organizational, cultural and other issues. They also argue for a greater recognition of DSS research in the IS field, and lament the fact that DSS research seems to have virtually disappeared from leading IS journals. The pioneers argue that we need to continue recognizing the multidisciplinary nature of the DSS field.

Table 2.1 Thematic analysis of pioneers' comments

Author/themes	Complexity of context	Sources of inspiration	Opportunistic view on technologies and theories	Future directions and challenges	Experience from the past	Importance of keeping "the big picture"	Relevance
Courtney	Everything is connected with everything else, at least in-so-far-as important problems are concerned			• Cognizant of social and cultural issues • Need to focus on individual and organizational perspectives, ethical issues and aesthetics	Avoid being driven by academic, rather than practical imperatives	• "Need to try to uncover hidden assumptions and different perspectives" • Current theories tend to be oversimplifying the complexity	Be especially careful in formulating problems. A good solution to the wrong problem may actually make it worse
Gray		Started out in management science and computer science and the techniques of these fields were pervasive in its beginnings	Innovation has to be the focus	• Data-driven DSS is still dominant paradigm; analytics coming back to the forefront • Focus on better DSS education and training	• GDSS learning is still current • New fields (such as business intelligence, competitive intelligence, knowledge management) build on past research	• The need for multidisciplinary approach • Better skills training to support such needs	• Moved past the elitist view... [to] the populist view... and user friendly vision • Knowledge transfer between academia and practice is still an issue

Table 2.1 (continued)

Author/themes	Complexity of context	Sources of inspiration	Opportunistic view on technologies and theories	Future directions and challenges	Experience from the past	Importance of keeping "the big picture"	Relevance
Holsapple		Some ground breaking theories from management science still relevant for future theoretical advancement	• New theories still to be discovered • Widespread in use and almost invisible, part of a bigger picture	Major impacts on productivity, agility, innovativeness, and reputation as part of organisational computing	IS researchers still not familiar enough with DSS principles, can benefit from cross-connections to DSS	Explore the dichotomy between individual performance and competitiveness	• Interrelated with newer IS expansions; • Major expansion of the IS discipline
Huber				Opportunities from unconventional use of technologies	Increased decision quality and timeliness		
Inmon	• The politics of DSS • Unstructured data • Business metadata • Non numerical visualization			Computerized DSS is still in its infancy			

Table 2.1 (continued)

Author/themes	Complexity of context	Sources of inspiration	Opportunistic view on technologies and theories	Future directions and challenges	Experience from the past	Importance of keeping "the big picture"	Relevance
Land	Understanding of group behaviour and design rationale is important		Provide clear explanations of the rationale and permit the decision makers to explore the decision space	Assistance of the facilitator may be needed to keep the design rationale clear		A DSS which is simply parachuted into the decision situation has little chance of being adopted	When approached in a deterministic view – could then be sidelined
McCosh		A tool which would help a manager or a business owner to do better or more business	. . . make sure it is flexible and understood by the company executive who has to use it	Need to spend more time on decision analysis and decision definition			
Scott Morton		. . . putting computing power in the hands of the managers was exciting	The ideas and concepts in the early 1970s, the technology at reasonable cost in the 1980s, still rarely used effectively	Need to be clear about the boundary between what computers can do well and what humans can do well	Still need a better understanding of the management of change		

Table 2.1 (continued)

Author/themes	Complexity of context	Sources of inspiration	Opportunistic view on technologies and theories	Future directions and challenges	Experience from the past	Importance of keeping "the big picture"	Relevance
Wagner			The "new" DSS is now a combination of art, technology, and psychology	The value of DSS is to "rehearse the future", not dealing with historical data	We have been pre-occupied with looking backwards rather than forward	Teaching understanding of the technology of DSS is important because if they don't understand "it" and see "it" they won't use "it"	
Watson			The technology may be new and vendors may hype the ideas as new, but the basic concepts have typically been around for quite a while	The greatest days for decision support are still ahead	Almost everything that is touted as "new" has significant antecedents	Exciting developments are real-time data warehousing, enterprise application integration (EAI), and enterprise information integration (EII)	

Table 2.1 (continued)

Author/themes	Complexity of context	Sources of inspiration	Opportunistic view on technologies and theories	Future directions and challenges	Experience from the past	Importance of keeping "the big picture"	Relevance
Whinston			Still in search of major conclusions	Hard to predict what should be the next focus		The field is driven by advances in technology and what people are able to get access to for solving their problems	

2.5 Conclusions

What are major conclusions from experiences with computerized DSS? Based on the literature analysis and reflections presented above, the field of DSS is still pretty relevant. Originating from different reference disciplines, DSS has expanded to be perceived as a multidisciplinary field. Since its origins as an "academic elite" discipline, DSS became a component of any management information system, enterprise resource planning, as well as personal computing tool. Some new terms have been "invented" as successors of the DSS advancements. Among others, business intelligence, knowledge management and various personalized work support tools inherited features originated from "good old ideas" that DSS researchers described in seminal work from 1970s to 1980s.

There is a strong belief that computerized DSS is still "in its infancy" in terms of its sophisticated use of all the opportunities that modern technologies create for more "ubiquitous, invisible and democratic" use of support any time and any place. The driving force behind development of new approaches to decision support still remains the user demand, and this demand should be recognized at all different levels from individuals to organizations and societies in face of solving social and even ethical problems of global magnitude.

A "good old principle" of user-centered design is most relevant to the development of modern DSS tools, which require all along collaboration between decision makers and systems designers. This principle drives development of systems, which are simple enough, but relevant to decision-makers real needs. It was suggested, that the best DSS bring to the surface underlying assumptions and hidden conflicts, which would be impossible without applying computational power and processing capabilities available thanks to modern technologies.

What are the issues associated with decision support that still need attention? From the scholarly perspectives, the lack of underlying theory and, as a result, limited academic impact is recognized as needing attention of future DSS researchers. However, the impact should not be a sole purpose of researchers, rather, the outcome of solid development of tools and techniques, which address real problems of real people.

Although recognized as a legitimate sub-field of information research and practice, DSS is still seen as "a side show", rather than an intrinsic focus of IS research. In this respect, the focus of IS research on informal systems, organizational politics, information management, human relations and competitive intelligence has as strong importance to the design of DSS, which fit demands of modern socio-technical systems. In the same way, research and teaching about decision-making and decision support should be an integral part of any business information systems education.

The basic research model studied by most of the traditional DSS research suggests a main effect of decision support capability on performance. Little has been done to identify contingencies that impact adoption of DSS or the moderators that influence the success of specific types of systems. The following emerging topics represent a sample:

a. Connected decision makers who are continually linked to decision support information and collaborative technologies including voice and video. Impact on quality of decisions, burnout of decision makers, deskilling decision-making jobs.
b. Real-time data collection and display. Impact of tracking employees and monitoring by managers, information overload, issues of trust and invasion of privacy.
c. Smart devices with built in decision automation. Impact on people, learned helplessness, feelings of intrusion into one's life, increased sense of dependence on technology.
d. Integrated, targeted marketing approaches that take interactions across multiple channels, past history, and predicted future behaviors into account. Marketing effectiveness, customers reaction to perceived invasions of their privacy.
e. Networks of sensors in field operations that allow for optimization of constrained resources, e.g., energy. Efficiency gains from such networks, and robustness of data-intensive settings.
f. "Connecting the dots" and integrating, analyzing, and acting on disparate information on customers, terrorists, drug compounds and molecules. Technology problem versus a human agent problem, degree of human intervention necessary.

There are new opportunities for enhancing decision support with data mining technologies. Some of these have led to rule oriented, automated decision systems that can be employed in real time applications. Interaction with social network systems is enabling a new level of decision support technologies in recommendation systems as well as collaborative decision systems. These tools are being used, for example, to forecast sales of cultural products such as movies and music (Davenport and Harris, 2009; Sharda and Delen, 2006).

The last few years have seen exciting developments in user interfaces. Cell phone inputs through SMS are becoming more common for at least some consumer DSS-type applications. Multi-touch interfaces such as that on the iPhone and iPad, and on the Microsoft Surface platform, are almost revolutionary in enabling entirely new ways of interaction with a DSS application. Many companies, for example, are developing image processing applications to provide purchasing-decision support on smart-phones while a customer is in a store. User interfaces are going to change significantly in the next few years (Kroeker, 2010). Their first use will probably be in gaming and consumer applications, but the business and DSS applications should be explored by DSS researchers.

A third category of technologies to impact DSS research and practice is the availability of massive data generated through RFID and other sensors. RFID tagging is already being used by some companies to make decisions in supply chain management to gain additional efficiency (Nambiar, 2009). RFID technology generates massive amounts of data that can be analyzed to achieve great insights into a company's environment, a major purpose for the very existence of business intelligence and decision support (e.g., Baars et al., 2008).

By now, we have created and studied many DSS, but the lessons learned from the past need more thorough and systematic codification to reduce the tendency to reinvent the practice of building DSS, losing the opportunity to capitalize on the fact that the field has a rich history with some seminal work performed by pioneers to whom we owe the position that DSS research and practice enjoys now. These reflections of pioneers can help understand the progress of the field of DSS to determine what has been learned before from the first hand experiences of those who stood at the roots of the discipline. Their vision for the future research needs resonates with the research efforts of new researchers and is well illustrated in the content of this book. This chapter presents the first attempt at systematic study of the field. It aims to lay the ground for future DSS researchers and practitioners to continue building the solid DSS foundation in order to achieve the dreams of the pioneers in efficient use of advanced technology to support "better ways of doing things in the 'real' world we all live and work in", and move faster in these directions with the "... pioneering attitude that makes forays into the intellectual wilderness."

Appendix: Brief Biographies of Interviewees

James F. Courtney Professor of Management Information Systems at Louisiana Tech University. He received his Ph.D. in Business Administration with a major in management science from the University of Texas at Austin in 1974. He is the co-developer of the Systems Laboratory for Information Management (1981), a software package to support research and education in decision support systems, co-author of Database Systems for Management (1992), and Decision Support Models and Expert Systems (1992).

Paul Gray Professor emeritus and Founding Chair of the Department of Information Science at Claremont Graduate University. He specializes in data warehousing, business intelligence, decision support systems, and knowledge management. He is the author/editor of 12 books, most recently Decision Support in the Data Warehouse with H.J. Watson. He is also the author of over 120 journal articles including three "first papers" in crime in transportation, in telecommuting, and in group decision support systems. He is the founding editor of the Communications of AIS. Paul received a Ph.D. in Operations Research from Stanford University.

Clyde W. Holsapple Rosenthal Endowed Chair in Management Information Systems at the University of Kentucky. His research focuses on supporting knowledge work, particularly in decision-making contexts. He has authored over 100 research articles. His many books include Foundations of Decision Support Systems (with Bonczek and Whinston, 1981), Decision Support Systems: A Knowledge-Based Approach, and the 2-volume Handbook on Knowledge Management. He received a Ph.D. from Purdue University in 1977. His dissertation was titled "Framework for a Generalized Intelligent Decision Support System".

George P. Huber Charles and Elizabeth Prothro Regents Chair in Business Administration, The University of Texas at Austin. His research focuses on decision making and effects of information technologies on organizations. He has authored over 100 articles. Huber published a pioneering public sector decision support application article (1969) co-authored with Charles Holt. Also, Huber wrote pioneering articles on behavioral issues associated with using DSS and GDSS. He received a Ph.D. from Purdue University in 1965.

William H. Inmon Bill Inmon, is recognized as the "father of the data warehouse" and co-creator of the "Corporate Information Factory. His work on concepts related to data warehouses began with a 1983 Computerworld article, "What Price Relational?" As an author, Inmon has written about a variety of topics on the building, usage, and maintenance of the data warehouse and the Corporate Information Factory. He has written more than 650 articles, many of them have been published in major computer journals such as Datamation, ComputerWorld, and Byte Magazine. In 1991 Inmon published a practical how-to guide titled Building the Data Warehouse. Check www.inmongif.com

Frank Land He started his career in computing with J. Lyons, in 1953, working on the pioneering LEO Computer first as a programmer and then as a systems analyst on business decision support applications. In 1967, he left industry to join the London School of Economics on National Computing Centre grant to establish teaching and research in systems analysis becoming Professor of Systems Analysis in 1982. He is a Fellow of the British Computer Society and was awarded a Fellowship of the AIS in 2001 and the AIS LEO Award in 2003.

Andrew M. Mccosh Eminent Scholar Department of Finance, College of Business Administration, Florida International University. He previously served on the faculties at Harvard, Columbia, the University of Edinburgh, the University of Manchester, and the University of Michigan. He has published research in the areas of innovation and business processes, ethics, decision support technology, and financial strategy. He received a DBA from Harvard Business School.

Michael S. Scott Morton Professor of Management at Sloan School of Management at the Massachusetts Institute of Technology. Scott Morton is concerned about organizational and structural changes that US firms must make in order to compete successfully in the global marketplace. He studied engineering at the University of Glasgow in Scotland and finished his studies at Carnegie-Mellon before obtaining his doctorate at the School of Business at Harvard University. His dissertation completed in 1967 was the first systematic study of a computerized management decision system.

Gerald R. Wagner In 1978, Jerry resigned from his position as tenured Professor and Head of Operations Research, College of Engineering, University of Texas at Austin. He then started his first software company Execucom, which became a leading force in DSS. Execucom sponsored the first DSS conference and started the DSS transactions. Execucom was acquired by GTE in 1984. Dr. Wagner is known for his software including IFPS, VisionQuest, Planners Lab and Web IQ. In 2003, he founded the International Academy for Advanced Decision Support (IAADS).

Hugh J. Watson Professor of MIS and a holder of a C. Herman and Mary Virginia Terry Chair of Business Administration in the Terry College of Business at the University of Georgia. He has authored 22 books and over 100 scholarly journal articles. He helped develop the conceptual foundation for decision support systems in the 1970s, researched the development and implementation of executive information systems in the 1980s, and most recently, specializes in BI and data warehousing. Hugh is a Fellow of the Association for Information Systems and The Data Warehousing Institute. He is the Senior Director of the Teradata University Network.

Andrew B. Whinston Hugh Roy Cullen Centennial Chair Professor in Information Systems at the Graduate School of Business in the University of Texas at Austin. He is also Professor in the departments of Economics and Computer Science. He is founding Editor-in-Chief of the Decision Support Systems journal. Whinston received his Ph.D. in Management from Carnegie Mellon University in 1962. He has authored seminal books in various disciplines. He has also published over 250 papers in leading academic journals in Economics, Business and Computer Science. Most of Dr. Whinston's research has been based at the Center for Research in Electronic Commerce.

References

Alter, S. L. (1980). *Decision Support Systems: Current Practice and Continuing Challenge*. Reading, MA: Addison-Wesley.

Baars, H., Kemper, H., Lasi, H., and Siegel, M. (2008). Combining RFID Technology and Business Intelligence for Supply Chain Optimization Scenarios for Retail Logistics. In Proceedings of the Proceedings of the 41st Annual Hawaii International Conference on System Sciences (January 7–10, 2008). HICSS. IEEE Computer Society, Washington, URL http://people.ischool.berkeley.edu/~glushko/IS243 Readings/RFID-and-BI.pdf

Bonczek, R. H., Holsapple, C. W., and Whinston, A. B. (1981). *Foundations of Decision Support Systems*. New York, NY: Academic Press.

Bush, V. (1945). As We May Think. *The Atlantic Monthly*, 176(1), July, pp. 101–108, URL http://www.theatlantic.com/unbound/flashbks/computer/bushf.htm

Caminer, D. T. (1997). LEO and Its Applications: The Beginning of Business Computing. *The Computer Journal*, 40(10), 585–597.

Codd, E. F., Codd, S. B., and Salley, C. T. (1993). Providing OLAP (On-Line Analytical Processing) to User-Analysts: An IT Mandate. Technical Report, E. F. Codd and Associates (Sponsored by Arbor Software Corporation).

Courtney, J. F. (2007). Reflections on Decision Support, posted at DSSResources.COM, May 21, 2007, URL http://dssresources.com/reflections/courtney/courtney05212007.html

Courtney, J. F., Jr., and Jensen, R. L. (1981, Spring). Teaching DSS with DBMS. *ACM SIGMIS Database*, 12(3), 7–11.

Davenport, T. H., and Harris, J. G. (2009). What People Want (and How to Predict It). *MIT Sloan Management Review*, 50(2), 23–31.

DeSanctis, G., and Gallupe, R. B. (1987, May). A Foundation for the Study of Group Decision Support Systems. *Management Science*, 33(5), 589–609.

Engelbart, D. C. (1962) Augmenting Human Intellect: A Conceptual Framework, October 1962, Air Force Office of Scientific Research, AFOSR-3233, URL www.bootstrap.org/augdocs/friedewald030402/augmentinghumanintellect/ahi62index.html

Gorry, A., and Scott Morton, M. S. (1971, Fall). A Framework for Information Systems. *Sloan Management Review*, 13(1), 56–79.

Gray, P. (1981). The SMU Decision Room Project. Transactions of the 1st International Conference on Decision Support Systems, Atlanta, GA, pp. 122–129.

Gray, P. (1983). *Guide to IFPS (Interactive Financial Planning System)*. New York, NY: McGraw-Hill Book Company.

Gray, P. (2007). Reflections on Decision Support, posted at DSSResources.COM, April 7, 2007, URL http://dssresources.com/reflections/gray/gray04072007.html

Holsapple, C. W. (2008) Reflections on Decision Support, posted at DSSResources.COM, April 27, 2008, URL http://dssresources.com/reflections/holsapple/holsapple04272008.html

Houdeshel, Ga. nd, and Watson, H. (1987, March). The Management Information and Decision Support (MIDS) System at Lockheed-Georgia. *MIS Quarterly*, 11(1), 127–140.

Huber, G. P. (1982). Group Decision Support Systems as Aids in the Use of Structured Group Management Techniques. Transactions of the 2nd International Conference on Decision Support Systems, San Francisco, CA, pp. 96–103.

Inmon, W. H. (1992). EIS and the Data Warehouse: A Simple Approach to Building an Effective Foundation for EIS. *Database Programming and Design*, 5(11), 70–73.

Kimball, R. (1994). DBMS Interview: The Doctor of DSS. *DBMS Magazine*, July 20.

Kroeker , K. L. (2010, February). Alternate Interface Technologies Emerge. *Communications of the ACM*, 53(2), 13–15.

Nambiar, A. N. (2009) RFID Technology: A Review of its Applications. In Proceedings of the World Congress on Engineering and Computer Science 2009, Vol. II, WCECS 2009, October 20–22, 2009, San Francisco, CA, USA. Available from URL: http://www.iaeng.org/publication/WCECS2009/WCECS2009_pp1253-1259.pdf

Power, D. J. (2002). *Decision Support Systems: Concepts and Resources for Managers*. Westport, CT: Greenwood/Quorum.

Power, D. J. (2007). A Brief History of Decision Support Systems. DSSResources.COM, URL http://DSSResources.COM/history/dsshistory.html, version 4.0, March 10, 2007.

Rinehart, G. (2006). A Brief History of Decision Support Systems, White Paper – URL http://decisioninterface.com/Documents/DSS%20History.pdf

Rockart, J. F. (1979). Chief Executives Define Their Own Data Needs. *Harvard Business Review*, 67, 2 March–April 1979, pp. 81–93.

Scott Morton, M. S. (1971). *Management Decision Systems; Computer-Based Support for Decision Making*. Boston, MA: Division of Research, Graduate School of Business Administration, Harvard University.

Scott Morton, M. S. (2007). Reflections on Decision Support, posted at DSSResources.COM, September 28, 2007, URL http://dssresources.com/reflections/scottmorton/scottmorton9282007.html

Scott Morton, M. S., and McCosh, A. M. (1968). Terminal Costing for Better Decisions. Harvard Business Review, 46, 3, May–June 1968, pp. 147–56.

Sharda, R., and Delen, D. (2006). Predicting Box Office Success of Motion Pictures with Neural Networks. *Expert Systems with Applications*, 30, 243–254.

Sprague, R. H., Jr., and Watson, H. J. (1979, Fall). Bit by Bit: Toward Decision Support Systems. *California Management Review*, XXII(1), 60–68.

Swanson, E. B., and Culnan, M. J. (1978, December). Document-Based Systems for Management Planning and Control: A Classification, Survey, and Assessment. *MIS Quarterly*, 2(4), 31–46.

Turoff, M. (1970). Delphi Conferencing: Computer Based Conferencing with Anonymity. *Journal of Technological Forecasting and Social Change*, 3(2), 159–204.

Turoff, M., and Hiltz, S. R. (1982). Computer Support for Group Versus Individual Decisions. *IEEE Transactions on Communications*, COM-30(1), 82–90.

Watson, H. J. (2007). Reflections on Decision Support, posted at DSSResources.COM, July 6, 2007, URL http://dssresources.com/reflections/hwatson/hwatson07062007.html

Further Readings

Gray, P. (2008). The Nature of Group Decision Support Systems. In Burstein F.C., W. Holsapple (Eds), *Handbook on Decision Support Systems: Basic Themes* (pp. 371–389). Berlin, Heidelberg: Springer.

Holsapple, C., and Whinston, A. (1996). *Decision Support Systems: A Knowledge-Based Approach*. St. Paul, MN: West Publishing.

Huber, G. P. (2007). Reflections on Decision Support, posted at DSSResources.COM, November 2, 2007, URL http://dssresources.com/reflections/huber/huber11022007.html

Inmon, W. H. (1990). *Using Oracle to Build Decision Support Systems*. Fort Bragg, CA: QED Press.

Inmon, W. H. (2007). Reflections on Decision Support, posted at DSSResources.COM, June 7, 2007, URL http://dssresources.com/reflections/inmon/inmon06072007.html

Kimball, R., Thornthwaite, W., Reeves, L., and Ross, M. (1998). *The Data Warehouse Lifecycle Toolkit*. New York, NY: Wiley.

Land, F. F. (1975). Evaluation of Systems Goals in Determining a Design Strategy for a Computer-Based Information System. *Computer Journal*, 19, 290–294.

Land, F. F. (2008). Reflections on Decision Support, posted at DSSResources.COM, March 16, 2008, URL http://dssresources.com/reflections/land/land03162008.html

Martin, D. (2008). David Caminer, a Pioneer in Computers, Dies at 92. *The New York Times*, June 29, 2008, URL http://www.nytimes.com/2008/06/29/technology/29caminer.html

McCosh, A. M. (2007). Reflections on Decision Support, posted at DSSResources.COM, December 19, 2007, URL http://dssresources.com/reflections/mccosh/mccosh12192007.html

McCosh, A. M., and Scott Morton, M. S. (1997). *Management Decision Support Systems*. London: Macmillan.

Scott Morton, M. S., and Stephens, J. A. (1968). The Impact of Interactive Visual Display Systems on the Management Planning Process. *IFIP Congress*, 2, 1178–1184.

Simmons, J. M. M. (1962). *LEO and the Managers*. London: Macdonald.

Wagner, G. R. (2007). Reflections on Decision Support, posted at DSSResources.COM, July 22, 2007, URL http://dssresources.com/reflections/gwagner/wagner07222007.html

Watson, H. „ Houdeshel, G., and Rainer, R. K., Jr. (1997). *Building Executive Information Systems and Other Decision Support Applications*. New York, NY: Wiley.

Whinston, A. (2009). Reflections on Decision Support, posted at DSSResources. COM, January 2.

Chapter 3
The Intellectual Structure of Decision Support Systems Research (1991–2004)

Sean Eom[1]

[1] Department of Accounting and MIS, Southeast Missouri State University, Cape Girardeau, MO 63701, USA, sbeom@semo.edu

List of Acronyms

ACA	Author Cocitation Analysis
DDM	Data-Dialogue-Model
DSS	Decision Support Systems
EMS	Electronic Meeting Systems
GSS	Group Support Systems
INSPIRE	INterneg Support Program for Intercultural REsearch
KB	Knowledge Base
MCDM	Multi Criteria Decision Making
MCDSS	Multiple-Criteria Decision Support Systems
MDS	Multidimensional Scaling
MIS	Management Information Systems
MS	Management Science
NSS	Negotiation Support Systems
OR	Operations Research
SAST	Strategic Assumptions Surfacing and Testing
SI-Nets	Semantic Inheritance Networks

3.1 Introduction

Before the term DSS had formally been used, there were many other similar terms to refer to the same or similar systems such as computer aided decision systems (Ferguson and Jones, 1969), computer based decision systems (Seaberg and Seaberg, 1973), computer based management decision systems (Sprague et al., 1974), decision calculus (Little, 1970), decision and information systems (King and Cleland, 1973), decision-information systems (Montgomery and Urban, 1970), decision oriented information systems (Boer, 1972), information and decision systems (Bonini, 1963), management information decision systems (Dickson, 1968), man-machine decision systems (Gerrity, 1971), man-machine planning systems (Vasarhelyi, 1977), and management support systems (Scott Morton, 1971). In 1994, several authors used the term decision support systems (Alter, 1974; Meador

D. Schuff et al. (eds.), *Decision Support*, Annals of Information Systems 14,
DOI 10.1007/978-1-4419-6181-5_3,

and Ness, 1974). Although the idea of using computers for making better decisions was published as early as 1963, the idea described by Ferguson and Jones (1969) is considered to be the first one discussing the basic idea of DSS in the DSS literature.

Over the past 40 years (1969–2008), the area of DSS has progressed toward becoming a solid academic discipline. It is in the process of solidifying its domain and demarcating its reference disciplines. This paper addresses the question of what constitutes DSS research today. This question can be answered by many different approaches. It is possible that each DSS researcher can provide his or her own perception-based views on DSS research. This study, however, aims to provide the collective field view of the intellectual structure of DSS through the empirical consensus of authors of 1,488 citing articles. These articles were published in 131 journals in DSS and MIS areas during the period of 1991–2004. It identifies the intellectual structure and major themes in DSS research, using multivariate analysis of an author cocitation matrix. The intellectual structure of an academic discipline refers to subspecialties/sub-domains within a particular discipline and how each of subspecialties is inter-related together.

3.2 Background

Within the managerial and organizational context, it was in the early 1950s when one of the first computers began to process payroll data. Since then, the study of computers and information systems has evolved continuously. Since the early 1970s, scholars in the management information systems (MIS)/decision support systems (DSS) areas have recognized the important roles computer-based information systems play in supporting managers in their semi-structured or unstructured decision making activities. For example, Gorry and Scott Morton (1971, p. 57) made the controversial claim that "Information systems should exist only to support decisions." Since then, there has been a growing amount of research in the area of DSS (Elam et al., 1986; Eom and Lee, 1990a; Farhoomand, 1987; Teng and Galletta, 1990). As Keen (1980) indicated in the early 1980s, it is necessary for information systems research to clarify reference disciplines and to build a cumulative tradition to become a coherent and substantive field. This is necessary for DSS research as well. In the DSS area, Eom et al. (1993) conducted an initial study to identify two areas of contributing disciplines (management science and multiple criteria decision making) and five subspecialties of DSS research (foundations, group DSS, database management systems, multiple-criteria DSS, marketing DSS, and routing DSS). Due to the restrictive nature of their data set (specific DSS applications only), their study failed to provide a comprehensive picture of DSS research subspecialties.

Several recent surveys have reported a macro-view of decision support systems development status and their evolution as an academic field. A study by Farhoomand (1987) reports that DSS has been one of the five top research themes and has shown steadily increasing acceptance among information systems researchers in the last 9 years (1977–1985). A recent survey, based on perceptions of a sample of MIS researchers, reports that almost one third of the respondents were conducting DSS research (Teng and Galletta, 1990). The results of another survey indicate that an increasing number of decision support systems have been developed and implemented in many for-profit and not-for-profit organizations in every functional area of decision making (Eom and Lee, 1990b). All these research efforts indicate that the fields of DSS have become an important part of computer-based information systems.

As a field of study continues to grow and becomes a coherent field, study of the intellectual development of the field is important. Culnan (1986, p. 156) stressed its importance in this way: "Researchers can benefit by understanding this process and its outcomes because it reveals the vitality and the evolution of thought in a discipline and because it gives a sense of its future. In a relatively new field such as MIS, this understanding is even more beneficial because it identifies the basic commitments that will serve as the foundations of the field as it matures." For DSS to become a coherent and substantive field, a continuing line of research must be built on the foundation of previous work. Without it, there may be good individual fragments rather than a cumulative tradition (1980). When speaking about a cumulative research tradition, Keen (1980, p. 18) emphasized the importance of reflecting upon research that has already been done: "It atrophies if it cuts itself off from curiosity, diversity, and reflection" and "Let us make sure we keep a few philosophers, historians, general systems theorists and social activists within our network; even if only to write useful survey papers."

A number of prior studies have been conducted to assess the extent of progress within these stages in the information systems area. Culnan (1986, 1987) and Cushing (1990) conducted examinations of the intellectual evolution and development of the MIS area. These authors concluded that significant progress had been made toward a cumulative research tradition in MIS and identified several groups of MIS research subfields. On the other hand, others perceived that MIS researchers felt that there was an overemphasis on transient topics and that there was continuing evidence of fragmentation and lack of both a cumulative research tradition and articulated MIS theories (Farhoomand, 1987; Teng and Galletta, 1990). Thus, there have been conflicting assessments as to the existence of a cumulative research tradition in the MIS area and the evolution of MIS as a field of scientific research. In the DSS area, several studies (Eom, 1995, 1996, 1998a, 1998b) conducted to identify the intellectual structure, cumulative tradition, and reference disciplines of DSS, up to 1995.

3.3 Data

The data for this study were gathered from a total of 1,488 citing articles in the DSS area over the past 14 years (1991–2004). These 1,488 articles were collected from DSS application and other articles. The number of citing articles can be an indicator of vitality of the DSS area. During the past 10 years, DSS researchers have published 984 articles at an average rate of 98.4 articles per year, while researchers published a total of 632 articles at an average rate of 31.6 articles per year in the previous two decades. The number of published articles has continuously increased every year over the past three decades. However, the number of published articles peaked in 1998 and then slowly decreased to 90 articles in 2004.

These 1,488 articles consist of specific DSS application articles and non-application articles. Specific DSS application articles were chosen by using the following three criteria: (1) A description of semi- or unstructured decisions; (2) A description of the human-computer interface and the nature of the computer-based support for decision makers' intuitions and judgments; and (3) A description of a data-dialogue-model system. The non-application articles were selected if they satisfy one of the following conditions: (1) It must discuss development, implementation, operation, impact, or DSS components. (2) For DSS articles related to contributing disciplines, they must be explicitly related to the development, implementation, operation, use, or impact of DSS or DSS components.

3.4 Research Methodology

This research is based on Author Cocitation Analysis (ACA). ACA can be defined as "a set of data gathering, analytical, and graphical display techniques that can be used to produce empirical maps of prominent authors in various areas of scholarship" (McCain, 1990). ACA is based on the assumptions that "bibliographic citations are an acceptable surrogate for the actual influence of various information sources" (McCain, 1986) and that the cocitation analysis of a field yields a valid representation of the intellectual structure of the field (McCain, 1984, 1990). Authors whose works are cited together frequently are interpreted as having close relationships between them. ACA is based on the assumptions that "cocitation is a measure of the perceived similarity, conceptual linkage, or cognitive relationship between two cocited items (documents or authors)" and "cocitation studies of specialties and fields yield valid representations of intellectual structure" (McCain, 1986).

ACA is the principal bibliometric tool to establish relationships among authors in an academic field. Thus ACA can identify subspecialties of a field and how closely each subgroup is related to each of the other subgroups. By establishing relationships among authors, ACA provides a basis of revealing the intellectual structure of literature and defining the principal subject (major area of subspecialties in an academic discipline and their contributing disciplines) through the empirical consensus of the majority of DSS article authors (Eom, 2009).

Using the cocitation rate of 25 with himself or herself in the period (1991–2004), the final author set of 119 authors is chosen. Roughly speaking, these chosen authors represent the authors of the top 1% of all published DSS research papers in terms of citation frequency. The raw cocitation matrix of 119 authors is analyzed by the factor, cluster, and multidimensional scaling procedures of SAS (statistical analysis systems) to ascertain the underlying structure of DSS research subspecialties.

3.5 Results of Multivariate Analysis

The outputs of ACA SAS procedures include rotated factor patterns, factor structure correlations, inter-factor correlations (factor procedure outputs), dendrogram (cluster procedure output), two-dimensional plots, and annotated three dimensional scatter plot (MDS procedure outputs). All outputs from the three procedures are basically producing identical outputs in terms of the resulting intellectual structure of the DSS field. The factor procedure output shows the final factor structure outcomes that list all factors extracted in the order of the size of variances explained by each factor, from the largest to smallest. On the other hand, the cluster analysis resulted in the dendrogram (tree graph). It shows how each of the authors in the study is combined into a new aggregate cluster until all authors are grouped into one final cluster (CL1). In other words, the dendrogram shows the process of forming a research subspecialty by combining authors based on Person's correlations coefficient, which is used as a measure of the perceived similarity, conceptual linkage, or cognitive relationship. Finally, the MDS procedures produce two-dimensional and three dimensional spatial representations of all authors under study. The MDS map shows inter-relationships among research subspecialties as well as the relationships among authors within a research subspecialty.

Factor analysis, cluster analysis, and multidimensional scaling are complementary techniques which use the identical dataset (cocitation matrix), but produce slightly different outputs. The outputs may provide us with a different aspect of identifying the intellectual structure of an academic field. The critical difference is that the cluster procedure shows the process of how the final cluster (CL1) is formed starting from original (N–1) clusters, where N is the number of variables. Comparison of the three solutions from the three multivariate analyses may provide some valuable information on the similarities and differences to help us reach a better interpretation of the results of multivariate analysis. Due to space limitations, this paper included the dendrogram and two-dimensional maps.

The cluster analysis resulted in the dendrogram (Fig. 3.1), which illustrates hierarchical clustering of seven groups of DSS researchers. Figure 3.1 shows both the cluster structure and the joining sequence. This figure shows how each of the authors in the study is combined into a new aggregate cluster until all 119 authors are grouped into the final cluster (CL1). However, the dendrogram is constructed to show only seven clusters of DSS research. Figure 3.1 shows, from the top, model management, user-interface/implementation, evaluation, foundations, multiple-criteria decision support systems (MCDSS)/negotiation support systems (NSS), and group support systems (GSS). The dendrogram also shows one more step of clustering procedures below the cutoff line, if an eight cluster solution is desirable.

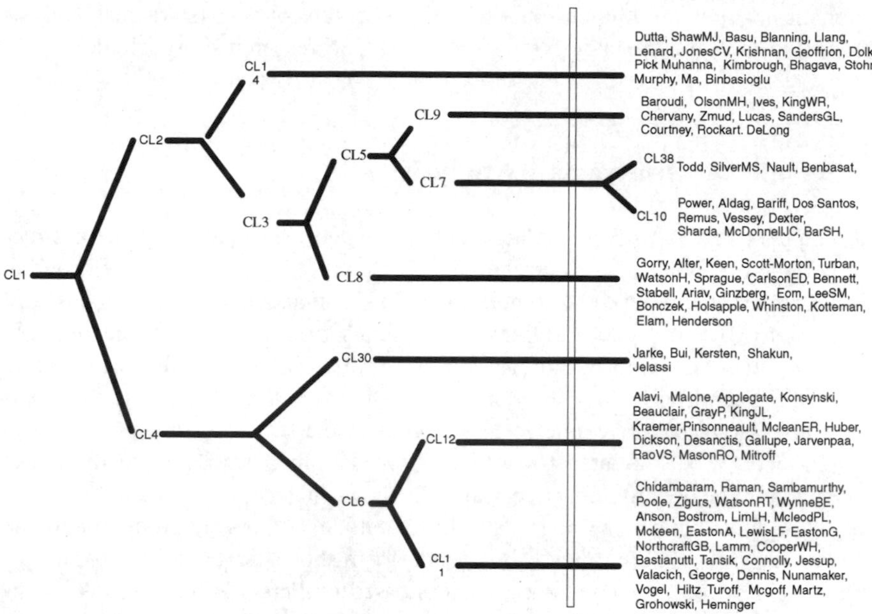

Fig. 3.1 Dendrogram depicting cluster structure and joining sequence (1991–2004)

The dendrogram shows a linkage among various clusters, and influence could be inferred based on the close examination of the works of authors in the clusters. The area of decision support systems (CL1) has two distinctive big branches (CL2 and CL4). Cluster 2 is divided into two branches (the model management cluster with no more branches and cluster 3). The cluster 3 braches into two clusters (the foundation cluster with no more branches and cluster 5 representing user-interface/implementation, and evaluation subspecialties). Cluster 4 consists of two clusters (the MCDSS/NSS cluster with no more branches and group support systems/electronic meeting systems cluster that has two more branches).

First, factors 7 and 8 in Table 3.1 did not appear as separate clusters in Fig. 3.1. Two authors (Vessey and Todd) with factor loadings greater than 0.7 belong to cluster 7. Rather than interpreting factors 7 with only two authors (Vessey and Todd) with factor loadings greater than 0.7 and factor 8 (Mason and Mitroff) as separate factors, It is more desirable to merge these authors to other clusters. In GSS, the cluster analysis suggests that GSS factor is a combination of two different clusters (cluster 11 and cluster 12). Second, authors can be loaded more than one factor, while each cluster contains only one unique author. No author can appear in more than one cluster. Therefore, cluster analysis output alone may not accurately reflect the contributions of each author to each area of DSS research subspecialties. For example, Mason and Mitroff significantly contributed to the user interface and group support systems area. Their work (Mason and Mitroff, 1981) on Strategic Assumptions Surfacing and Testing (SAST) was the model Applegate

Table 3.1 Comparison of the results of factor and cluster analyses

Factor solution	Corresponding cluster solution
Factor 1 Group support systems	Cluster 6
Factor 2 Model management	Cluster 14
Factor 3 Foundations	Cluster 8
Factor 4 Evaluation	Cluster 7
Factor 5 User interface	Cluster 9
Factor 6 MCDSS/NSS	Cluster 30
Factor 7 Unnamed	Part of cluster 7
Factor 8 Unnamed	Part of cluster 6

used to develop automated support for stakeholder identification and assumption surfacing module of PLEXSYS groupware (Applegate, 1986). Their 1973 article on "a program for research on management information systems" (Mason and Mitroff, 1973) laid the strong foundation for research on individual difference, user interfaces, and implementation research. Nonetheless, cluster analysis does not show any of their contributions to other DSS research subspecialties except only one area (GSS).

Group Support Systems (GSS): Cluster6/Factor 1 appears to define group decision support systems (GDSS), group support systems (GSS) and electronic meeting systems (EMS). Fifty-eight of all DSS scholars (48%) were clustered into factor 1. The authors in the GSS/EMS factor account to 36.14% of the common variance. GDSS/GSS/EMS have become the most vibrant area of DSS research during the period of investigation. Since the 1990s, approximately one half of all the authors selected for this study have been in the area of GDSS/GSS/EMS. The bulk of research in computer support of the group is concerned with providing foundations (Dennis et al., 1988; DeSanctis and Gallupe, 1987), conducting empirical research to identify the relationships among new constructs and group outcomes (Connolly et al., 1990; Gallupe et al., 1988; Watson et al., 1988; Zigurs et al., 1988) and integration of prior empirical studies using quantitative (Benbasat and Lim, 1993), qualitative (Dennis et al., 1990; George et al., 1990), and theoretical approaches (DeSanctis and Poole, 1994).

Model Management: Cluster 14/Factor 2 appears to represent model management. Since 1975, model management has been researched to encompass several central topics (see Table 3.2). The authors in the model management factor can be broadly classified into the following three broad areas: model representation; model manipulation; and modeling approach/modeling system developments.

Foundations: Cluster 8/Factor 3 seems to represent the foundations of DSS. During the first two decades (1969–1989) of DSS research, a large number of authors (18 out of 67) were loaded to the foundation factor with factor loadings greater than 0.7. Since 1990, the authors loaded to the foundation factor remain the same number. The relative proportion and substantiality of the foundation factor have decreased from 28.77 to 18.7%, in terms of percent of variance explained by this factor. The intellectual structure of DSS emerged in this study during the

Table 3.2 Issues in model management

Issues	Approach	Researchers
Model representation	Semantic inheritance networks (SI-Nets)	Elam et al. (1980)
	Knowledge abstraction	Dolk and Konsynski (1984) and Konsynski and Dolk (1982)
	Predicate calculus	Bonczek et al. (1980, 1981b, 1987)
	Relational	Blanning (1982, 1984, 1985)
	Models as data	Lenard (1986, 1993)
	Embedded language	Bhargava and Kimbrough (1993)
	Structured modeling	Geoffrion (1987)
Model manipulation/integration	Structured modeling	Geoffrion (1987)
	Graph-based approach	Basu and Blanning (1994), Greenberg and Maybee (1981), Liang (1988) and Muhanna (1994)
	Relational approach	Blanning (1985)
	Models as components of KB and integration as inference	Banerjee and Basu (1993), Binbasioglu and Jarke (1986), Bonczek et al. (1981a), Dutta and Basu (1984), Kottemann and Dolk (1992), Krishnan (1991) and Ma et al. (1989)
	Machine learning	Shaw et al. (1988)
	Object-oriented model integration	Dempster and Ireland (1991)
Modeling approach/systems development	Subscript-free modeling languages	Lin et al. (2000)
	Graph-based modeling	Jones (1995)
	Modeling by example	Angehrn (1991)
	Visual interactive modeling systems	Beroggi (2001)
	Expert systems-embedded active modeling systems	Dolk and Kridel (1991)
	Automatic formulation of optimization models	Binbasioglu and Jarke (1986), Bu-Hulaiga and Jain (1988), Krishnan (1988, 1990), Muhanna and Pick (1988) and Murphy and Stohr (1986)

two investigation periods (1969–2004) vividly tells us that Sprague, Keen, Carlson, Scott-Morton, H. Watson, Alter, Gorry, etc. laid the strong foundation and built the skeleton of the intellectual structure of the DSS research. Nevertheless, their influences have been decreasing over the past two decades.

Cluster 8/Factor 3 also includes authors in design of DSS (Ariav and Ginzberg, 1985; Cats-Baril and Huber, 1987; Gorry and Scott Morton, 1971; Keen and Scott Morton, 1978; Silver, 1990; Sprague, 1980; Sprague and Carlson, 1982). DSS design is the process of identifying the key decisions through decision analysis and specifying the requirements of each DSS component in order to support key decisions identified through decision analysis. Some notable contributions include Ariav and Ginzberg (1985). They presented a systemic view DSS design, based on the conventional systems theoretic taxonomy for describing the major aspects of a system: environment, role, components, architecture (arrangement of components), and resources. Besides, a number of empirical studies were conducted to test the existing DSS design frameworks/theory such as Igbaria and Guimaraes (1994), who empirically tested the outcomes of user involvement in DSS development. This established the positive relationship between user involvement and several measures of system success A contingency model of DSS design methodology was developed by Arinze (1991) to help DSS developers select an appropriate methodology out of several methodologies of data-driven, process driven (Keen and Scott Morton, 1978; Sprague and Carlson, 1982), decision-driven (Stabell, 1983), and systemic paradigms (Ariav and Ginzberg, 1985).

Others began to investigate new lines of research questions such as stimulus-based DSS, which can criticize the user. This idea was termed as the conversational framework of DSS, as opposed to the traditional passive DSS framework in which DSS provides a set of operations research (OR) management science (MS) tools. A design theory of vigilant executive information systems is outlined to provide rigorous and valid guidance to EIS design. It is presented as an approach of building executive information systems (Walls et al., 1992). Vigilance is defined as "the ability of an information system to help executive remain alertly watchful for weak signals and discontinuities in the organizational environment relevant to emerging strategic threats and opportunities" (Walls et al., 1992, p. 36).

Evaluation: Cluster 8/Factor 4 seems to represent the evaluation of DSS. The evaluation of DSS is concerned with analyzing the costs and benefits of decision support systems before and after DSS development and implementation. The value of DSS can be measured by eight methodologies: (1) decision outputs; (2) changes in the decision process; (3) changes in managers' concepts of the decision situation; (4) procedural changes; (5) classical cost/benefit analysis; (6) service measures; (7) managers' assessment of the system's value; and (8) anecdotal evidence (Keen and Scott Morton, 1978). Authors under this factor, however, have primarily investigated the effects of DSS on the quality of decisions, user attitudes toward DSS, and decision confidence.

Aldag and Power (1986) conducted a laboratory study on the effects of computerized decision aids on the quality of decision. This study was based on the review of a number of prior research papers. In doing so, individual differences are incorporated as an independent variable to find correlations of attitude toward the decision aid to individual-difference indices. The result of Aldag and Power's study detected no significant differences in performances, although user attitudes toward the computer-based decision aid were favorable and users gained more decision confidence.

Sharda et al. (1988) reviewed the results of four representative case studies, six field studies, three field tests, and 11 laboratory studies. Field and laboratory test based studies reached inconclusive results with regard to the positive impacts of DSS users over the users without DSS. Further, Sharda et al. (1988)

conducted an experimental investigation using an executive decision making game. They discovered that the groups with DSS made significantly more effective decisions, examined more alternatives, and exhibited a higher confidence level in their decisions than their non-DSS counterparts.

Todd and Benbasat (1991, 1992) conducted numerous laboratory experiments and concluded that the use of a decision aid may result in effort savings, but not improved decision performance. In other words, DSS may help the decision maker be more efficient, but not more effective. Therefore, they suggested that DSS designers consider the decision maker's trade-off between improving decision quality and conserving effort. The cost-benefit theory generally views problem solving as a trade-off between the effort to make a decision and the accuracy of the outcome, regardless of the characteristics of the tasks that must be performed.

Cognitive fit theory developed by Vessey (1991, 1994) and Vessey and Galletta (1991) specifically provide a useful guideline for the designers of decision support systems for tasks involving graphical and/or tabular representation of data in the decision making process. However, there are a large number of DSS applications that do not critically depend on the use of tables or graphs (e.g., optimization model based DSS). Vessey and Galletta (1991) argue that supporting the task with the appropriate display format leads to minimization of both effort and error. Therefore, system designers should concentrate on determining the characteristics of the tasks that problem solvers must address, and supporting those tasks with the appropriate problem representation and support tools.

User-Interface/Implementation: Cluster 9/Factor 5, User Interface/Implementation, is a new factor that emerged in this study. The design, implementation, and evaluation of information systems are an integrated and inseparable process. DSS implementation research aims to systematically identify factors which will influence the implementation success of DSS so that those critical factors can be managed effectively. This factor includes authors those who studied the success measures of MIS/DSS. There are several milestones in DSS implementation research in chronological sequence.

- A path analytical model examining individual differences and MIS success (Zmud, 1979) based more than 100 empirical studies in the 1970s
- An analysis of 22 studies up to 1981 to examine User involvement and MIS success (Ives and Olson, 1984)
- A path analytic model to examine user involvement, system usage, and user's satisfaction (Baroudi et al., 1986)
- A field study examining decision context (semi-structured or unstructured) and DSS success (Sanders and Courtney, 1985)
- A meta analysis of 144 implementation research examining User factors and DSS success (Alavi and Joachimsthaler, 1992)
- A broad research methodology (Actor-Network Theory) based implementation research (Walsham and Sahay, 1999)

Individual Differences and MIS Success: Zmud (1979) synthesized the literature of more than 100 empirical studies by examining the effects of a number of cognitive, personality, demographic, and situational variables upon information processing and decision behavior. His conclusion (individual differences do exert a major force in determining MIS success) was later refuted by Huber (1983, p. 567), who concluded that "the currently available literature on cognitive styles is an unsatisfactory basis for deriving operational guidelines for MIS and DSS designs" and "further cognitive style research is unlikely to lead to operational guidelines for MIS and DSS designs."

Ives and Olson's review of research found conflicting relationships between user involvement and various measures of MIS success and presented a descriptive model of user involvement in which user involvement, system quality, and system acceptance were major constructs. A later study of Baroudi et al. (1986) demonstrated that user involvement in the development of information systems will enhance both system usage and the user's satisfaction with the system. Further, the study provides evidence that the user's satisfaction with the system will lead to greater system usage. Subsequent meta-analysis of Alavi and Joachimsthaler (1992) confirmed the findings of Baroudi et al. (1986) and suggested that user factors (cognitive style, personality, demographics, user-situational variables) do impact DSS success. It also suggested that the user-situational variables (involvement, training and experience) are more important than cognitive styles and personality.

Another approach drawn from contextualism is introduced using actor network theory (Callon, 1986a, b; Latour, 1987; Law, 1992). Walsham and Sahay (1999) applied a new research method (actor network theory) to explain why geographical information systems (GIS) were not successfully implemented in India via examining the fundamental attitudes, perception, and social structure. They provide an in-depth analysis of a major GIS initiative from a particular Indian government ministry. Using a qualitative case study, they presented a new interesting information system implementation context. This could not have been explained by other implementation research approaches such as individual differences of human actors (Zmud, 1979), organizational and task environmental factors (Sanders and Courtney, 1985), and user factors (Alavi and Joachimsthaler, 1992). Using actor-network theory, they assert that the GIS technology, a non-human actor, enforces values of its developers which to some extent are, at odds with the value of the countries where it is implemented and the cultural assumptions. Consequently, the GIS technology served to constrain its own diffusion and implementation in India.

MCDSS/NSS: Factor 6 seems to represent two groups of authors – Multiple Criteria Decision Support Systems (MCDSS) and negotiation support systems (NSS). The first group represents MCDSS researchers as defined by (Bui, 1984; 1987; Jarke, 1986; Jelassi and Foroughi, 1989; Jelassi et al., 1985). An MCDSS can be defined as an MCDM model embedded DSS to solve various semistructured and unstructured decisions involving multiple attributes or multiple objectives or both. According to Zeleny (1982, p. 17), the term "multiple criteria decision making" (MCDM) indicates a concern with the general class of problems that involve multiple attributes, objectives, and goals. Attributes are the characteristics of objects in the real world. These attributes can be specified "in relative independence from the decision maker's needs or desires." (Zeleny, 1982, p. 15). Objectives, which are "closely identifiable with a decision maker's needs and desires," specify (1) a set of attributes (or an attribute) and (2) "directions of improvement or preferences along individual attributes or complexes of attributes." (Zeleny, 1982, p. 15).

MCDSS can be broadly categorized into the following: data-oriented MCDSS (Jelassi et al., 1985) utilizing multiattribute decision making models; model-oriented MCDSS utilizing multiple objective decision making models (Eom et al., 1987), and MCDM model embedded Group DSS (Bui and Jarke, 1984). MCDSS intend to provide the necessary computerized assistance to decision makers in such a way that the decision makers are encouraged to explore the support tools available. Integration of MCDM into DSS has long been advocated by the researchers in both areas. The founding fathers of DSS such as Keen and Scott Morton (1978, p. 48) believe that the multiple criteria decision problem is at the core of decision support and "a marriage between MCDM and DSS promises to be practically and intellectually fruitful." Since MCDM inherently necessitates a simultaneous comparison of the large number of decision criteria and alternatives, which demand a complex array of information, an integration of MCDM with DSS is inevitable. The rationale may be that MCDM models can be useful tools for DSS problem solving, while DSS helps maintain and retrieve MCDM models for the repeated usage. Indeed, Weistroffer and Narula (1997) argued that efficient and user-friendly DSSs are crucial for successfully solving real-world MCDM problems.

In the area of NSS, most of MCDSS researchers are in fact NSS researchers too, because the essential element of both systems is MCDM models. NSS researchers built systems such as MEDIATOR (Jarke et al., 1987), multi-attribute NSS with market signaling (Bui et al., 2001), NSS for hostage crisis management (Wilkenfeld et al., 1995), NegocIAD based on a multi-agent architecture from distributed artificial intelligence (Espinasse et al., 1997), and INSPIRE (INterneg Support Program for Intercultural Research) (Kersten and Noronha, 1999). INSPIRE is a Web-based asynchronous NSS generator/shell. Others proposed a theoretical model that seeks to improve negotiation outcomes in terms of the following five dependent variables – time to settlement, satisfaction, distance from efficient frontiers, distance from Nash solution (fairer solution), and confidence with solution (Lim and Benbasat, 1992).

3.6 Results of Multi-dimensional Scaling Analysis

While cluster analysis shows a detailed structure of clusters, multidimensional scaling (MDS) procedures produces several two-dimensional and three-dimensional maps. The maps show a geometric representation of the relationships among all authors in a Euclidean space (ordinary two- or three-dimensional space).

Figure 3.2 presents a two-dimensional MDS map. The vertical axis represents dimension 1 (group support systems) and the horizontal axis represents dimension 2 (model management). Each author is represented by an asterisk (*) in the two

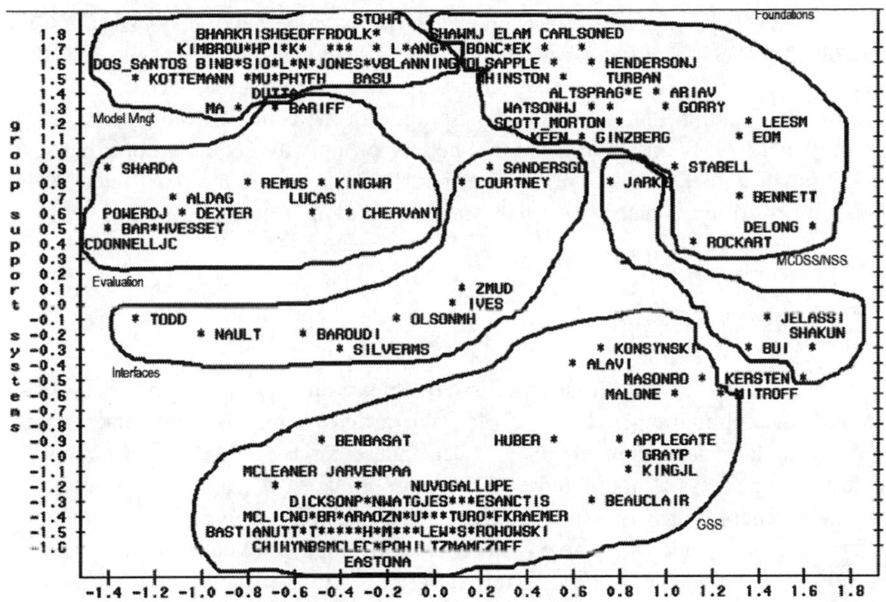

Fig. 3.2 Two dimensional MDS map (Note: 12 observations hidden. 141 label characters hidden)

dimensional Euclidian space. The boundaries of each DSS subspecialty are drawn manually using the results of factor and cluster analyses.

Using an analogy, the DSS field can be compared to a tree that has two major branches. The first branch consists of 4 sub-branches of foundations, model management, interfaces, and evaluation. The second branch has two sub-branches of group support systems and MCDSS/NSS. Adding an imaginary diagonal line from the lower left corner points extending to the upper right corner, we see there are two big branches above and below the diagonal line.

The proximities within a subspecialty: The placement of authors on the center of each DSS subspecialty, as represented by the boundary line, means that those authors are linked with a substantial portion of the author set, with relatively high correlations. For example, see the placement of Dennis, Nunamaker, Vogel, and Gallupe on the map. Dennis is hidden. Nunamaker, Vogel, and Gallupe are placed all together with the label (NUVOGALLUPE) in the center of the GDSS subspecialty group.

The proximities between subspecialties: In the figures representing group support systems on the X2 axis and model management on the X1 axis, placement near the periphery represents a more focused linkage. This is illustrated by the model management researchers (Blanning, Bonczek, Whinston, and Holsapple) located in the upper-right hand area. The best way to interpret this two-dimensional map is to add a diagonal line starting at the left bottom point (–2, –2) to the right upper point (2, 2). The diagonal line divides all of the subspecialties into two groups of interrelated subspecialties. The first group, below the diagonal line, consists of GSS and MCDSS/NSS. The second group, above the diagonal line, represents all other areas (model management, foundations, evaluation, and user-interfaces). The location of the founding fathers, especially Sprague in the center of the groups above the diagonal line, seems to indicate that he has strongly and equally contributed to model management, evaluation, and user interfaces areas. On the other hand, Keen and Scott-Morton are placed near the evaluation and interfaces groups.

3.7 Limitations

This research has several limitations. First, this research data cover only 1991–2004. Second, the bibliographic database of citing articles contains only model-based DSS, excluding data-oriented DSS. Third, the research method of bibliometrics includes a weakness of not including rising stars in the field. Some great ideas from new researchers flourish to form a research subspecialty. Some perish. However, ACA will not include those new researchers until their publications are cited frequently to a certain level. Fourth, the empirical map of prominent DSS authors presented here is based on the selection criteria of using the minimum number of co-citation frequency we used. We fully acknowledge the numerous contributions of all the other authors who were not selected in the final author set. Despite the limitations, the DSS research subspecialties that appeared in this study represent the collective field view of the intellectual structures of DSS over the period of 1991–2004.

3.8 Conclusions

We have documented the intellectual structure of DSS during the period of 1991–2004. The intellectual structure of any academic field must be understood as an on-going developmental process of past, present, and future. This paper overviews the accomplishments of the DSS field. It also attempts to answer the question of what DSS is today and what DSS research constitutes. When comparing the results of the previous investigation period (1969–1989) (Eom and Farris, 1996), this research clearly shows that the DSS area is solidifying its domain. Over the period of 1969 through 1989, DSS research had mainly concentrated on each component of (data/model/dialogue/decision maker) specific DSS. Over the past 15 years (1990–2004), the domain of DSS research has expanded from the data-dialogue-model (DDM) emphasis to include Keen and Scott Morton's DSS framework emphasizing design, implementation, and evaluation (Keen and Scott Morton, 1978) and group support systems and electronic meeting systems. Besides, DSS research subspecialties that have emerged in this study, not reported in this paper, reflect the influence of a wide range of reference disciplines from which good ideas, theories, methodologies, philosophical bases, and assumptions are adopted or borrowed. The DSS reference disciplines include cognitive science, psychology, management science, systems science, communication science, organizational science, and multiple criteria decision making.

References

Alavi, M., and Joachimsthaler, E. A. (1992). Revisiting DSS Implementation Research: A Meta-Analysis of the Literature and Suggestions for Researchers. *MIS Quarterly*, 16(1), 95–116.

Aldag, R. J., and Power, D. J. (1986). An Empirical Assessment of Computer-Assisted Decision Analysis. *Decision Sciences*, 17(4), 572–588.

Alter, S. L. (1974). *Eight Case Studies of Decision Support Systems*. Cambridge, MA: Center for Information Systems Research, Sloan School of Management, MIT.

Angehrn, A. A. (1991). Modeling by Example: A Link between Users, Models and Methods in DSS. *European Journal of Operational Research*, 55(3), 296–308.

Applegate, L. M. (1986). *Idea Management in Organization Planning*. Unpublished Ph.D. Dissertation, University of Arizona, Tucson, AZ.

Ariav, G., and Ginzberg, M. J. (1985). DSS Design: A Systemic View of Decision Support. *Communications of the ACM*, 28(10), 1045–1052.

Arinze, B. (1991). A Contingency Model of DSS Development Methodology. *Journal of Management Information Systems*, 8(1), 149–166.

Banerjee, S., and Basu, A. (1993). Model Type Selection in an Integrated DSS Environment. *Decision Support Systems*, 9(1), 75–89.

Baroudi, J. J., Olsen, M. H., and Ives, B. (1986). An Empirical Study of the Impact of User Involvement on Systems Usage and Information Satisfaction. *Communications of the ACM*, 29(3), 232–238.

Basu, A., and Blanning, R. W. (1994). Metagraphs: A Tool for Modeling Decision Support Systems. *Management Science*, 40(12), 1579–1600.

Benbasat, I., and Lim, L. -H. (1993). The Effects of Group, Task, Context, and Technology Variables on the Usefulness of Group Support Systems: A Meta-Analysis of Experimental Studies. *Small Group Research*, 24(4), 430–462.

Beroggi, G. E. G. (2001). Visual-Interactive Decision Modeling (Videmo) in Policy Management: Bridging the Gap between Analytic and Conceptual Decision Modeling. *European Journal of Operational Research*, 128(2), 338–350.

Bhargava, H. K., and Kimbrough, S. O. (1993). Model Management: An Embedded Languages Approach. *Decision Support Systems*, 10, 277–299.

Binbasioglu, M., and Jarke, M. A. (1986). Domain Specific DSS Tools for Knowledge-Based Model Building. *Decision Support Systems*, 2(3), 213–223.

Blanning, R. W. (1982). A Relational Framework for Model Management in Decision Support Systems. In G. W. Dickson (Ed.), *Decision Support Systems-82 Transactions* (pp. 16–28). San Francisco, CA.

Blanning, R. W. (1984). Conversing with Management Information Systems in Natural Language. *Communications of the ACM*, 27(3), 201–207.

Blanning, R. W. (1985). A Relational Framework for Join Implementation in Model Management Systems. *Decision Support Systems*, 1(1), 69–81.

Boer, G. A. (1972). A Decision Oriented Information System. *Journal of Systems Management*, 23(10), 36–39.

Bonczek, R. H., Holsapple, C. W., and Whinston, A. B. (1980). The Evolving Roles of Models in Decision Support Systems. *Decision Sciences*, 11(2), 337–356.

Bonczek, R. H., Holsapple, C. W., and Whinston, A. B. (1981a). *Foundations of Decision Support Systems*. New York, NY: Academic Press.

Bonczek, R. H., Holsapple, C. W., and Whinston, A. B. (1981b). A Generalized Decision Support System Using Predicate Calculus and Network Data Base Management. *Operations Research*, 29(2), 263–281.

Bonczek, R. H., Holsapple, C. W., and Whinston, A. B. (1987). The Evolution of MIS to DSS: Extension from Data Management to Model Management. In M. J. Ginzberg, W. R. Reitman, and E. A. Stohr (Eds.), *Decision Support Systems: Proceedings of the NYU Symposium on Decision Support Systems, New York, 21–22 May 1981* (pp. 61–78). Amsterdam; New York, NY; Oxford: North-Holland Publishing Company.

Bonini, C. P. (1963). *Simulation of Information and Decision Systems in the Firm*. Englewood Cliffs, NJ: Prentice Hall.

Bu-Hulaiga, M., and Jain, H. K. (1988). An Interactive Plan-Based Procedure for Model Integration in DSS. Paper presented at the 21st Annual Hawaii International Conference on System Sciences Kailua-Kona, HI.

Bui, T. X. (1984). Building Effective Multiple Criteria Decision Support Models: A Decision Support System Approach. *Systems, Objectives, Solutions*, 4(1), 3–16.

Bui, T. X. (1987). *Co-Op: A Group Decision Support System for Cooperative Multiple Criteria Decision Making* (Vol. 290). Berlin: Springer.

Bui, T. X., and Jarke, M. A. (1984). A DSS for Cooperative Multiple Criteria Group Decision Making. In Proceedings of the 5th International Conference on Information Systems (pp. 101–113). Tucson, AZ.

Bui, T. X., Yen, J., Hu, J., and Sankaran, S. (2001). A Multi-Attribute Negotiation Support System with Market Signaling for Electronic Markets. *Group Decision and Negotiation*, 10(6), 515–537.

Callon, M. (1986a). The Sociology of an Actor-Network: The Case of the Electric Vehicle. In M. Callon, J. Law, and A. Rip (Eds.), *Mapping the Dynamics of Science and Technology* (pp. 19–34). London: Macmillan Press.

Callon, M. (1986b). Some Elements of a Sociology of Translation: Domestication of the Scallops and the Fishermen of St Brieuc Bay. In J. Law (Ed.), *Power, Action and Belief. A New Sociology of Knowledge?* (pp. 196–229). London: Routledge and Kegan Paul.

Cats-Baril, W. L., and Huber, G. P. (1987). Decision Support Systems for Ill-Structured Problems: An Empirical Study. *Decision Sciences*, 18(3), 350–372.

Connolly, T., Jessup, M., and Valacich, J. S. (1990). Effects of Anonymity and Evaluative Tone on Idea Generation in Computer-Mediated Groups. *Management Science*, 36(6), 689–703.

Culnan, M. J. (1986). The Intellectual Development of Management Information Systems, 1972–1982: A Co-Citation Analysis. *Management Science*, 32(2), 156–172.

Culnan, M. J. (1987). Mapping the Intellectual Structure of MIS, 1980–1985: A Co-Citation Analysis. *MIS Quarterly*, 11(3), 341–353.

Cushing, B. E. (1990). Frameworks, Paradigms, and Scientific Research in Management Information Systems. *Journal of Information Systems*, 4(2), 38–59.

DeSanctis, G., and Gallupe, B. (1987). A Foundation for the Study of Group Decision Support Systems. *Management Science*, 33(5), 589–609.

DeSanctis, G., and Poole, M. S. (1994). Capturing the Complexity in Advanced Technology Use: Adaptive Structuration Theory. *Organization Science*, 5(2), 121–147.

Dempster, M. A. H., and Ireland, A. M. (1991). Object-Oriented Model Integration in a Financial Decision Support System. *Decision Support Systems*, 7(4), 329–340.

Dennis, A. R., George, J. F., Jessup, L. M., Nunamaker, J. F., Jr., and Vogel, D. R. (1988). Information Technology to Support Electronic Meetings. *MIS Quarterly*, 12(4), 591–624.

Dennis, A. R., Nunamaker, J. F., Jr., and Vogel, D. R. (1990–1991). A Comparison of Laboratory and Field Research in the Study of Electronic Meeting Systems. *Journal of Management Information Systems*, 7(3), 107–135.

Dickson, G. W. (1968). Management Information Decision Systems. *Business Horizons*, 11(6), 17–26.

Dolk, D. R., and Konsynski, B. R. (1984). Knowledge Representation for Model Management Systems. *IEEE Transactions on Software Engineering*, SE-10(6), 619–628.

Dolk, D. R., and Kridel, D. J. (1991). An Active Modeling System for Econometric Analysis. *Decision Support Systems*, 7(4), 315–328.

Dutta, A., and Basu, A. (1984). An Artificial Intelligence Approach to Model Management in Decision Support Systems. *IEEE Computer*, 17(9), 89–97.

Elam, J. J., Henderson, J. C., and Miller, L. W. (1980). Model Management Systems: An Approach to Decision Support in Complex Organizations. In E. R. McLean (Ed.), Proceedings of the First International Conference on Information Systems (pp. 98–110). Philadelphia, PA.

Elam, J. J., Huber, G. P., and Hurt, M. E. (1986). An Examination of the DSS Literature (1975–1985). In E. R. McLean and H. G. Sol (Eds.), *Decision Support Systems: A Decade in Perspective* (pp. 239–251). Amsterdam, North-Holland: Elsevier Science.

Eom, S. B. (1995). Decision Support Systems Research: Reference Disciplines and a Cumulative Tradition. *Omega: The International Journal of Management Science*, 23(5), 511–523.

Eom, S. B. (1996). Mapping the Intellectual Structure of Research in Decision Support Systems through Author Cocitation Analysis (1971–1993). *Decision Support Systems*, 16(4), 315–338.

Eom, S. B. (1998a). The Intellectual Development and Structure of Decision Support Systems (1991–1995). *Omega*, 26(5), 639–658.

Eom, S. B. (1998b). Relationships Between the Decision Support System Subspecialties and Reference Disciplines: An Empirical Investigation. *European Journal of Operational Research*, 104(1), 31–45.

Eom, S. B. (2009). *Author Cocitation Analysis: Quantitative Methods for Mapping the Intellectual Structure of an Academic Discipline*. Hershey, PA: Information Science Reference.

Eom, S. B., and Farris, R. (1996). The Contributions of Organizational Science to the Development of Decision Support Systems Research Subspecialties. *Journal of the American Society for Information Science*, 47(12), 941–952.

Eom, H. B., and Lee, S. M. (1990a). Decision Support Systems Applications Research: A Bibliography (1971–1988). *European Journal of Operational Research*, 46(3), 333–342.

Eom, H. B., and Lee, S. M. (1990b). A Survey of Decision Support System Applications (1971–April 1988). *Interfaces*, 20(3), 65–79.

Eom, S. B., Lee, S. M., and Kim, J. K. (1993). The Intellectual Structure of Decision Support Systems (1971–1989). *Decision Support Systems*, 10(1), 19–35.

Eom, H. B., Lee, S. M., Snyder, C. A., and Ford, N. F. (1987–1988). A Multiple Criteria Decision Support System for Global Financial Planning. *Journal of Management Information Systems*, 4(3), 94–113.

Espinasse, B., Picolet, G., and Chouraqui, E. (1997). Negotiation Support Systems: A Multi-Criteria and Multi-Agent Approach. *European Journal of Operational Research*, 103(2), 389–409.

Farhoomand, A. F. (1987). Scientific Progress of Management Information Systems. *Data Base*, 18(4), 48–56.

Ferguson, R. L., and Jones, C. H. (1969). A Computer Aided Decision System. *Management Science*, 15(10), B550–B561.

Gallupe, R. B., DeSanctis, G., and Dickson, G. W. (1988). Computer-Based Support for Group Problem-Finding: An Experimental Investigation. *MIS Quarterly*, 12(2), 277–296.

Geoffrion, A. M. (1987). An Introduction to Structured Modeling. *Management Science*, 33(5), 547–588.

George, J. F., Easton, G. K., Nunamaker, J. F., Jr., and Northcraft, G. B. (1990). A Study of Collaborative Group Work with and Without Computer-Based Support. *Information Systems Research*, 1(4), 394–415.

Gerrity, T. P., Jr. (1971). Design of Man-Machine Decision Systems: An Application to Portfolio Management. *Sloan Management Review*, 12(2), 59–75.

Gorry, G. A., and Scott Morton, M. S. (1971). A Framework for Management Information Systems. *Sloan Management Review*, 13(1), 55–70.
Greenberg, H. J., and Maybee, J. S. (1981). *Computer Assisted Analysis and Model Simplification*. New York, NY: Academic Press.
Huber, G. P. (1983). Cognitive Style as a Basis for MIS and DSS Design: Much Ado About Nothing? *Management Science*, 29(5), 567–579.
Igbaria, M., and Guimaraes, T. (1994). Empirically Testing the Outcomes of User Involvement in DSS Development. *Omega*, 22(2), 157–172.
Ives, B., and Olson, M. H. (1984). User Involvement and MIS Success: A Review of Research. *Management Science*, 30(5), 580–603.
Jarke, M. A. (1986). Knowledge Sharing and Negotiation Support in Multiperson Decision Support Systems. *Decision Support Systems*, 2(1), 93–102.
Jarke, M. A., Jelassi, M. T., and Shakun, M. F. (1987). Mediator: Towards a Negotiation Support System. *European Journal of Operational Research*, 31(3), 314–334.
Jelassi, M. T., and Foroughi, A. (1989). Negotiation Support Systems: An Overview of Design Issues and Existing Software. *Decision Support Systems*, 5(2), 167–181.
Jelassi, M. T., Jarke, M. A., and Stohr, E. A. (1985). Designing a Generalized Multiple Criteria Decision Support System. *Journal of Management Information Systems*, 1(4), 24–43.
Jones, C. V. (1995). Development in Graph-Based Modeling for Decision Support. *Decision Support Systems*, 13(1), 61–74.
Keen, P. G. W. (1980). MIS Research: Reference Disciplines and a Cumulative Tradition. In E. R. McLean (Ed.), Proceedings of the First International Conference on Information Systems (pp. 9–18). Philadelphia, PA.
Keen, P. G. W., and Scott Morton, M. S. (1978). *Decision Support Systems: An Organizational Perspective*. Reading, MA: Addison-Wesley.
Kersten, G. E., and Noronha, S. J. (1999). Www-Based Negotiation Support: Design, Implementation, and Use. *Decision Support Systems*, 25(2), 135–154.
King, W. R., and Cleland, D. I. (1973). Decision and Information Systems for Strategic Planning. *Business Horizons*, 16, 29–36.
Konsynski, B. R., and Dolk, D. R. (1982). Knowledge Abstractions in Model Management. In: Decision Support Systems-82 Transactions (pp. 187–202). San Francisco, CA.
Kottemann, J. E., and Dolk, D. R. (1992). Model Integration and Modeling Languages: A Process Perspective. *Information Systems Research*, 3(1), 1–16.
Krishnan, R. (1988). Automated Model Construction: A Logic Based Approach. *Annals of Operations Research*, 21, 195–226.
Krishnan, R. (1990). A Logic Modeling Language for Automated Model Construction. *Decision Support Systems*, 6(2), 123–152.
Krishnan, R. (1991). Pdm: A Knowledge-Based Tool for Model Construction. *Decision Support Systems*, 7(4), 301–314.
Latour, B. (1987). *Science in Action: How to Follow Engineers and Scientists Through Society*. Cambridge, MA: Harvard University Press.
Law, J. (1992). Notes on the Theory of the Actor-Network: Ordering, Strategy and Heterogeneity. *Systems Practice*, 5(4), 379–393.
Lenard, M. L. (1986). Representing Models as Data. *Journal of Management Information Systems*, 2(4), 36–48.
Lenard, M. L. (1993). An Object-Oriented Approach to Model Management. *Decision Support Systems*, 9(1), 67–73.
Liang, T. -P. (1988). Development of a Knowledge-Based Model Management System. *Operations Research*, 36(6), 846–863.
Lim, L. -H., and Benbasat, I. (1992–1993). A Theoretical Perspective of Negotiation Support Systems. *Journal of Management Information Systems*, 9(3), 27–44.
Lin, S. -Y. E., Schuff, D., and St. Louis, R. D. (2000). Subscript-Free Modeling Languages: A Tool for Facilitating the Formulation and Use of Models. *European Journal of Operational Research*, 123(3), 614–627.

Little, J. D. C. (1970). Models and Managers: The Concepts of a Decision Calculus. *Management Science*, 16(8), B466–B485.

Ma, P. -C., Murphy, F. H., and Stohr, E. A. (1989). Semantic Structures in Linear Programs. In Proceedings of the 22nd Annual Hawaii International Conference on System Sciences (Vol. III, pp. 459–466): IEEE Computer Society Press, Los Alamitos, CA.

Mason, R. O., and Mitroff, I. I. (1973). A Program for Research on Management Information Systems. *Management Science*, 19(5), 475–487.

Mason, R. O., and Mitroff, I. I. (1981). *Challenging Strategic Planning Assumption: Theory, Cases, and Techniques*. New York, NY: John Wiley and Sons.

McCain, K. W. (1984). Longitudinal Author Cocitation Mapping: The Changing Structure of Macroeconomics. *Journal of the American Society for Information Science*, 35(6), 351–369.

McCain, K. W. (1986). Cocited Author Mapping as a Valid Representation of Intellectual Structure. *Journal of the American Society for Information Science*, 37(3), 111–122.

McCain, K. W. (1990). Mapping Authors in Intellectual Space: A Technical Overview. *Journal of the American Society for Information Science*, 41(6), 433–443.

Meador, C. L., and Ness, D. N. (1974). Decision Support System: An Application to Corporate Planning. *Sloan Management Review*, 15(2), 51–68.

Montgomery, D., and Urban, G. (1970). Marketing Decision-Information Systems: An Emerging View. *Journal of Marketing Research*, 7(2), 226–234.

Muhanna, W. A. (1994). Symms: A Model Management System That Supports Reuse, Sharing and Integration. *European Journal of Operational Research*, 72(2), 214–243.

Muhanna, W. A., and Pick, R. A. (1988). Composite Models in Symms. In Proceedings of the 21st Hawaii International Conference on System Sciences (Vol. III, pp. 418–427): IEEE Computer Society Press, Los Alamitos, CA.

Murphy, F. H., and Stohr, E. A. (1986). An Intelligent System for Formulating Linear Programs. *Decision Support Systems*, 2(1), 39–47.

Sanders, G. L., and Courtney, J. F. (1985). A Field Study of Organizational Factors Influencing DSS Success. *MIS Quarterly*, 9(1), 77–93.

Scott Morton, M. S. (1971). *Management Support Systems: Computer Based Support for Decision Making*. Cambridge, MA: Division of Research, Harvard University.

Seaberg, R. A., and Seaberg, C. (1973). Computer Based Decision Systems in Xerox Corporate Planning. *Management Science*, 20(4), 575–584.

Sharda, R., Bar, S. H., and McDonnell, J. C. (1988). Decision Support System Effectiveness: A Review and Empirical Test. *Management Science*, 34(2), 139–159.

Shaw, M. J., Tu, P. -L., and De, P. (1988). Applying Machine Learning to Model Management in Decision Support Systems. *Decision Support Systems*, 4(3), 285–305.

Silver, M. S. (1990). Decision Support Systems: Directed and Non-directed Change. *Information Systems Research*, 1(1), 47–70.

Sprague, R. H., Jr. (1980). A Framework for the Development of Decision Support Systems. *MIS Quarterly*, 4(4), 1–26.

Sprague, R. H., Jr., and Carlson, E. D. (1982). *Building Effective Decision Support Systems*. Englewood Cliffs, NJ: Prentice Hall.

Sprague, R. H., Jr., Sasaki, M., and Sato, M. (1974). *Computer Based Management Decision Systems: Conceptual Structure and a Prototype System*. Honolulu, HI: Japan-American Institute of Management Science.

Stabell, C. B. (1983). A Decision Oriented Approach to Building Decision Support Systems. In J. L. Bennett (Ed.), *Building Decision Support Systems* (pp. 221–260). Reading, MA: Addison-Wesley.

Teng, J. T. C., and Galletta, D. F. (1990). MIS Research Directions: A Survey of Researcher's Views. *Data Base*, 21(3/4), 1–10.

Todd, P. A., and Benbasat, I. (1991). An Experimental Investigation of the Impact of Computer Based Decision Aids on the Decision Making Processes. *Information Systems Research*, 2(2), 87–115.

Todd, P. A., and Benbasat, I. (1992). The Use of Information in Decision Making: An Experimental Investigation of the Impact of Computer-Based Decision Aids. *MIS Quarterly*, 16(3), 373–393.

Vasarhelyi, M. A. (1977). Man-Machine Planning Systems: A Cognitive Style Examination of Interactive Decision Making. *Journal of Accounting Research*, 15(1), 138–153.

Vessey, I. (1991). Cognitive Fit: A Theory-Based Analysis of the Graphs Versus Tables Literature. *Decision Sciences*, 22(2), 219–240.

Vessey, I. (1994). The Effect of Information Presentation on Decision Making: A Cost-Benefit Analysis. *Information and Management*, 27(2), 103–119.

Vessey, I., and Galletta, D. (1991). Cognitive Fit: An Empirical Study of Information Acquisition. *Information Systems Research*, 2(1), 63–84.

Walls, J. G., Widmeyer, G. R., and El Sawy, O. A. (1992). Building an Information System Design Theory for Vigilant Eis. *Information Systems Research*, 3(1), 36–59.

Walsham, G., and Sahay, S. (1999). Gis for District-Level Administration in India: Problems and Opportunities. *MIS Quarterly*, 23(1), 39–65.

Watson, R. T., DeSanctis, G., and Poole, M. S. (1988). Using a Gdss to Facilitate Group Consensus: Some Intended and Unintended Consequences. *MIS Quarterly*, 12(3), 463–478.

Weistroffer, H. R., and Narula, S. C. (1997). The State of Multiple Criteria Decision Support Software. *Annals of Operations Research*, 72(1), 299–313.

Wilkenfeld, J., Kraus, S., Holley, K. M., and Harris, M. A. (1995). Genie: A Decision Support System for Crisis Negotiations. *Decision Support Systems*, 14(4), 369–391.

Zeleny, M. (1982). *Multiple Criteria Decision Making*. New York, NY: McGraw-Hill.

Zigurs, I., Poole, M. S., and DeSanctis, G. (1988). A Study of Influence in Computer-Mediated Group Decision Making. *MIS Quarterly*, 12(4), 625–644.

Zmud, R. W. (1979). Individual Differences and MIS Success: A Review of the Empirical Literature. *Management Science*, 25(10), 966–979.

Chapter 4
Ethical Decision-Making and Implications for Decision Support

John R. Drake[1], Dianne J. Hall[2], and Teresa Lang[3]

[1] Eastern Michigan University, Ypsilanti, MI 48197, USA, john.drake@emich.edu
[2] Auburn University, Auburn, AL 36849, USA, dhall@auburn.edu
[3] Columbus State University, Columbus, GA 31907, USA, lang_teresa@colstate.edu

4.1 Introduction

In an effort to support ethical decision-making using information systems, it is paramount that researchers (1) accurately determine what ethical perspectives individuals hold, (2) understand how those perspectives affect decision-making in situations compounded by ethical issues, and (3) work toward designing decision support systems (DSS) that can facilitate decision-making in relation to these issues. However, little headway has been made in this area. There is little consistency in ethical perspective research, particularly in relation to how ethical perspectives impact the decision-making process or, more basically, how to identify those perspectives. In addition, research in decision support systems has only recently begun to explore behavioral and human characteristics as integral parts of the process that supports decision-making. The purpose of this chapter is to discuss a framework for analyzing the impact of ethical perspectives on decision making, identify instruments useful for identifying such perspectives, and to provide guidance for the decision support system design issues specific to decision-making contexts with an ethical component.

4.2 Background

Studies of ethical perspectives and resulting behaviors are common in areas of philosophy, psychology, theology, and other behaviorally oriented disciplines. Those studies, which often seek to guide proper behavior in given situations, reside in the area of normative ethics. Business disciplines, on the other hand, are more likely to revolve around descriptive ethics. This subset of ethics seeks to identify, explain, and predict behavior. Decision support technologies can guide behavior through suggestion and or serve to inform the decision maker such that the individual decides on the appropriate behavior for a given situation (Silver, 1991). However, such guidance will be less effective if the underlying ethical foundations of the decision maker are unknown or poorly understood.

D. Schuff et al. (eds.), *Decision Support*, Annals of Information Systems 14,
DOI 10.1007/978-1-4419-6181-5_4,

Unfortunately, an individual's ethical leanings may be difficult to uncover. There are four major obstacles that must be overcome before ethical decision-making research can advance substantially. First, it is difficult to discern what one individual regards as his or her primary belief system because different problems may lead to different ethically oriented solutions. For example, utilitarianism is an ethical belief system that is founded on the principle of "the greatest good for the greatest number" (Mills, 1863). A storekeeper may decide to price basic necessities (e.g., milk, bread) at a loss during an economic downturn. This act may be considered utilitarian. Other products that some may consider basic necessities (e.g., meat, vegetables), however, may not be reduced. This would not be considered utilitarian. This inconsistency is not only true with individuals, but with organizations as well. In an examination of code of ethics for Association for Computing Machinery (ACM), Wheeler (2003) identified numerous ethical guidelines but not a fundamental standard. It was, rather, an amalgamation of ethical perspectives. Research has confirmed the lack of a consistent ethical belief system (e.g., McDonald and Pak, 1996).

The second obstacle is that individuals often compartmentalize ethical beliefs, using different perspectives under different contexts. For instance, consider the shopkeeper example above. During difficult economic times, the shopkeeper demonstrates a measure of utilitarianism evident in the store's pricing structure. As an individual, however, this shopkeeper may also engage in altruistic behavior (Lewes, 1853), such as donating cash or services to a food kitchen. When viewed from a shopkeeper frame, utilitarianism is the predominant belief. Viewed through an individual frame, altruism becomes predominant. Individuals may also change perspective dependent on their social surroundings. For example, they may be altruists at church, egoists with friends, and utilitarian at work. This compartmentalization has also been supported by research (e.g., Grover and Hui, 1994).

The third obstacle is that people sometimes act in a manner that is contrary to their espoused beliefs. The shopkeeper above, for instance, may claim to be concerned with affordability of basic necessities and, on the surface, appears to act in a utilitarian fashion by reducing the prices. However, that same store may have overpriced items that allow the shopkeeper to maintain a profit. Individuals may profess to believe one thing, yet act contrary to that belief. The existence of discrepancies between ideal behavior and actual behavior is well noted in psychological research (Higgins, 1997). The difference may be attributed to unconscious influences or conscious deviations. A study on value beliefs and decision outcome showed that individuals claimed to have beliefs that were not consistently represented in subsequent tasks (Hall and Davis, 2007). That difference may be attributable to the desire to "say the right thing" and the desire to "do the right thing" which are not always compatible. Regardless, this discrepancy makes predicting an individual's actions based on their ethical beliefs problematic in that a researcher cannot ask individuals what they believe and then be able to accurately predict their behavior.

The fourth obstacle is that individuals often demand different standards of ethical behavior for different groups of people, making it difficult to judge ethical beliefs from third person perspectives. In the United States, for instance, it is not unusual to hold public figures or others in a position of authority to higher standards than others; however, social norms drive what is considered ethical. For example, one study found that the ethical attitude of high level employees had an effect on the ethical behaviors of lower-level managers (Jackson, 2000). Another study found that questionable sales practices against competitors were viewed less negatively than the same practices against employees or customers (Abratt and Penman, 2002). Furthermore, individuals often believe they are more ethical than other people (Morgan, 1993; O'Clock and Okleshen, 1993).

Despite the problems listed above, ethics researchers have explored various means of analyzing ethical perspectives and the decision-making process. However, the obstacles show the difficulties in applying and interpreting pure empirical methodologies in relation to ethically based scenarios. One way to begin to focus the research, and in turn begin to mitigate some of these difficulties, is to apply a framework for ethical decision-making. Frameworks allow researchers to focus on particular behaviors or contexts. One applicable framework is the model developed by Jones (1991).

In the following sections, this chapter explores some of the instruments used in ethics research in terms of Jones' (1991) issue-contingent model of ethical decision-making in organizations. First, a brief summary of Jones' issue-contingency model is provided. Next, a review of instruments designed to measure each concept in the model is analyzed. From this analysis, implications for decision support research are explored.

4.2.1 The Ethical Decision-Making Process: A Jones Perspective

Jones' (1991) issue-contingent model of ethical decision-making in organizations (see Fig. 4.1) largely builds upon Rest's (1979) four component decision-making model. This model is a simplified view of single event moral decision-making processes and eliminates how morality is developed over time and many of the complexities that arise in cognitive decisions. This simplicity makes it ideal for use as a foundation for investigating ethical perspectives and its impact on behavior.

Although Jones (1991) uses the terms ethics and morals interchangeably, he defines the existence of a moral issue as a situation in which voluntary action will have consequences to others. He then defines an ethical decision as being one that is morally and legally acceptable to the community at large. The individual who is interpreting and acting is called the moral agent whether that person recognizes the moral issues embedded in the decision context or not. We also adopt these definitions for the purpose of the following discussion. While Jones does not adopt a particular moral standard for defining what is and what is not a moral issue, he recognizes that a person must recognize that an issue is morally based for the framework to be applicable. This is the first step of the process.

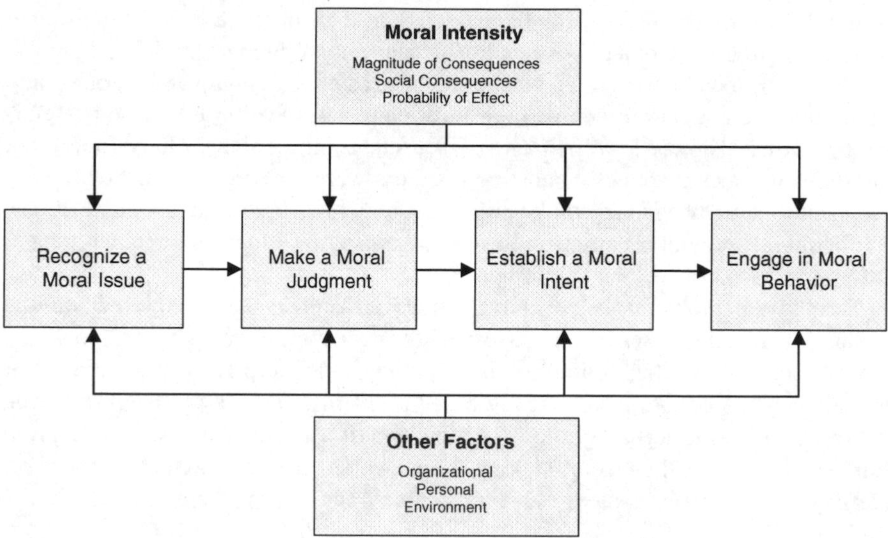

Fig. 4.1 Adapted from Jones' (1991) issue-contingent model of ethical decision making in organizations

This step is particularly difficult to model in a DSS. How can a DSS "recognize" a moral issue? Would the organization define moral issue or would the decision maker? Further, what effect does the developer's moral perspective have on the development of the DSS (Fleischmann and Wallace, 2005)? A framework would guide the answers these questions and improve development of a morally aware DSS or decision environment.

Once a person recognizes an issue as moral, he or she must make a moral judgment. Kohlberg's (1976) model of moral development suggests that individuals use different levels or stages of reasoning when making judgments about a moral issue. An individual's ability to recognize the moral dilemma, formulate assumptions and hypotheses regarding the context, and develop actionable alternatives is largely dependent on his or her individual characteristics, understanding of the situation, and biases. This indicates that an individual may not act consistently even when confronted by similar situations and will consider the individual characteristics of the issue when deciding on appropriate behavior. It is here that Jones' (1991) model differs. Previous models which he synthesized, including those by Rest (1986), Trevino (1986), Hunt and Vitell (1986), Dubinsky and Loken (1989), and Ferrell and Gresham (1985), do not include the explicit characteristics of the moral issue and therefore imply that ethical behavior is consistent across context. In Jones' (1991) model, judgment of the context is the second step and establishes the behavior the individual deems appropriate for that specific moral issue.

As this second step relates to DSS development, the modeler must determine what the judgment should be and how to incorporate it into the system. Hall and

Davis' system (2007) was based on values, which are internalized beliefs based on actions perceived as ethical. To facilitate interpretation of an event from a different perspective, that system prompted the user to consider a context from opposing perspectives. To help a decision-maker judge an ethical context, a similar approach could be used. For instance, the system could be programmed to recognize an ethical pattern (e.g., utilitarian) and could prompt the user to consider the context from a different ethical pattern (e.g., altruistic). Subsequently, a range of appropriate action could be suggested that are based on a mix of ethical dispositions. This would facilitate the next step in the process.

Closely following this judgment is the establishment of intent to behave morally (step three). Intentions, in terms of social psychology, represent a cognitive evaluation about what an individual intends to do in a particular context. A decision that a behavior is "correct" is, however, not the same as a decision to act upon that correct behavior. Organizational factors such as group dynamics, authority factors, social norms, and socialization processes may influence individuals to act in a manner that is inconsistent with their initial intention. Any number of things can limit intentions from being actualized, including fatigue, frustration, distractions, unexpected difficulties, etc. (Rest, 1986). The last step is to engage in moral behavior. This step is clearly individual specific. The DSS may guide the decision maker toward a morally "correct" action, but the individual must initiate the action.

Each of these four components, Jones argues, is influenced by the moral intensity of the issue. According to Jones, moral intensity represents "a construct that captures the extent of issue-related moral imperative in a situation" (1991, p. 372). Essentially, this construct captures the hierarchical relationship of moral issues in their importance and relevancy to each individual. The goal of this concept is to capture proportionality in moral responsibility. Jones identifies six potential components of this construct: magnitude of consequences, social consensus, probability of effect, temporal immediacy, proximity, and concentration of effect.

The six components could be incorporated into a DSS to refine the system. Although many require subjective interpretation, their inclusion may further the process. For instance, again consider the shopkeeper. A decision to reduce prices on some products but not others has consequences that he may not consider. He may consider the decision solely from a temporal profit perspective (immediate break even) but may not consider the social consensus (willingness or not to pay more for non-essential items), probability of losing/gaining customers, overall balance of reduced products (magnitude of consequence), and so on. Simply raising one's awareness regarding information has been shown to modify behavior (Wade-Benzoni et al., 2002).

Other things that impact the analysis of the situation and the eventual action include organizational, individual, and environmental factors. Jones (1991) identified several organizational factors that often complicate individual ethical behavior by creating structural barriers or creating hierarchy relationships that influence individuals away from their intentions. It may also instill a groupthink mentality, which directly effects judgment on particular moral issues. Trevino (1986) proposed a number of individual factors (e.g. ego strength, field dependence, locus of control, etc.) that may influence the relationship between moral judgment and moral action. Other environmental factors may include difficulty to complete a behavior or emergency situations that complicate a decision (Rest, 1986).

The above discussion illustrates how complicated even a seemingly simple framework can become. Each of the processes in Jones' (1991) model are confounded by one factor – the decision-maker and his or her interpretation of the environment, the situation, and the potential ramifications of action. Thus, it becomes important to identify means by which the individual ethical characteristics of an individual can be measured such that that person's potential biases may be mediated by decision support technology.

4.3 Measuring Ethical Decision-Making Components

For each of the ethical decision-making processes identified above and for moral intensity, we review various instruments designed to capture the construct and examine if gaps exist in that domain. When identifying instruments, we focus on those that are more than a single question and those that have been validated in more than one study.

4.3.1 Recognition of a Moral Issue

Measuring the recognition of a moral issue entails more than just a simple yes/no question. Because individuals may invest in any number of ethical beliefs systems (Forysth, 1980), a simple yes/no answer does not afford the researcher any opportunity to delve into the reasoning behind the answer. Study participants who answer "no" to whether they believe a particular issue is moral may have a complex and sophisticated moral system that is founded on a different standard than that of the researcher who wrote the question and different from other participants who identified the issues as moral. If this is the case, an individual with different ethical beliefs may genuinely believe they are acting morally and yet appear immoral in the eyes of the research project.

To overcome this problem, it is necessary to establish the ethical beliefs of the individual within the context of the issue before establishing recognition of an issue as moral. A variety of instruments have attempted to capture ethical belief systems. Forysth (1980) designed and tested the ethics position questionnaire to assess the degree of idealism and relativism individuals adopt. Four distinct ethical perspectives were related to the degree that an individual was idealistic and/or relativistic in their ethical beliefs. These four ethical ideologies were (1) situationalism, (2) absolutism, (3) subjectivism, and (4) exceptionism. The instrument showed strong reliability and validity. However, it proved poor at predicting ethical judgments of various scenarios, showing at times large differences in male and female participants with the same ethical ideology. While gender is known to affect ethical behavior (e.g., Fleischman and Valentine, 2003), it alone may not be responsible for the differences noted. It is likely that the difference is also attributable to Jones' (1991) contention that ethical decision-making is issue contingent and that broad based ethical ideologies may be inappropriate for recognizing moral issues.

Reidenbach and Robin (1988, 1990) developed and refined a normative ethical beliefs scale based on a variety of ethical theories. In their studies, a search of ethics literature suggested five ethical philosophies: deontology, utilitarianism, relativism, justice, and egoism. Performing a factor analysis on the item stems in the first study yielded vastly different factor structures for each scenario. The factor structure bore little resemblance to the a priori judgment of normative ethical beliefs. In the second study, factor analysis reduced the five ethical philosophies to three dimensions – justice, relativism, and contractualism – with a greatly reduced number of item stems for each dimension. These dimensions serve as a starting point for further investigation, but may not fully capture the complexities of normative ethical beliefs that pertain to recognizing an issue as moral.

A more recent study attempts to empirically identify moral awareness of moral issues (Jordan, 2009). In this study, business professionals were asked to indicate important issues from a vignette. Participants were also asked to identify strategic and moral issues contained in the vignettes. From these results, the Moral Awareness in Business Instrument (MABI) provided a two-factor solution, suggesting a strategic versus moral division in awareness of moral issues. The author posited that her moral label in this investigation might not be what the participants in the study consider moral or what other researchers may consider moral, illustrating the complexity of researcher-designed scenarios.

4.3.2 Make a Moral Judgment

In Jones' model, moral judgment consists of the identification of what the correct response to a moral issue should be. One of the more popular measures of moral judgment comes from the Kohlberg's theory of cognitive moral development (1981). According to Kohlberg (1981, 1986), judgment consists of two parts which are (1) the structure of the moral reasoning, and (2) the content of the reasoning. Cognitive moral theory focuses on the former of these two. This theory postulated that moral judgment evolves over time through six stages. In stage 1, individuals focus on pain and punishment as the primary means of decisions. In Stage 2, individuals obey rules to further their self-interests. At stage 3, individuals adopt the norms of his or her peers. In stage 4, the individuals adopt moral standards of society. At stage 5, individuals become aware of that some values are optional and that people conform to social norms through an implied contract. At stage 6, individuals choose universal principles and follow them. Kohlberg developed an interview technique to determine which of the six stages an individual uses when making a moral judgment. Because of the time intensive nature of Kohlberg's data gathering techniques, Rest (1979) developed the Defining Issues Test (DIT), which attempts to classify moral judgment into Kohlberg's six stages with short vignettes and follow-up questionnaire.

Although the DIT is a well documented instrument, it explicitly attempts to identify reasoning patterns, not conclusions. Moral judgment, as Jones describes it, evaluates moral issues at a specific instant in time irrespective of what developmental stage an individual uses in his or her reasoning. Various research efforts suggest that moral reasoning is related to moral behavior, but is not the only factor (Elm and Weber, 1994). Referring back to Kohlberg's theory, we see that *content* is also an important factor in judgment. The process of evaluating a moral issue depends on the ethical belief system of the participant. Ethical evaluations based on ethical beliefs systems (e.g. utilitarian, justice, etc.) have been shown to mediate the influence of moral intensity on moral evaluations (May and Pauli, 2002). This suggests that ethical belief systems are an important factor in moral judgments. Just as identifying an issue as moral depends on the ethical belief system an individual holds, so too does the content of a moral judgment. Individuals may agree that an issue has moral relevance to it, but come to completely different moral judgments. For example, an altruist may believe sacrificing him or herself for the sake of society is morally good, whereas an egoist may consider it morally repugnant. Both could see the decision as a moral issue and would be operating on ethical principles (Kohlberg's stage 6), but come to completely different judgments.

4.3.3 Establish a Moral Intent

In Jones' (1991) ethical decision-making model, moral intent is equivalent to the concept of intentions found in the theory of reasoned action and the theory of planned behavior (Ajzen, 1991). Because intent is issue specific, a simple vignette with specific questions in regard to the intended behavior is sufficient and consistent with prior research. These questions may take any form from open-ended (e.g., "What would you do in this situation?") to a Likert scale (e.g., "How strongly do you believe that Sue took the correct action in this situation, with 1 being Strongly Disagree and 7 being Strongly Agree?").

4.3.4 Engage in Moral Behavior

The final outcome of the ethical decision-making process is notoriously difficult to measure because individuals are generally not forthcoming about engaging in immoral behavior (Trevino, 1992). While single statement questions exist for this construct, no multi-statement instruments could be found. Further, a researcher must balance whether the answer represents the espoused action or the real action. This is a situation where separate analysis of the participant's ethical foundation, intention development process, and a task requiring a moral action would be valuable.

4.3.5 Moral Intensity and Other Factors

Since Jones proposed the concept of moral intensity, various researchers have included this construct in their research efforts. In various studies, a single statement was developed to reflect each of the six components of moral intensity (Singhapakdi et al., 1996). In other studies, two statements were developed to reflect each of the six components (Frey, 2000; May and Pauli, 2002). In another, a vignette was used (Chia and Lim, 2000). Throughout these studies moral intensity was shown to be closely related awareness, but no reliable multi-dimensional structure was found for moral intensity.

Other instruments for measuring ethics include organization ethical climate, such as the ethical positions questionnaire, which captures the work climate in which someone operates (Victor and Cullen, 1988) and the Corporate Ethical Values (Hunt et al., 1989). Instruments designed to capture single values include the love of money scale (Tang and Chui, 2003). This scale captures how much individuals are motivated by money. Tang's research has shown that motivation by money leads to unethical behavior.

The more we understand about how an individual recognizes and reacts to moral issues, the more we are able to incorporate that cognitive map into a DSS designed to help decision-makers work through morally charged contexts. Understanding how moral intensity, personal factors, environmental factors, and organizational factors impact ethical decision-making enables DSS designers to observe patterns in users, mitigate organizational issues, and highlight appropriate guidelines.

4.3.6 Measuring Ethical Decision Processes

Jones' (1991) model of issue-contingent ethical decision-making provides researchers with an invaluable starting point for understanding the ethical decision process. Understanding this process will allow researchers to design better ethics-based decision support systems that support multiple perspectives while avoiding toxic decision processes resulting in unethical behavior. However, as the above discussion illustrates, while much research has been done on many aspects of ethical decision-making, there has yet to be a foundational ethical instrument that can be tested and modified to strengthen ethical decision-making research.

One gap identified above is the inadequate means of measuring individual ethical perspectives. Business ethics researchers have an opportunity to develop instruments that better capture an individual's ethical perspective in a given context. In particular, there is a need for an instrument that can capture normative ethical perspectives within descriptive categories for enhanced prediction of behavior in various issue contingent contexts. Such an instrument should include values, issue recognition, judgment, intention, and behavior regardless of age, gender, education, and cultural background. One promising instrument integrates issues specific contexts with personal ethical perspectives used to make the ethical decisions (Drake et al., 2009), thereby combining personal factors with moral judgment into a single instrument. This better establishes common ethical reasoning approaches to various issues.

O'Fallon and Butterfield (2005) conducted a comprehensive review of empirical ethical decision-making literature and found that while a number of articles were published during their timeframe, no consistent use of instruments were noted. Further, there was little consistency among the articles in terms of dependent and independent variables, methodologies, or techniques. Findings were likewise inconsistent. Therefore, further development of ethical decision-making instruments within a framework similar to Jones' (1991) for the descriptive side of ethics may be beneficial.

Recently, Weber and McGivern (2009) validated an instrument to assess moral reasoning. Using two scenarios with different contexts enabled the researchers to mitigate the context-specific issues of ethical decision-making. They were able to demonstrate that the participants choose a resolution that was consistent with their moral reasoning, and that the moral reasoning of the two groups (agree/disagree with the action) was different. While moral reasoning in and of itself is not valued in

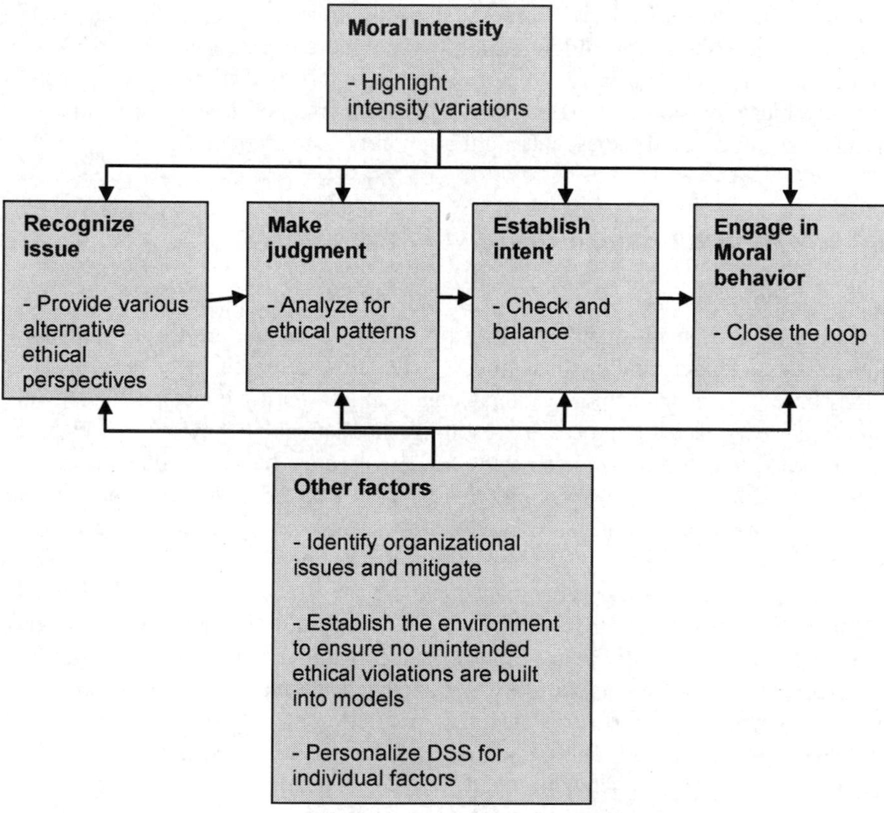

Fig. 4.2 DSS design

Jones' (1991) model, reasoning processes play into the decision process and should be acknowledged in a decision support design. Specific issues to be addressed by an ethically-based DSS are shown in Fig. 4.2. Although Jones' model would flow throughout, it would primarily be active in the areas of providing alternative ethical perspectives and identifying organizational issues.

4.4 Decision Support Considerations

As decision support technologies evolve, things that were once impossible are now common-place. For instance, the idea that a machine can reason is no longer on the fringe of reality. Artificial intelligence is a common component within support technology. The ability to program machines to support complex decisions through reasoning and fuzzy logic allows decision support technology designers to consider embedding value and ethical support for multiple perspectives. Technology is trending toward human characteristics; programming it to represent multiple perspectives is a logical step forward.

Consider, for example, the common framework in intelligent agents known as the Belief-Desire-Intention (BDI) model. The Belief-Desire-Intention (BDI) model is a frequently studied model for those working in agent systems (Rao and Georgeff, 1995). Put simply, an agent acts to achieve a goal (desire) by performing specific acts (intentions). Desires and intentions are based on the agent's underlying beliefs, which are similar to the non-agent usage of the word in that those beliefs affect how the agent perceives or acquires information. Although these beliefs may be updated as the environment changes, the foundation of the beliefs remains reasonably constant. For instance, an agent may believe that the organization sells only one subset of product because its task requires only that it be aware of that product. Another agent may work with other products, thus believing a different product structure exists. Although the product subset of either agent may change, the over-arching product base for that system does not. Because agents generally have a different set of underlying beliefs, each agent may represent a different perspective.

The BDI model has been applied in various contexts; notably, its applicability to a multi-perspective decision system has been demonstrated (Hall et al., 2005). Their paper extends the Unbounded Systems Thinking (UST) model (Mitroff and Linstone, 1993) with the BDI model. In their demonstrative system, agents were created that represented individual stakeholders and their individual value system and characteristics that paralleled the technical, organizational, and personal perspectives of the UST model. Their simulation indicated that the demonstrative system performed the same task as its human counterparts, arrived at a similar conclusion, but introduced less subjectivism in the decision.

In a similar fashion, agents can be programmed with ethical beliefs. These agents can then work with decision makers to interpret the situation, recognize moral issues, and can recommend action (suggestive guidance) or encourage the decision maker to explore other alternatives (informative guidance). When multiple agents are used that each represent an ethical standard, the decision maker's biases may be reduced as he or she reaps the benefits of multiple perspectives during the decision making task. Agent technology is becoming more commonplace as a tool for DSS facilitation.

Decision support for multiple perspectives should lead to better decisions (Hine and Goul, 1998). It has been found that value focused thinking can be mitigated through DSS components designed to introduce alternative perspectives when making decisions (Courtney, 2001; Hall and Davis, 2007; Hall and Paradice, 2007). To expand on Hall's work, researchers could consider various ethical perspectives and its effect on decision support systems as suggested by Courtney (2001). By highlighting alternative ethical perspectives, DSS components can increase issue awareness and recognition, leading to better organizational decisions with fewer unethical behaviors. To that end, understanding which ethical perspectives and which stages of moral development are employed most often and which ethical perspectives lead to various outcomes could greatly improve the design of a DSS.

Given the numerous ethical dilemmas and unethical behavior that regularly makes news, the idea of implementing ethical support into a decision support technology is clearing going to be more important as organizations seem to minimize unethical behavior. While literature shows that ethics and ethical behavior are routinely researched, it will be difficult to make much headway without a consistent framework and instruments on which to build validated constructs.

This chapter discussed the need for measuring ethical decision-making process in order to better understand how to design decision support systems that supports ethical decisions. Jones' issue-contingent decision-making model provided a framework for discussing the status of various instruments designed to assess various factors in the decision-making process. From this review, it is apparent that a number of opportunities for further research that would add to our understanding of ethical decision making with respect to decision support.

References

Abratt, R., and Penman, N. (2002). Understanding Factors Affecting Salespeople's Perceptions of Ethical Behavior in South Africa. *Journal of Business Ethics*, *35*(4), 269–280.

Ajzen, I. (1991). The Theory of Planned Behavior. *Organizational Behavior and Human Decision Processes*, *50*, 179–211.

Chia, A., and Lim, S. M. (2000). The Effects of Issue Characteristics on the Recognition of Moral Issues. *Journal of Business Ethics*, *27*(3), 255–269.

Courtney, J. F. (2001). Decision Making and Knowledge Management in Inquiring Organizations: A New Decision-Making Paradigm for DSS. *Decision Support Systems Special Issue on Knowledge Management*, *31*(1), 17–38.

Drake, J. R., Hall, D. J., and Lang, T. (2009, Novmber 14–16). Ethical Perspectives of Business Students: Development of a New Instrument. Paper presented at the Decision Sciences Institute 40th Annual Meeting, New Orleans, LA.

Dubinsky, A. J., and Loken, B. (1989). Analyzing Ethical Decision Making in Marketing. *Journal of Business Research*, *19*(2), 83–107.

Elm, D., and Weber, J. (1994). Measure Moral Judgment: The Moral Judgment Interview or the Defining Issues Test? *Journal of Business Ethics*, *13*(5), 341–355.

Ferrell, O. C., and Gresham, L. G. (1985). A Contingency Framework for Understanding Ethical Decision-Making in Marketing. *Journal of Marketing*, *49*(3), 87–96.

Fleischman, G., and Valentine, S. (2003). Professional's Tax Liability and Ethical Evaluations in an Equitable Relief Innocent Spouse Case. *Journal of Business Ethics*, *42*(1), 27–44.

Fleischmann, K. R., and Wallace, W. A. (2005). A Covenant with Transparency: Opening the Black Box of Models. *Communications of the ACM*, *48*(5), 93–97.

Forysth, D. (1980). A Taxonomy of Ethical Ideologies. *Journal of Personality and Social Psychology*, *39*(1), 175–184.

Frey, B. (2000). The Impact of Moral Intensity on Decision Making in a Business Context. *Journal of Business Ethics*, *26*(3), 181–195.

Grover, S., and Hui, C. (1994). The Influence of the Role Conflict and Self-Interest on Lying in Organizations. *Journal of Business Ethics*, *13*(4), 295–303.

Hall, D. J., and Davis, R. A. (2007). Engaging Multiple Perspectives: A Value-Based Decision-Making Model. *Decision Support Systems*, *43*(4), 1588–1604.

Hall, D. J., Guo, Y., Davis, R. A., and Cegielski, C. (2005). Extending Unbounded Systems Thinking with Agent-Oriented Modeling: Conceptualizing a Multiple-Perspective Decision-Making System. *Decision Support Systems*, *41*(1), 279–295.

Hall, D. J., and Paradice, D. B. (2007). Investigating Value-Based Decision Bias and Mediation: Do You Do as You Think? *Communications of the ACM*, *50*(4), 81–85.

Higgins, E. T. (1997). Beyond Pleasure and Pain. *American Psychologist*, *52*(12), 1280–1300.

Hine, M., and Goul, M. (1998). The Design, Development, and Validation of a Knowledge Based Organizational Learning Support System. *Journal of Management Information Systems*, *15*(2), 119–152.

Hunt, S., and Vitell, S. (1986). A General Theory of Marketing Ethics. *Journal of Macromarketing*, *6*(1), 5–16.

Hunt, S., Wood, V., and Chonko, L. (1989). Corporate Ethical Values and Organizational Commitment in Marketing. *Journal of Marketing*, *53*(3), 79–90.

Jackson, T. (2000). Management Ethics and Corporate Policy: A Cross-Cultural Comparison. *Journal of Management Studies*, *37*(3), 349–369.

Jones, T. M. (1991). Ethical Decision Making by Individuals in Organizations: An Issue-Contingent Model. *Academy of Management Review*, *16*(2), 366–395.

Jordan, J. (2009). A Social Cognition Framework for Examining Moral Awareness in Manager's and Academics. *Journal of Business Ethics*, *84*(2), 237–258.

Kohlberg, L. (1976). Moral Stages and Moralization: The Cognitive-Development Approach. In T. Lickona (Ed.), *Moral Development and Behavior: Theory, Research, and Social Issues* (pp. 31–53). New York, NY: Holt, Rinehart, and Winston.

Kohlberg, L. (1981). *Essays on Moral Development* (Vol. 1). San Francisco, CA: Harper and Row.

Kohlberg, L. (1986). A Current Statement on Theoretic Issues. In S. Modgil and C. Modgil (Eds.), *Lawrence Kohlberg: Consensus and Controversy*. Philadelphia, PA: The Falmer Press.

Lewes, G. H. (1853). *Compte's Philosophy of the Sciences*. London: George Bell and Sons.

May, D., and Pauli, K. (2002). The Role of Moral Intensity in Ethical Decision Making. *Business and Society*, *41*(1), 84–117.

McDonald, G., and Pak, P. (1996). It's All Fair in Love, War, and Business: Cognitive Philosophies in Ethical Decision Making. *Journal of Business Ethics*, *15*, 973–996.

Mills, J. S. (1863). Utilitarianism. In R. C. Solomon, C. W. Martin, and W. Vaught (Eds.), *Morality and the Good Life: An Introduction to Ethics Through the Classical Sources* (Vol. 5). Boston, MA: McGraw-Hill.

Mitroff, I. I., and Linstone, H. A. (1993). *The Unbounded Mind: Breaking the Chains of Traditional Business Thinking* (1st ed.). New York, NY: Oxford University Press.

Morgan, R. (1993). Self and Co-worker Perceptions of Ethics and Their Relationships to Leadership and Salary. *Academy of Management Journal*, *36*(1), 200–214.

O'Clock, P., and Okleshen, M. (1993). A Comparison of Ethical Perceptions of Business. *Journal of Business Ethics*, *12*, 677–687.

O'Fallon, M. J., and Butterfield, K. D. (2005). A Review of the Empirical Ethical Decision-Making Literature: 1996–2003. *Journal of Business Ethics*, *59*(4), 375–413.

Rao, A. S., and Georgeff, M. P. (1995, June 12–14). BDI Agents: From Theory to Practice. Paper presented at the First International Conference on Multi-Agent Systems, San Francisco, CA.

Reidenback, R., and Robin, D. (1988). Some Initial Steps Toward Improving the Measurement of Ethical Evaluations of Marketing Activities. *Journal of Business Ethics*, *7*(11), 871–879.

Reidenback, R., and Robin, D. (1990). Toward the Development of a Multidimensional Scale for Improving Evaluations of Business Ethics. *Journal of Business Ethics*, *9*(8), 639–653.

Rest, J. (1979). *Development in Judging Moral Issues*. Minneapolis, MN: University of Minnesota Press.

Rest, J. (1986). *Moral Development: Advances in Research and Theory*. New York, NY: Praeger.

Silver, M. S. (1991). Decisional Guidance for Computer-Based Decision Support. *MIS Quarterly*, *15*(1), 105–122.

Singhapakdi, A., Vitell, S., and Kraft, K. (1996). Moral Intensity and Ethical Decision-Making of Marketing Professionals. *Journal of Business Research*, *36*(3), 245–255.

Tang, T., and Chui, R. (2003). Income, Money Ethic, Pay Satisfaction, Commitment, and Unethical Behavior: Is the Love of Money the Root of Evil for Hong Kong Employees? *Journal of Business Ethics*, *46*(1), 13–30.

Trevino, L. (1986). Ethical Decision Making in Organizations: A Person-Situation Interactionist Model. *Academy of Management Review*, *11*(3), 601–617.

Trevino, L. (1992). Experimental Approaches to Studying Ethical-Unethical Behavior in Organizations. *Business Ethics Quarterly*, *2*(2), 121–136.

Victor, B., and Cullen, J. (1988). The Organizational Bases of Ethical Work Climates. *Administrative Science Quarterly*, *33*(1), 101–126.

Wade-Benzoni, K. A., Hoffman, A. J., Thompson, L. L., Moore, D. A., Gillespie, J. J., and Bazerman, M. H. (2002). Barriers to Resolution in Ideologically Based Negotiations: The Role of Values and Institutions. *Academy of Management Review*, *27*(1), 41–57.

Weber, J., and McGivern, E. (2009). A New Methodological Approach for Studying Moral Reasoning Among Managers in Business Settings. *Journal of Business Ethics*, *92*(1), 149–166.

Wheeler, S. (2003). An Analysis of the Association for Computing Machinery (ACM) Code of Ethics. *ACM SIGCAS Computers and Society*, *33*(3), 2.

Chapter 5
Web and Mobile Spatial Decision Support as Innovations: Comparison of United States and Hong Kong, China

James B. Pick[1]

[1] University of Redlands, Redlands, CA 92373, USA, james_pick@redlands.edu

5.1 Introduction

The objective of this chapter is to analyze the adoption and diffusion of web-based and mobile-based spatial decision support (WMSDS) in organizations on an exploratory basis; test the usefulness of adoption and diffusion models empirically based on case studies of organizations in Hong Kong, China, and in the U.S.; evaluate issues, controversies, and constraints to WMSDS; and consider future trends. Web and mobile spatial services are a rapidly growing, innovative part of GIS, supportable to users having only a web browser or inexpensive mobile device (Peng and Tsou, 2003; Lopez, 2004; Li, 2007; Simon et al., 2007; Drummond et al., 2007b; Sugumaran and Sugumaran, 2007). Studies in web and mobile GIS have so far concentrated on the spatial design, GIS procedures, technical configurations, and applications (Ray, 2007; Li and Longley, 2006; R. Sugumaran et al., 2007; Sugumaran and Sugumaran, 2007; Kingston, 2007; Harkins and Lawton, 2007; Gup, 2007; Mendoza et al., 2009), but have not empirically analyzed the effectiveness of spatial decision making, assessed WMSDS relative to stage of adoption and diffusion, or compared findings from two countries. Everett Rogers (2003) introduced adoption-diffusion theory, which explains the sequence and stages of technology innovation. This theory and the related user-diffusion theory are applied to understand spatial decision support relative to the innovation stage at which web and mobile spatial decision services with WMSDS are adopted and diffused. The future potential and opportunities for research in WMSDS are discussed.

5.1.1 Background

Geographic information systems (GIS) utilize geo-referenced data bases and spatial modeling tools to analyze problems, model spatial phenomena, and support operational and management activities. A spatial decision system (SDS) is a GIS that accesses spatial modeling and statistical tools to support semi-structured or unstructured organizational decisions. As web and mobile technologies have

D. Schuff et al. (eds.), *Decision Support*, Annals of Information Systems 14,
DOI 10.1007/978-1-4419-6181-5_5,

exploded in usage, spatial decision support tools increasingly can be utilized on these platforms. One of the features of GIS and of WMSDS is spatial analysis, which utilizes spatial statistics, comparison of spatial layers, spatial distances and buffer zones, and other algorithms and models involving space to reach solutions to problems.

WMSDS is of recent origin and is considered in this study as an innovation. There is a need to apply conceptual theories to better understand WMSDS and anticipate its future. Adoption/diffusion theory (Rogers, 2003) posits attributes of an innovation that help to explain its stage of technology adoption. The theory of adoption requires pioneers that are early in an exponential growth which transitions into diffusion of the innovation to a broader user base through communications, social networking, and channels of innovation, with deeper knowledge of the innovation and more variety of uses (Robertson and Gatignon, 1986). Use-diffusion theory (Venkatesh and Shih, 2005), which builds on Rogers' ideas, focuses in more depth on how diffusion can occur in a high quality manner so that users realize the use they anticipate and over time become satisfied with the technology and appreciative of its impact and future potential. Use-diffusion introduces more social and personal determinants, divides users into categories related to intensity and generality of use, and considers more thoroughly outcomes of innovation. The present study is based on these theories in assessing stages of spatial decision making by the organization, its users, and clients/customers.

Web-based and mobile-based spatial decision support (WMSDS) is part of a broad and growing trend towards internet-based spatial applications and services (Drummond et al., 2007b). The latter have been widely used only since 2000 (Drummond et al., 2007a; Pick, 2008). Currently WMSDS is moving past the geospatial and IS communities and becoming standard with the consuming public, social networking users, and citizens engaged in public participation with governments.

WMSDS can be provided through a variety of networking channels to users having only a web browser or inexpensive mobile device (Lopez, 2004; Zhao et al., 2007; Sugumaran et al., 2007; Drummond et al., 2007a). Mobile applications can be connected to GPS and wireless communications, so that spatial information passes back and forth between mapping and other servers and the mobile devices. For instance, utility personnel in the field can do maintenance based on centralized maps of utility infrastructure assets in the field. Using such technology, they can update information, enter new information, perform analyses, and communicate the information back and forth with a centralized system (Meehan and Huntsman, 2007). WMSDS can be integrated into large scale information technology systems, to an extent that they sometimes lose their identity as separate applications (Rizos and Drane, 2004).

So far, research in web-based and mobile GIS has concentrated on the spatial design, GIS procedures, technical configurations, and applications (Peng and Tsou, 2003; Lopez, 2004; Li, 2007; Simon et al., 2007; Drummond et al., 2007a), but little on their broad architecture, organizational aspects, management, standards, costs and benefits, strategies, and adoption and diffusion.

Additionally, previous studies have not analyzed multiple case studies, nor compared findings from two culturally different countries. The present study fills these gaps, in order that management can assess its own opportunities or deficiencies, and better evaluate whether or not to commit to this decision making approach.

5.1.2 Issues, Controversies, Problems

The position of this paper emphasizes WMSDS as an innovation in an adoption and diffusion context. In contrast to other studies, it examines in depth the determinants of adoption and diffusion, which can be favorable or unfavorable. Another difference with prior studies is the international comparative framework, which is between the U.S. and Hong Kong, China.

Much of the prior research concerned highly technical aspects of WMSDS such as infrastructure, telecommunications, server design, and spatial representations (Lopez, 2004; Drummond et al., 2007a; Brimicombe and Li, 2006; Zhao et al., 2007). Previous studies of applications emphasize the technology and software application and project management aspects of WMSDS (Ray, 2007; Drummond et al., 2007a; Kingston, 2007; Harkins and Lawton, 2007; Gup, 2007; Sugumaran et al., 2007). There is a gap that can be partly filled by the organizational and adoption and diffusion viewpoints.

A reason for a paucity of prior studies is that WMSDS has only had widespread adoption for 5 years. The major consumer platforms for web-based spatial decision-making were introduced in 2005 and included Google Map/Earth, Microsoft Virtual Earth, and Yahoo Maps. At onset, they did not include decision tools, so the advent of widespread web- and mobile platforms with decision-making capabilities occurred only within the past 2–4 years. The recency of the innovation has so far constrained published academic studies. Several conferences have stimulated broader interest occasionally touching on organizational aspects, for instance the National Science Foundation TeraGrid Workshop on Cyber GIS in 2010.

The specific objectives of the present study are (1) to analyze literature on web and mobile spatial decision making, (2) to examine models for adoption and diffusion of spatial web and mobile services, (3) to test research propositions that are largely based on adoption-diffusion theory, on an exploratory basis, through interviews in Hong Kong and the U.S., and (4) to evaluate the usefulness of the adoption-diffusion and use-diffusion models for WMSDS. The full interview protocol covers the topic areas of how organizations, develop, configure and implement spatial web and mobile services; who the users are for the services; what their application are; what is the web and/or mobile architecture of the applications; who decides on the architecture and how has it changed; what standards are utilized; spatial decision support, costs and benefits; strategies for deploying these services; and their impact on competitive advantage. The interviews were transcribed and the results analyzed.

The research will benefit other researchers by filling in gaps on the advantages of WMSDS, adjustment to it, user friendliness of WMSDS, development process, strategic/competitive importance, and cross-country comparison. The conceptual model and empirical findings should be useful in complementing more technical studies or in testing and expanding the present research with larger samples and different methodologies. The project will benefit practitioners in the real world by providing benchmark results for a variety of organizations and industries. A manager can compare his/her company with a cross section of other organizations on web- and mobile-based spatial decision support. The manager can gain context by understanding the differences between the U.S. and Hong Kong, China.

5.2 Theories of Adoption and Diffusion

This section sets the background on adoption and diffusion theories, which are then utilized to formulate a conceptual model of WMSDS. The theories of adoption and diffusion of innovations are drawn from the work of Rogers (1962, 2003) and from subsequent studies that have further developed the theory (Shih and Venkatesh, 2004; Venkatesh and Shih, 2005; Dewan et al., 2009). The theories can be applied to any innovation, i.e. ranging across such areas as major scientific breakthroughs, agricultural methods, health discoveries, and information technology advances. The theories concern perceived innovation, that is, as seen in the eyes of its potential adopters and current users.

The theories incorporate innovation, its use, communications that spread it, constraints on use, types of use, and social influences. Adoption-diffusion theory (Rogers, 1962, 2003) focuses on the influences on adoption, attributes that favor it, adopters, and on sequences and rates of adoption. Diffusion is the spread of the innovation more widely through communications and expanding knowledge of it. Diffusion is especially influential in the middle and late stages of the adoption-diffusion process.

Adoptions in the real world tend to follow a normal curve of frequencies. At first there are only a few early adopters, followed by a period of rapidly increasing frequency until, in the late period, adoptions peak, frequencies lower and eventually taper off to zero. Empirical studies of various innovations have confirmed innovation frequencies follow a normal curve (Rogers, 2003). A consequence is that the cumulative number of adoptions follows an S-shaped, or sigmoid curve, which starts slowly, accelerates, and slows, eventually reaching a plateau on number of adopters.

Rogers (2003) considered the adoption of an innovation in a social and communication context. After early adopters accepted the innovation, it is communicated to others through social channels. Eventually it diffuses to a significant number of adopters in the social system, who experience varied levels of satisfaction. Diffusion refers to the process in which users of the innovation develop additional knowledge and new patterns of use experience. In this way, the diffuser gains enhanced degree of use (Robertson and Gatignon, 1986; Shih and Venkatesh, 2004).

Five attributes that favor adoption have been identified and shown empirically to account for a high proportion of adoption-diffusion project variance. They are relative advantage, compatibility, complexity, trialability, and observability (Rogers, 2003).

- *Relative advantage*. It refers to how much advantage the innovation provides versus the prior technology. Rogers posited that if an innovation has high relative advantage, its rate of adoption will be high.
- *Compatibility*. It represents the compatibility of the innovation with the experiences, values, and needs of the potential adopters. An innovation might be path-breaking technically but fall short on compatibility.
- *Complexity*. It is the degree of difficulty to use and understand an innovation (Rogers, 2003). Ease of use would speed up adoption. The technology acceptance model (TAM) has confirmed ease of use as important (Davis, 1989, 1993). Complex innovations necessitate more time in learning and education.
- *Trialability*. It is extent to which an innovation lends itself to be pilot tested. With high trialability, adoption will occur more quickly (Rogers, 2003).
- *Observability*. It is the visibility of the innovation to the society using it. If an innovation is more observable, communication will be faster about it, leading to a higher rate of adoption.

Rogers posited that communication channels are essential for the adoption process. For instance, an iPod can be communicated through the channels of text messaging and social networking; a car innovation through the web and dealer networks. The theory can include change agents who specialize as professionals in promoting the diffusion of an innovation. The role of change agents is sometimes taken by opinion leaders i.e. persons very visible and well known in a field whose favoring of an innovation impacts a large number of people. If opinion leaders are prominent in promoting an innovation, then the theory posits a 2-step diffusion process, (1) from the innovation to the opinion leader, and (2) from the opinion leader to the user.

In contrast to adoption-diffusion theory that emphasizes stages of adoption and diffusion, the use-diffusion model focuses on diffusion, rate of use, and variety of use (Shih and Venkatesh, 2004). Early and middle stages of adoption of a technology transition to the late stage, characterized by diffusion of that technology. Diffusers may fall in different categories by rates of use and variety of use. The use of the technology over time leads to outcomes of diffusion. As seen in Fig. 5.1, the determinants of use-diffusion (U/D) are grouped in social, technological, personal, and external dimensions (Shih and Venkatesh, 2004). The social dimension encompasses factors in the user's social setting that influence pattern of use. It might include technology training in the community, competitive or cooperation arrangements, or normal means of communications. The technological dimension includes the sophistication of hardware and/or software, the associated technologies, and the data storage capacities. The personal dimension emphasizes characteristics of the individual that favor or discourage use, such as ease or difficulty of use, educational

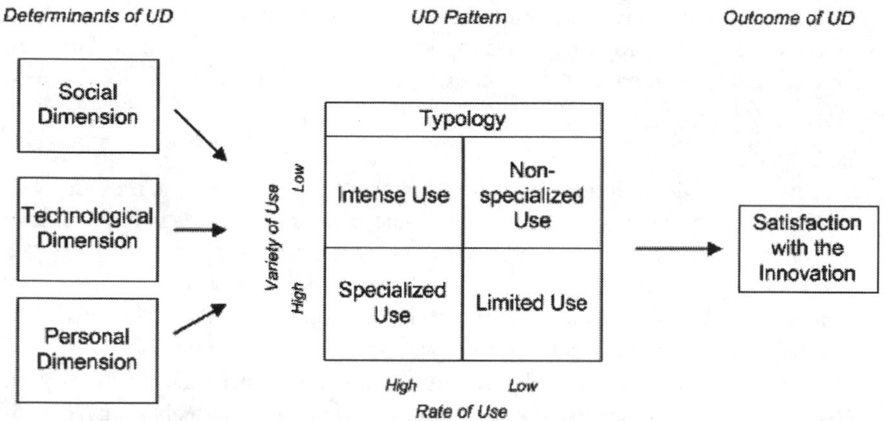

Fig. 5.1 Use diffusion generic model (source: Shih and Venkatesh, 2004)

background, and concept of privacy. The external dimension embodies factors external to the individual and his/her social setting, such as access to global technology, exposure to worldwide media, and the economy in the broad region.

The typology of use is cross-classified by rate of use and variety of use. Rate of use refers to how frequently the innovation is utilized. Variety of use measures the different uses of an innovative product or service.

The use-diffusion generic model (Shih and Venkatesh, 2004) shows the four use-diffusion types in the center of the diagram in Fig. 5.1. Determinants impact type of diffusion-user. The outcomes are satisfaction with the technology, perceived use of the technology, and interest in use of new technologies. In contrast to Rogers' model, the use-diffusion one is not driven by rate of adoption. Rather, the innovation has already succeeded in achieving adoption, so the user's focus shifts to the determinants of diffusion leading to higher quality of use, variety of use, and eventually to the outcomes. Diffusion occurs in the context of the community social system surrounding the organization. Use-diffusion theory has the advantages of emphasizing diffusion determinants, distinguishing types of users, and providing for varied outcomes

Adoption-diffusion theory is most applicable to WMSDS in the early and middle stages, while use-diffusion theory is most relevant in the late, mature stages of diffusion of WMSDS. The reason is that through adoption, a user experiences the innovation for the first time, but is not ready to differentiate his/her use more. Later on, Use-diffusion theory focuses on attributes favoring diffusion and rates of diffusion (Shih and Venkatesh, 2004).

Web-based and mobile-based spatial technologies are perceived by users as innovations. The study justification is that they have appeared only in the last decade and are considered currently by the vast majority of users as the introduction of something new. For that reason, it is more likely that adoption-diffusion theory will apply, since the innovations have not yet progressed yet to a full diffusion phase.

5.3 Research Propositions

The research propositions are as follows:

1. There are significant advantages the web and mobile SDS over the traditional SDS approach.
2. The WMSDS innovation helps the organization competitively.
3. The organization can adjust well to the innovation of WMSDS.
4. The innovation is user-friendly for customers and internal users.
5. In development, the WMSDS innovation is prototyped or piloted in small segments.
6. The WMSDS innovation is visible within and outside the organization.
7. WMSDS differs in its innovation features between the U.S. and Hong Kong.

Although an entire similarly designed study of WMSDS could not be found, each research question can be supported by prior literature. Each of the first six propositions relate to an attribute of A/D theory. A/D is chosen over U/D for reasons given at the end of the last section. The last proposition does not relate directly to A/D theory, but instead posits there are cross-country differences in adoption and diffusion.

5.3.1 There Are Significant Advantages to the Web and Mobile SDS over the Traditional SDS Approach

Studies have reported positive or mixed advantages of WMSDS over traditional SDS (Kraak, 2004; Evans et al., 2004; Lopez, 2004; Rizos and Drane, 2004; Shiode et al., 2004; Bapna and Gangopadhyay, 2005; Kingston, 2007; Ray, 2007; Li, 2007; Mendoza et al., 2009; Zhang and Li, 2005). In studies of positive advantages, participatory web-based decision-making was beneficial in deciding on locations of nuclear waste disposal sites (Evans et al., 2004); web-based GIS for oversize vehicles on state highways in Delaware reduced permitting time and processing costs and improved safety (Ray, 2007); the WMSDS approach effected better utility vehicle routing versus prior routing methods (Mendoza et al., 2009); and time-critical web-based GIS decision-making benefited by enhanced data sharing and heterogeneous sources (Zhang and Li, 2005). Another logical-conceptual study reasoned that web-based and mobile-based mapping has benefits over paper due to causes including enhanced visualization, improved search capability, hyperlinking, and better access to attributes (Kraak, 2004). Mixed advantages and disadvantages were reported for web-based GIS to assist in analysis of vehicle crashes (Bapna and Gangopadhyay, 2005) and for a web-based environment-on-call (EoC) system for Manchester, England city government (Kingston, 2007). Several broad studies found advantages for web-based and mobile-based SDS for safety services, consumer portals, enterprise applications (Lopez, 2004); vehicle control and services, emergency services, electronic payments, travel (Rizos and Drane, 2004);

advertising, instant messaging, real-time tracking (Shiode et al., 2004); and mobile applications (Li, 2007). For the latter, growth in public skepticism of the application was disadvantageous. Overall, the literature points to advantages.

The proposition relates in A/D theory to the attribute of *relative advantage*.

5.3.2 The WMSDS Innovation Helps the Organization Competitively

Most literature studies have concerned government organizations. Although not competing financially, government organizations compete for attention and prominence among peer governments. Lopez (2004) pointed out the competitive advantages for wireless carriers in integrating their customer relationship management and field operations with customers and suppliers. Other studies reported that WMSDS benefitted governments (Bapna and Gangopadhyay, 2005; Ray, 2007). In an overview of competitive and market benefits of mobile GIS (Li, 2007), many advantages were reported.

The proposition relates in A/D theory to the attribute of *relative advantage*.

5.3.3 The Organization Can Adjust Well to the Innovation of WMSDS

Good internal adjustment by important governmental stakeholders was reported for a web-based prototype spatial system for vehicle crashes (Bapna and Gangopadhyay, 2005). The state government of Delaware adjusted well to a heavy vehicle routing application (Ray, 2007). On the other hand, in WMSDS for time-critical applications, organizations were concerned about unsatisfactory reliability, security, performance, and semantic interoperability (Zhang and Li, 2005). Since most of the present study cases are not time-critical, we posit that organizations will adjust well.

The proposition relates in A/D theory to the attribute of *compatibility*.

5.3.4 The Innovation Is User-Friendly for Customers and Internal Users

Studies reported moderate to high user-friendliness of WMSDS applications (Bapna and Gangopadhyay, 2005; Ray, 2007; Kingston, 2007). Where there were issues, they tended to be ones of psychology (Bapna and Gangopadhyay) and trust/confidence (Kingston, 2007). These behavioral issues are expected to be overcome with more user training experience, and familiarity. The proposition is aligned with the deep sentiment in the literature of need to improve user friendliness.

The proposition relates in A/D theory to the attribute of *complexity*.

5.3.5 In Development, the WMSDS Innovation Is Prototyped or Piloted in Small Segments

In a prior study that used prototyping (Bapna and Gangopadhyay, 2005), a web-based SDSS for commercial motor vehicle crashes was developed as a prototype for the State of Maryland; it was beneficial in pointing to drawbacks that can be worked on in full implementation. In another study (Ray, 2007) prototyping was not used but the whole system was tested. However, there was a delivery delay due to insufficient tools and user interfaces to test the full implementation.

Thc proposition relates in A/D theory to the attribute of *trialabiliy*.

5.3.6 The WMSDS Innovation Is Visible Within and Outside the Organization

Some studies have reported visibility of WMSDS applications inside and outside the organization (Bapna and Gangopadhyay, 2005; Kingston, 2007; Li, 2007), while others report visibility only on the inside (Rizos and Drane, 2004; Scheibe et al., 2006; Ray, 2007). None reports visibility only on the outside. We posit that most WMSDS applications will be visible both within and outside the organization.

The proposition relates in A/D theory to the attribute of *observability*.

5.3.7 WMSDS Differs in Its Innovation Features Between the US and Hong Kong

We could not locate comparative literature on differences in WMSDS use between countries. However, there are many studies of WMSDS in the U.S. (e.g. Bapna and Gangopadhyay, 2005; Scheibe et al., 2006; Ray, 2007; Sugumaran et al., 2007) and in the UK (e.g. Evans et al., 2004; Kingston, 2007), but we cannot identify country differences between them. In the information systems literature, many cross-country comparisons have confirmed significant country differences, for instance in electronic collaboration research (Lefebvre et al., 2006; Reinig et al., 2008; Lowry, 2010, to mention only a few). An extensive worldwide study of technology differences (Dutta and Mia, 2007) showed that although the U.S and Hong Kong are world leaders in technology, with U.S. ranked 7th in networked readiness index and Hong Kong ranked 12th among 122 nations, for key indicators of per capita mobile phone subscribers and per capita broadband subscribers Hong Kong exceeded the U.S. Both these factors are important for WMSDS.

Because of their underlying infrastructure differences, the present study proposes that differences in WMSDS will be found between the U.S. and Hong Kong.

5.4 Methodology

The case study research strategy consists of the definition of the focus of the study, framework construction, data collection, and case analysis. The case study method (Yin, 1994) is utilized to evaluate the development and implementation of spatial web and mobile services; the users; their applications; architecture; spatial web and mobile decision making; standards; costs and benefits; strategies; and differences between two nations.

5.4.1 Case Studies

This research is performed through case studies of 14 organizations, half in Hong Kong, China, and half in the U.S. They are mostly medium to large-sized, and drawn from business and government. The organizations were selected based on a convenience sample. The reason is that most organizations using WMSDS restrict access of academic interviewers. This is especially true for private business, which has proprietary and confidentiality reasons to exclude academic researchers. Twenty one organizations were approached, of which 14 agreed to participate in the survey. There were either one or two interviewees per organization, for a total of 19 interviewees. When two interviewees were interviewed, they were interviewed together, but the person speaking was noted on the transcript.

For each firm, an in-person or telephone interview of up to 2 h was conducted with one or two executive(s) or manager(s) responsible for spatial web and spatial mobile applications. If this executive/manager did not know certain questionnaire areas, an interview was requested of one other management or technical person at the organization. If the interviewee granted consent, the interview was audio recorded. The recording was transcribed and the transcript used in the case analysis. The investigator also took handwritten notes that were utilized in the analysis. The interviewees were given the option to remain anonymous. Two organizations elected anonymity and are referred to as Digital Mobile Device Leader (DMDL) and U.S. Federal Security Agency (FSA).

5.5 Findings

Findings mostly support the research propositions. WMSDS provided advantages over traditional client-server and desktop platforms. Most organizations adjusted to WMSDS innovation, although some reported user resistance and managerial stress leading to turnover. Users for all organizations indicated easier use for WMSDS versus antecedents. Prototyping/piloting was standard for system development for half the cases. Visibility of the innovation was moderate overall and keyed to extent of external utilization. WMSDS was a significant competitive factor for a fifth of the organizations, all of which were large businesses. There were significant differences in WMSDS between the two countries, in particular greater spatial data constraints in Hong Kong, more WMSDS software customization in Hong Kong, and increased mobile spatial decision support effectiveness in the U.S. The findings demonstrate that the adoption/diffusion model is useful for WMSDS.

The detailed findings of the case analysis are seen in Tables 5.1 and 5.2. Although there is not space in this paper to detail each of the 14 cases, this section examines the overall findings in more detail and especially concentrates on the findings for comparative results between the U.S. and Hong Kong, since those differences are heretofore unknown.

5.5.1 Decision Support

For the 14 cases, decision support varies quite a lot between internal and external users. The latter are mostly the general public but sometimes client users, such as for the Hong Kong firms, Star Vision and Map King. For Map King, the client users apply web- and mobile-based GIS solutions mostly for transportation applications in other southeast Asian countries. Areas of spatial decision making also vary considerably among the 14 cases. For instance, the U.S. Federal Security Agency (FSA) applies a combination of web-based and mobile-based GIS to make decisions on the location of agents in the field and their proximities to each other and to other assets. The users are managers or specialized field agents. The manager-interviewee stated: "I would say it would have to be a 70:30 split between managers and agents in the field.... There's a subset of agents that are called intelligent agents that can either be intelligence managers like myself or [field] agents who are detailed to the intelligence department. And I would say managers and those agents I just mentioned would be most prolific users of mapping applications that we create here in this department. Whereas agents in the field don't necessarily have a need to access the mapping services constantly, they do have access to them."

At UC Irvine, public users make low-level decisions on campus locations based on a web-based map. At Hong Kong Government Lands Division, web-based GIS is utilized internally for city planning decisions based on demographic and economic data. Overall, the GIS basis for uses tend to be evenly spread between a narrow to wide ranges of map layers and data attributes. Regarding whether the WMSDS application was proprietary or open, about 53% were proprietary and the others open.

5.5.2 Findings on Differences Between US WMSDS and Hong Kong WMSDS for the Case Organizations

Analysis of the interview responses resulted in three major areas of differences for SDS between the U.S. and Hong Kong organizations in the sample. They are the following.

Table 5.1 Summary of case study findings on spatial decision support, data characteristics, and adoption stage, United States

Firm	Decision support	Propietary	Range of map layers and data attributes	Stage in adoption/ diffusion	Support for propositions					
					Proposition 1	Proposition 2	Proposition 3	Proposition 4	Proposition 5	Proposition 6
Bexar County, Texas	Staff. DS at low level for tax and property, cap projects	N	Wide	Early+	+	NA	+	+		
	Public. foreclosures	N		Early	+	NA	+	+		+
Digital Mobile Device Leader (DMDL)	Staff. No.	NA	Wide	NA						
	Outside users. DS for individual path decisions			Middle	+	+	+	+	+	+
GeoNav	Staff. No WMSDS									
	Outside users. no, WMSDS in planning but not ready									
US Federal Security Agency (FSA)	Staff. new users need time	Y	Wide	Early	+	NA	+	+		

Table 5.1 (continued)

					Support for propositions					
Firm	Decision support	Propietary	Range of map layers and data attributes	Stage in adoption/ diffusion	Proposition 1	Proposition 2	Proposition 3	Proposition 4	Proposition 5	Proposition 6
Lamar Advertising	Staff. MIS for sales reps on proposal generation. Mixes web-based and hardcopy	Y	Narrow	Middle	+	+	+	+	+	+
City of Tacoma	Staff. Long-range planners in Economic Development Department who decide on relationships of infrastructure, demographics, etc. for planning reports. Some people in city manager's office request and user maps for decision. Fire Department for support uses on decisions	N	Wide	Early	+	NA	+	+	+	+

Table 5.1 (continued)

Firm	Decision support	Propietary	Range of map layers and data attributes	Stage in adoption/ diffusion	Support for propositions					
					Proposition 1	Proposition 2	Proposition 3	Proposition 4	Proposition 5	Proposition 6
	Public. Gov Me application has 100 layers and used by general public. Especially population with developers and real estate professionals who need to know what is the spatial arrangement of infrastructure	N	Wide	Early	+	NA	+	+	+	+
UC Irvine	Staff. A few faculty using it for educational decision-making. People in the campus data center to decide on spatial arrangements of servers and other equipment in the center	Y	Narrow	Early to mid	+	+	+	NA	+	NA

Table 5.1 (continued)

Firm	Decision support	Propietary	Range of map layers and data attributes	Stage in adoption/ diffusion	Support for propositions					
					Proposition 1	Proposition 2	Proposition 3	Proposition 4	Proposition 5	Proposition 6
	Educational clients. Used by select lobbyists, consultants, politicians for decision making	Y	Narrow	Early	NA	NA	NA	NA	NA	NA
	Public. Widely used for campus maps on the UCI website. Used for low level individual decision making	N	Narrow	Mid	+	+	+	+	+	+

NA = Not available.
+ in cell = proposition supported; Blank in cell = proposition not supported.

Table 5.2 Summary of case study findings on spatial decision support, data characteristics, and adoption stage, Hong Kong

Firm	Decision support	Propietary	Range of map layers and data attributes	Stage in adoption/ diffusion	Support for propositions					
					Proposition 1	Proposition 2	Proposition 3	Proposition 4	Proposition 5	Proposition 6
Centamap (subsidiary of CentaLine)	Staff. Use some web-based information for MIS not for decision support	Y	NA							
	Public. Used for low level individual decision making	N	Wide	Middle	+	+	+	+		
Hong Kong Air Cargo Terminals Ltd. (HACTL)	Staff. May support low level individual WMSDS	Y	Narrow	Early	+		+	+		
Hong Kong govern-ment/Lands division	Staff. Applied for social applications. Searching done based on demographic data. Some planning decisions utilize this information	N	Mid	Middle	+	NA		+		

Table 5.2 (continued)

Firm	Decision support	Propietary	Range of map layers and data attributes	Stage in adoption/ diffusion	Support for propositions					
					Proposition 1	Proposition 2	Proposition 3	Proposition 4	Proposition 5	Proposition 6
	Public. No. However, data sold to selected other organizations	Y	NA	NA	NA	NA	NA	NA	NA	NA
Hong Kong govern-ment/slopes division	Staff. Location potential landslide areas for mitigation e.g. areas near squatters.	N	Narrow	Middle	+	NA				+
Map King	Staff. No WMSDS use									
	Clients. Corporations apply it for routing decisions	Y	Narrow	Middle	+	+	NA	NA	+	
	Public. Used for online mapping. Low level individual decision making	N	Wide	Middle	+	+	+	+	+	+

Table 5.2 (continued)

Firm	Decision support	Propietary	Range of map layers and data attributes	Stage in adoption/ diffusion	Support for propositions					
					Proposition 1	Proposition 2	Proposition 3	Proposition 4	Proposition 5	Proposition 6
Star vision	Staff. Web mapping done internally for managing the firm's map server and public website			NA	+	+		+		+
	Clients. Corporations manage vehicle tracking and do fleet management. Small firms do personal spatial tracking for customers	Y	Narrow	Middle	+	+	+	+		
Hong Kong yellow pages	Staff. No WMSDS use									
	Public. Used for decisions on spatial location	Y	Narrow	Middle	+	+	+	+	+	+

NA = Not available.
+ in cell = proposition supported; Blank in cell = proposition not supported.

5.5.2.1 Difference in Systems Development of Web-Based SDS

In U.S. half of organizations used a prototyping/piloting approach, while in Hong Kong, almost entirely the organizations utilized traditional systems development. The reason in the case sample is that Hong Kong organizations do more development and building of spatial web services, rather than subscribing to an outside web service. Since their users prefer the Chinese language, the Hong Kong firms are compelled to do development in-house, as external web service providers presently cannot satisfy Chinese language quality for these users.

For cases of prototyping in the U.S., commercial software or outside services for web development were provided to the in-house development team at the beginning, so internet software development was minimized and the team could focus on the application. For instance, City of Tacoma subscribed to Business Analyst Online, which is a web service emphasizing business and socio-demographic information for counties, cities, and small areas, which is offered by and hosted at ESRI Inc., a leading GIS software company. For Bexar County, commercial website creation software was given to departments for ease in constructing websites. Websites were built for location and volume of foreclosures, tax and property changes over time, locations of traffic signs and traffic counting devices, and for locations of capital building projects. In these cases, prototyping was done with the encouragement of management and reduced risk.

In another case, prototyping was present in the software culture. For Digital Mobile Device Leader (DMDL), spatial web mapping started as an independent entrepreneurial, creative and very small firm, with highly talented web developers. They preferred prototyping, and that tradition has carried through to much larger DMDL that purchased their firm. At DMDL, the prototyping is done in a compressed time frame involving many meetings of users and specialist developers and rapid weekly code updating. The manager-respondent put it this way: "Well basically we have a product manager who is tasked with doing some research interfacing either with third parties, business partners, and/or business groups with [DMDL] to understand how whatever we're building interfaces with the devices or if it's a standalone then how it interfaces with customers.... We present to the development team our requirements through the use case and show them our books... And then they come back with a proposal. We're an agile group, so we are very quick.... And every week we have a demo to show progress and then after four weeks of coding.. so there's one week of planning, four weeks coding that are done and we're done with the project and have no more features and then go into quality assurance."

5.5.2.2 Difference in WMSDS Application Areas

For the Hong Kong sample, application areas for WMSDS and other spatial web-related applications predominantly comprise (1) public city mapping, (2) transportation/logistics, and (3) Hong Kong government internal uses for demographic analysis, planning, and environmental assessment.

For the US sample, application areas were much more diverse including high performance athletic training, real-time public safety by a security agency, providing mapping for small utilities, enabling sales reps to put together sales reports with maps, providing dozens of attributes on a city spatial web, offering public online campus maps, and mapping physically a large data center for IT specialists.

There is an underlying interpretation of the difference. In the U.S., due to freedom of information, free or low government data costs, government initiatives to provide boundary files and coverages, and the many private data gathering firms which provide data that are georeferenced, there is a much wider variety of data available at low cost than in Hong Kong. The spatial land areas being covered are much larger, contributing further to diversity of data and applications.

One contributing factor to the difference in SDS application areas is that the Chinese central government severely restricts GIS use for the business sector in China. It is illegal for private enterprises and private citizens to use digital spatial data. Hence WMSDS is almost entirely restricted to use in the government sector. Hong Kong Special Administrative Region is exempted from the restrictions within Hong Kong. As a result Hong Kong GIS firms and government departments in the sample mainly support coverages and data in urban Hong Kong. Its total land area is 428 square miles and urban land area is 85.38 square miles. The region's population in 2008 was 6.98 million (Hong Kong Special Administrative Region Government, 2009). Thus the focus of Hong Kong organizations is nearly entirely on the exempted Hong Kong Special Administrative Region, rather than mainland China.

The implication is that the spatial web can be more powerfully populated with data in the U.S. Since there is such a huge amount and variety of spatial and associated attribute data, U.S. organizations would need to spend more time prioritizing what data are essential for a particular project.

A second contributing factor to WMSDS application areas is language differences. Since the handover of Hong Kong to China in 1993, Chinese has become more prevalent versus English in business and on the street. Hence, global standard software that uses language is evaluated in Hong Kong for robust Chinese language capabilities. To satisfy Hong Kong users, GIS software needs to have language and ground accuracy on naming, addressing, and attribute data. For instance, for many buildings in Hong Kong, there are different street addresses on four sides of the building, whereas in the U.S. a single building would have one address. The 4-sided addresses must have language accuracy in Chinese and English. Accuracy from outside global providers is considered insufficient by Hong Kong respondents, who believe that Google Earth/Maps and Yahoo Maps do not accurately support Hong Kong either spatially or in some language features, reducing adoption by Chinese language users.

5.5.2.3 3-D Applications

There is greater emphasis in Hong Kong, versus U.S., on 3-D applications for GIS infrastructure. Hong Kong is one of the densest locations on earth, a high rise and mid rise city.

Its density is 16,303 persons/square mile Hong Kong Special Administrative Region, and 131,532 persons/square mile in its urban part. This compares with 2,122 persons/square mile in the New York Combined Metropolitan Area (Forstall et al., 2009). The implications are that since Hong Kong land coverages are so limited, use of the same base maps is more likely, while spatial referencing is more likely to be 3-D.

Effective GIS for infrastructure and other WMSDS applications for the built environment have to consider 3-D capabilities as a necessity, much more than the U.S. cities. For WMSDS, 3-D decision models are beginning to be developed, as seen in the Hong Kong/Slopes and Centamap cases.

Hence the smaller players from Hong Kong in web-based mapping have opportunities in that market, even versus global giants. The global giants have no better attribute and digital boundary files than the locals. The locals also can do a better job on mapping of the 3-D complexity of Hong Kong, especially real estate and telecomm firms, since they already have the data on where people reside in the vertical dimension.

5.6 Outcomes for the Research Propositions

5.6.1 There Are Significant Advantages to the Web and Mobile SDS Over the Old Approach?

Supported. Two major advantages were identified.

(a) Ability to reach large public audiences. This is a familiar advantage of web-based applications in general. However, because of the spatial data and spatial analysis, it is generally not as easy to implement as text-based or simple imagery-based. It was present for four Hong Kong and four U.S. organizations.
(b) Improved centralization of planning, design, and implementation of WMSDS solutions. The advantages to organizations is that development of web-based applications need not be repeated by many diverse and decentralized offices. It was present for four Hong Kong and four U.S. organizations.

For one case, the Hong Kong Government Lands Division, centralization was set as a goal, with the expected benefit that information could be made available and shared across departments, but the respondent reported that department walls and required personnel rotations were barriers that prevented centralization from being realized. The rotations are required by the Hong Kong Government to reduce corruption. The interviewee explained: “Because in government we have to rotate, like me, you won’t be working one area for a very long time because in Hong Kong, especially in government, we have some rules to prevent people to have corruption. They don’t suggest people stay in one post for a long time so we have to change post. Once changing post, the tacit knowledge may not be kept."

5.6.2 WMSDS Innovation Helps the Organization Competitively

Supported. Ninety three percent of organizations reported the spatial web helped it competitively, and

Ninety three percent of organizations reported the web- and mobile-based spatial decision support was helping competitively, although this was a mixture of WMSDS by the organization and by individuals in the public. Fifty-seven percent of cases reported WMSDS was helping it or a client competitively, but not for individuals in the public.

5.6.3 The Organization Can Adjust Well to the Innovation of WMSDS

Partly supported. Largely, the case organizations adjusted well, but there were three exceptions are in the U.S. Lamar Advertising and City of Tacoma had turnover of the original spatial web champion, due to resistance and tensions. The Federal Security Agency experienced significant resistance by some users. The behavioral mechanisms in the three problematic cases are unexplained and the causation needs to be studied in more depth.

5.6.4 The Innovation Is User-Friendly for Customers and Internal Users

Supported for 13 of 14 cases. The exception is the FSA, which encountered some problems, since the developers, who are internal employees, had to learn GIS from scratch. This was partly due to the requirement for federal security clearances and necessity for knowledge of the unit's activities.

5.6.5 In Development, the WMSDS Innovation Is Prototyped or Piloted in Small Segments

The innovations largely underwent a traditional system development process. The reason might be the need for robust applications for widespread public use. The three exceptions are in the U.S. At City of Tacoma and Bexar County, outside spatial web services or website-creation software were used, relieving much of the county's burden and responsibility for development. At DMDL, the spatial web development division came from an entrepreneurial, creative and very small firm that was purchased. Its highly talented web developers, who moved to DMDL, continued to use a prototyping approach.

5.6.6 The WMSDS Innovation Is Visible Within and Outside the Organization?

WMSDS was visible, inside for half the cases, and outside for the other half. The popularity of WMSDS applications for the public makes WMSDS innovation especially visible on the outside. On the inside, visibility depends on maturity stage of adoption/diffusion and on how widespread it is organizationally.

5.6.7 WMSDS Differs in Its Innovation Features Between the US and Hong Kong

Supported. It differs in three respects:

(a) *Systems development.* Hong Kong case organizations utilize traditional systems development, while U.S. case organizations use half prototyping, half traditional.

(b) *Application areas for WMSDS.* Hong Kong case organizations apply WMSDS predominantly for city mapping for the public, transportation and logistics, and government internal professional-based uses, while U.S. case organizations are much more diverse in uses, including real-time security and safety for federal agents, multi-layer spatial web for a city, online campus maps, mapping the interior of a large-scale data center, evaluating a federal educational program, and collecting/analyzing data on high performance athletes.

    Hong Kong case businesses do not have access to digital spatial information on mainland China. It is prohibited in mainland China for that information to be used or distributed except by Chinese government (federal, provincial, local) or by a tiny handful of business organizations given permission. Thus, with respect to China, businesses in Hong Kong are excluded from digital boundary information for the mainland's 3,694,939 square miles of land. The organizations can have access to digital boundary data from most governments around the world and to worldwide private sources of data. This restriction constrains the scope of much of the effort for GIS in Hong Kong, and also leads to market saturation of GIS applications for Hong Kong. It influences the types of SDS that can be developed by these organizations.

    Hong Kong since the 1997 handover to China has emphasized Chinese as well as English. To be widely adopted, public spatial websites in Hong Kong must have robust Chinese language features. Global web software like Google Earth, Google Maps, and Yahoo Maps are competitively disadvantaged, opening niches for smaller Chinese providers. This differs from the U.S. where the large web services providers are a source of competition.

(c) There is greater emphasis in Hong Kong, versus U.S., on 3-D applications for GIS infrastructure. Effective GIS for infrastructure and other WMSDS applications for the built environment has to include 3-D capabilities as a necessity, more than the US

5.7 Case Findings and the Usefulness of the Research Models of Adoption and Use

As mentioned earlier, the A/D model is more relevant, since it focuses on adoption which characterizes the early and middle stage of the WMSDS innovation, which is only 5 years old. The correspondence with the five attributes of adoption-diffusion of relative advantage, compatibility, complexity, trialability, and observability (Rogers, 2003) for the fourteen cases are examined following the outcomes of the research questions, which reveal whether these attributes were or were not present.

As seen in Tables 5.1 and 5.2, each case was assigned to a stage of the A/D model based on respondent's description of extent of adoption and diffusion. Overall the WMSDS applications were 40% in the early and 60% in the middle adoption-diffusion stages. None was in an advanced stage. Hong Kong was more advanced in adoption-diffusion, with 88% in the middle stage, versus 30% middle for the U.S. The more stage-advanced WMSDS in Hong Kong might reflect its generally higher level of mobile and internet usage versus the U.S.

The Adoption Diffusion (A/D) model has been the useful one in this case study analysis. This can be demonstrated in the six right-hand columns of Tables 5.1 and 5.2, which indicate which research propositions were supported. As mentioned earlier, the research propositions correspond to the five A/D attributes as follows: *relative advantage* (propositions 1 and 2), *compatibility* (proposition 3), *complexity* (proposition 4), *trialability* (proposition 5), and *observability* (proposition 6). In the A/D model, at least two of the five determinants are evident in the cases. All five determinants are present for four cases. The most common missing determinants were trialability and observability. In trialability, only about half of cases used prototyping or piloting, so it was generally lower. On observability, the WMSDS applications available to the general public, about half, have been visible, while those utilized internally much less so. Compatibility was high in 86% of cases. Complexity was evident as an attribute for all cases except Hong Kong Government/Slopes. The Slopes respondent pointed out it was overburdened with standards which changed frequently and also that its users were mostly professional engineers and technical officers, so applications turned out to be quite complex. Since Slopes' WMSDS users are predominantly internal to the Hong Kong government, it can succeed presently with complexity. However, would potentially turn into a problem if Slopes were to open up public use. Finally relative advantage was evident in all the cases. Overall, the A/D determinants were medium to high and were associated with adoption. The actual status of adoption-diffusion was early to middle stage, so the cases mostly support the A/D model.

The Use-Diffusion (U/D) model is less useful because the fourteen cases were all in the early and middle stages, whereas U/D is more relevant to late stage. U/D would have the advantage of including social, personal, technological, and external determinants and more varied outcomes that would go beyond those analyzed for the A/D framework. In a more complete study, additional determinants can be added as survey items, especially technological and external ones In sum, although the A/D model is more suitable for the present research sample, for a large sample with greater presence of innovations in the late stage, a combination of A/D and U/D models would seem appropriate.

5.8 Future Trends

Emerging and future trends in web- and mobile based spatial decision support are considered from the standpoints of technology, decision support, privacy-ethical-legal issues, and international compatibility. The implications and opportunities of the present study and the trends discussed lead to several suggested areas for future research in WMSDS.

5.8.1 Technology and Data

GIS and other spatial technologies are trending towards greater spatial referencing, mobility, ubiquity, cloud computing, massive spatial server centers, and more powerful national cyber infrastructures (Li, 2007; Drummond et al., 2007b). Changes will increase the prevalence and power of WMSDS.

For attribute data to be accessible to GIS and WMSDS, more pervasive spatial referencing needs to occur. Spatial referencing is provision of locational coordinates to a record. In the future a higher proportion of data in government and industry will have this referencing, allowing it to be mapped and spatially analyzed. This is especially relevant for semi-structured or unstructured real-time decisions, where delays in referencing would compromise the decisions. As certain types of WMSDS become ubiquitous, people and society will interact with their environment in new ways. A simple example is decision-making on intra-metropolitan travel. In the future mobile workers, such as those in utility maintenance or sales teams, will be continually aware of the locations of other members of the team, as well as of customers, competitors, offices, other facilities, traffic conditions, obstacles and barriers, and contours of market forces. Decisions can made on the fly in relation to this whole complex. Caution and controls will be needed to avoid privacy and ethical incursions.

Mobile devices such as 4-G cell phones and beyond will support powerful broadband, and much stronger local and/or cloud-based processing capacity. A counter-trend is the reduction in screen size for most mobile devices. Although still possible with tiny screens, WMSDS is hampered in its visual aspects, implying map simplification. Breakthroughs in mobile ergonomics such as the iPad could offset this trend with "fold-out" features.

The rapidly growing WMSDS use today depends on the expansion of broadband throughout the world. It along with geo-referencing will support powerful WMSDS even in impoverished and least-developed countries and regions. Cloud computing refers to a client system accessing full-fledged software package or applications residing remotely on a server. Its predicted expansion will enable access to WMSDS on portable and mobile devices worldwide, with the caveat of small screen sizes.

Along with cloud computing is the trend towards massive centralized server farms, which are virtualized and able to fine-tune cloud and client-server applications. The essential data management component of WMSDS will tend in the future to reside on centralized server farms.

The U.S. federal government has underway a project to develop national cyber infrastructure, involving supercomputers and next generation broadband. This huge project will help underpin WMSDS in the U.S. government, defense industry, national labs, and academic R&D.

Most WMSDS applications today, including those researched in this study involve simple modeling and spatial analysis. For instance, U.S. city public websites often map several attributes, perhaps in percentage form, in real time. Companies display maps with business feature locations such as sites for advertising e.g. Lamar Advertising, warehouse contents such as Hong Kong Air Cargo Terminals Ltd., or road and satellite images, such as for Google maps. Presently the sophistication of WMSDS decision spatial models is limited. The future trend is towards more sophisticated and complex modeling, optimization, simulation, and spatial analysis. Spatial analysis is insufficiently utilized today even within intensive spatial development groups such as those for metropolitan county governments. It will require more education, training, R&D, and encouragement for spatial analysis to become prevalent for WMSDS applications. It is known that spatial analysis in business often adds a marginal accuracy to decision making leading to economic gain (Pick, 2008), so a more spatially analytic WMSDS would be beneficial.

WMSDS applications are likely to become more interactive. In the cases, the users did not interactively manipulate the GIS functionality beyond the standard web-based or mobile-based features, and also did not have capability to enter data. The trend among vendors is to offer more WMSDS interactivity, so spatial decision makers can readily alter spatial models and supplement, correct, or change data. This is seen today in mobile-based utility industry applications, in which field personnel while working on infrastructure enter and modify centralized spatial and attribute data that are utilized in maintenance and repair (Meehan and Huntsman, 2007).

As WMSDS becomes more diffused, privacy, ethical, and legal boundaries that are being tested in other segments of spatial technologies will arise as constraints on use. For instance, real-time decisions can be made with WMSDS by managers to guide transportation operators who waiver off course. If a truck driver's location during a break time is questionable, what are the rights of the company and driver regarding his/her privacy? What is the right of government to have access to, and make decisions based on internet service providers' cell phone locational information in its massive customer base? It is likely that these technologies may alter legal and ethical boundaries of decision-making. It will take time for organizations to develop policies and courts to rule on the difficult gray areas posed by WMSDS boundary questions.

International comparative differences in WMSDS such as those seen between the U.S. and Hong Kong are likely to become important. For instance, government regulation as well as intellectual property rights to land area digital coverages will differ between nations and need to be resolved. Language differences will become even more prominent as WMSDS spreads worldwide. Differences in street addressing, place designations, and census designations will hamper worldwide WMSDS unless better standards are achieved.

5.9 Conclusion

This chapter has examined web- and mobile-based spatial decision support in the context of adoption and diffusion. WMSDS is viewed as an innovation, since it has been present for only about a half a decade. Findings from structured interviews of fourteen case studies of WMSDS use by private-sector and governmental organizations in the United States and Hong Kong indicate that WMSDS is perceived as improved relative to the prior traditional approaches to spatial decision making. The firms have both external-public and internal applications for WMSDS. The stage of adoption and diffusion of the innovation is early to middle. Resistance to use is present in about 15% of cases. Web-based access to WMSDS is more extensive than mobile-based. This might be due to the bandwidth, reliability, and display differences between fixed and mobile platforms.

The adoption and diffusion models are shown to be useful in understanding the trajectories of use of the technologies. The determinants of A/D are shown to be relevant to the case sample, while UD's determinants, use typologies, and outcomes would be helpful for understanding late stage applications. U/D is recommended for future expanded research samples that include mature, late stage WMSDS.

Future trends discussed indicate applications of wide variety that are more complex, interactive, and helpful to spatial decision making. Among the barriers and constraints anticipated are those of privacy, ethics, law, intellectual property, government restrictions, and language. However, it is likely the critical mass will be achieved so these technologies will become a global part of future decision support.

References

Bapna, S., and Gangopadhyay, A. (2005). A Web-Based GIS for Analyzing Commercial Motor Vehicle Crashes. *Information Resources Management Journal*, 18(3), 1–12.

Brimicombe, A., and Li., Y. (2006). Mobile Space-Time Envelopes for Location-Based Services. *Transactions in GIS*, 10(1), 5–23.

Davis, F. D. (1989). Perceived Usefulness, Perceived Ease of Use, and User Acceptance of Information Technology. *MIS Quarterly*, 13(3), 319–340.

Davis, F. D. (1993). User Acceptance of Information Technology: System Characteristics, User Perceptions, and Behavioral Impacts. *International Journal of Man-Machine Studies*, 38, 318–339.

Dewan, S., Dale, G., and Kraemer, K. L. (2009). Complementarities in the Diffusion of Personal Computers and the Internet: Implications for the Global Digital Divide. *Information Systems Research*. published online in advance, June 12.

Drummond, J., R. Billen, E. João, and D. Forrest (Eds.) (2007a). *Dynamic and Mobile GIS*. Boca Raton, FL: CRC Press.

Drummond, J., João, E., and Billen, R. (2007b). Current and Future Trends in Dynamic and Mobile GIS. In J. Drummond, R. Billen, E. João, and D. Forrest (Eds.), *Dynamic and Mobile GIS* (pp. 289–300). Boca Raton, FL: CRC Press.

Dutta, S., and Mia, I. (2007). *The Global Information Technology Report 2006–2007*. New York, NY: Palgrave McMillan.

Evans, A. J., Kingston, R., and Carver, S. (2004). Democratic Input Into the Nuclear Waste Disposal Problem: The Influence of Geographical Data on Decision Making Examined Through a Web-Based GIS. *Journal of Geographical Systems*, 6(2), 117–132.

Forstall, R. L., Greene, R. P., and Pick, J. B. (2009). Which are the Largest? Why Published Lists of Major Urban Areas Vary So Greatly. *Tijdschrift Voor Economische en Sociale Geografie*, 100(3), 277–297.

Gup, A. (2007) 3 steps in one hour: Building a business intelligence application with the ArcWeb Services JavaScript API. *ArcUser*, March, 52–55. Available at www.esri.com

Harkins, K., and Lawton, M. (2007) Real-Time Tracking of the Washoe County, Nevada, 2006, General Election. *ArcNews*, Summer. Available at www.esri.com

Hong Kong Special Administrative Region Government. (2009). *Hong Kong: The Facts*. Hong Kong: Information Services Department, Hong Kong Special Administrative Region Government.

Kingston, R. (2007). Public Participation in Local Policy Decision-Making: The Role of Web-Based Mapping. *The Cartographic Journal*, 44(2), 138–144.

Kraak, M.-J. (2004). The Role of the Map in a Web-GIS Environment. *Journal of Geographical Systems*, 6(2), 83–90.

Lefebvre, E., Lefebvre, L. A., Hen, G. L., and Mendgen, R. (2006). Cross-Border e-Collaboration for New Product Development in the Automotive Industry. In J. F. Nunamaker Jr. and R. O. Briggs (Eds.), *Proceedings of the 39th Annual Hawaii International Conference on System Sciences* (Vol. 1). Washington, DC: IEEE Computer Society.

Li, Q. (2007). Opportunities in Mobile GIS. In J. Drummond, R. Billen, E. João, and D. Forrest (Eds.), *Dynamic and Mobile GIS* (pp. 19–34). Boca Raton, FL: CRC Press.

Li, C., and Longley, P. (2006). A Test Environment for Location-Based Services Applications. *Transactions in GIS*, 10(1), 43–61.

Lopez, X. R. (2004). Location-Based Services. In H. Karimi and A. Hammad (Eds.), *Telegeoinformatics: Location-Based Computing and Services* (pp. 171–188). Boca Raton, FL: CRC Press.

Lowry, P. (2010). Proposing the Online Community Self-Disclosure Model: The Case of Working Professionals in France and the UK Who Use Online Communities. *European Journal of Information Systems*, 19, 181–195.

Meehan, B., and Huntsman, J. M. (2007). *Empowering Electric and Gas Utilities with GIS*. Redlands, CA: ESRI Press.

Mendoza, J. E., Medaglia, A. L., and Velasco, N. (2009). An Evolutionary-Based Decision Support System for Vehicle Routing: The Case of a Public Utility. *Decision Support Systems*, 46, 730–742.

Pick, J. (2008). *Geo-Business: GIS in the Digital Organization*. New York, NY: Wiley.

Peng, Z.-R., and Tsou, M.-H. (2003). *Internet GIS: Distributed Geographic Information Services for the Internet and Wireless Networks*. New York, NY: Wiley.

Ray, J. J. (2007). A Web-Based Spatial Decision Support System Optimizes Routes for Oversize/Overweight Vehicles in Delaware. *Decision Support Systems*, 43, 1171–1185.

Reinig, B. A., Briggs, R. O., and De Vreede, G. J. (2008). A Cross-Cultural Investigation of the Goal-Attainment-Likelihood Construct and Its Effect on Satisfaction with Technology Supported Collaboration. In R. Sprague (Ed.), *Proceedings of 41st Hawaii International Conference on System Sciences*. Washington, DC: IEEE Computer Society.

Rizos, C., and Drane, C. (2004). The Role of Telegeoinformatics in ITS. In H. Karimi and A. Hammad (Eds.), *Telegeoinformatics: Location-Based Computing and Services* (pp. 315–347). Boca Raton, FL: CRC Press.

Robertson, T. S., and Gatignon, H. (1986). Competitive Effects on Technology Diffusion. *Journal of Marketing*, 50, 1–12.

Rogers, E. M. (1962). *Diffusion of Innovations* (1st ed). New York, NY: Free Press.

Rogers, E. M. (2003). *Diffusion of Innovations* (5th ed.). New York, NY: Free Press.

Scheibe, K. P., Carstensen, L. W., Jr., Rakes, T. R., and Rees, L. P. (2006). Going the Last Mile: A Spatial Decision Support System for Wireless Broadband Communications. *Decision Support Systems*, 42, 557–570.

Shih, C.-F., and Venkatesh, A. (2004). Beyond Adoption: Development and Application of a Use-Diffusion Model. *Journal of Marketing*, 68, 59–72.

Shiode, N., Li, C., Batty, M., Longley, P., and Maguire, D. (2004). The Impact and Penetration of Location-Based Services. In H. Karimi and A. Hammad (Eds.), *Telegeoinformatics: Location-Based Computing and Services* (pp. 349–366). Boca Raton, FL: CRC Press.

Simon, R., Frohlich, P., and Anegg, H. (2007). *Transactions in GIS*, 11(5), 783–794.

Sugumaran, R., Ilavajhala, S., and Sugumaran, V. (2007). Development of a Web-Based Intelligent Spatial Decision Support System (WEBISDSS). In B. Hilton (Ed.), *Emerging Spatial Information Systems and Applications* (pp. 184–202). Hershey, PA: Idea Group Publishing.

Sugumaran, V., and Sugumaran, R. (2007). Web-Based Spatial Decision Support Systems (WebSDSS): Evolution, Architecture, Examples, and Challenges. *Communications of the Association for Information Systems*, 19, 845–875, Article 40.

Venkatesh, A., and Shih, C.-F. (2005) An Investigation of Theories of Diffusion in The Global Context: A Comparative Study of the U.S., Sweden, and India. CRITO research Paper November. Irvine, CA: University of California Irvine, Center for Research on Information Technology in Organizations.

Yin, R. K. (1994). *Case Study Research: Design and Methods* (2nd Ed.). Thousand Oaks, CA: SAGE Publications.

Zhang, C., and Li, W. (2005). The Roles of Web Feature and Web Map Services in Real-Time Geospatial Data Sharing for Time-Critical Applications. *Cartography and Geographic Information Science*, 32(4), 269–383.

Zhao, P., Yu, G., and Di, L. (2007). Geospatial Web Services. In B. Hilton (Ed.), *Emerging Spatial Information Systems and Applications* (pp. 1–35). Hershey, PA: Idea Group Publishing.

Chapter 6
Knowledge Management Capability in Education

Jeremy Hodges[1] **and Ronald Freeze**[2]

[1] Embry-Riddle Aeronautical University, Daytona Beach, FL, USA, jeremy.hodges@erau.edu
[2] Emporia State University, Emporia, KS, USA, rfreeze@emporia.edu

6.1 Introduction

A recent focus on Knowledge Management Capability (KMC) has emerged among the subjects of organizational management (Holsapple and Wu, 2008). A principal reason for this emergence is the need for managers at all levels, in all industries, to unlock the potential of their organizational members by reducing barriers to knowledge acquisition, storage, presentation, and application (Freeze and Kulkarni, 2008). In an age of high-speed information exchange, it is essential for managers to understand the factors related to KMC within their industry and particularly in their organization (Oltra, 2005).

Knowledge Management Capability is the potential of an organization to acquire, store, present, and apply knowledge (Freeze and Hodges, 2009). The overall organizational KMC is divided into three areas: Lessons Learned, Expertise, and Knowledge Documents (Freeze and Hodges, 2009; Freeze and Kulkarni, 2008). These three KMC areas are unique and comprised of specific internal processes due to differences stemming from the attributes of the type of knowledge (tacit or explicit) associated with each KMC area.

From 2002 to 2004, Kulkarni and Freeze (2008) developed, validated, and refined a Knowledge Management Capability Assessment (KMCA) which was administered to three large business units within a Forture-50 manufacturing company. This assessment successfully identified scale items, factors, and the three areas associated with KMC formulation. Their instrument validation highlighted specific knowledge processes (KPs), as reflective constructs, and provided insight into KMC for a mechanistic organization. The KPs studied in the KMC relationship were acquisition, storage, presentation, and application. KMC was not modeled as a construct in this study.

The uniqueness of each KMC area indicated the possibility that the KMC construct is built from a number of KMC areas and is therefore formative in nature. Studies using the KMCA, an instrument that provides one-time measurements of KMC at an organizational level, indicated a need for future research into the possible formative nature of KMC (Freeze and Kulkarni, 2008). The refinement of the KMCA led to the initial validation of the instrument's transferability to additional contexts and indicated support for its use to assess KMC in various industries. Since

D. Schuff et al. (eds.), *Decision Support*, Annals of Information Systems 14,
DOI 10.1007/978-1-4419-6181-5_6, © Springer Science+Business Media, LLC 2011

KMC is believed to be measureable across all industries, this study's contributions focused on strengthening the transferability of the KMCA by applying it in another domain and investigating KMC representation as a formative construct.

The layout of this chapter first addresses the call for action in the study context, education. We then examine the basics of KMC through defining knowledge, knowledge processes and the KMC constructs. A presentation of our conceptual KMC model as a formative construct along with the theoretical justification as a third-order representation will follow. The study's methodology used to extend the KMCA into the educational domain is presented in the next section. Results, future trends and conclusions drawn from the study conclude this chapter.

6.2 Educational Background

The interest in KMC led to a call to study knowledge management (KM) in an educational organization (Milam, 2001). Applications of innovative business practices, including those employing codified processes for managing soft assets, such as knowledge, are lacking in the education industry (Kidwell et al., 2000). To effectively prepare students for the fast pace of information sharing, education practitioners need to be able to effectively acquire, store, present, and apply accurate and time-specific information for students. Efficient KM in education can provide a wide-ranging impact on society. Educational organizations, according to the United States Bureau of Labor Statistics (USBLS) (2008), employ over 3,100,000 people in the United States in over 150,000 schools, colleges, universities, professional and technical training organizations, and educational support service companies. This industry needs managers who can harness and apply their organization's knowledge assets. These numbers are a driver representing the overall scope of need for effective and efficient KM.

In January 2008, in the forward of "On Learning: The Future of Air Force Education and Training", then United States Air Force (USAF) commander of Air Education and Training Command General William Looney stated that it was necessary to develop an enterprise-wide infrastructure to capture the most critical asset: Knowledge (AETC, 2008). This initiative underpins the importance of understanding and applying KM principles, recognizing that there is a direct need in the education industry. Evaluation of KMC in educational organizations, such as those in Air Education and Training Command, can provide the first steps toward the development of an enterprise-wide knowledge infrastructure.

Answering the call to study KMC in education, Hodges (2009) embarked on the case presented here to administer an updated KMCA within a Department of Defense educational organization, verifying three KMC areas in addition to examining KMC as a formative construct (theoretical development in succeeding sections). The investigation of generic KPs in education concluded practical steps for developing specific capabilities. The building of KPs was addressed by modeling specific KMC areas, to show where exact improvements can be pursued. The multi-dimensional nature of these formative KPs indicates the existence of areas that can be significant in building an organizationally complete and optimal KMC. Jarvis et al. (2003) guided the KMCA extension to facilitate the investigation of KMC in a formative manner.

6.3 Knowledge Management Capability Background

The building of KMC theoretically starts with understanding the various representations of knowledge. With an understanding of knowledge representations, the movement of knowledge from entity to entity requires further understanding of the knowledge processes and how they may differ from context to context accordingly. Finally, an overall KMC encompasses all of the knowledge representations and knowledge processes.

6.3.1 Defining Knowledge

Numerous descriptions of knowledge are found in the literature relating to organizational management. For the purpose of this study, the definition provided by Tsoukas (2005) is applied as "the capability members of an organization have developed to draw distinctions in carrying out their work, in particular concrete contexts, by enacting a set of generalizations whose application depends upon historically evolved collective understanding" (Tsoukas, 2005, p. 120). Knowledge is socially constructed within the shared experiential context of those who have participated in its creation. Knowledge development in a social context thus contains tacit and explicit knowledge types.

Tacit knowledge is characterized by an array of scholar-practitioners as hard-to-describe, unobservable, and experienced based (Polanyi, 1966; Nonaka and Takeuchi, 1995). Tacit knowledge is gained through implicit learning processes, and in an educational application is considered to be a mechanism for using intuition (Burke and Sadler-Smith, 2006). In most references, tacit knowledge is considered immeasurable unless it can be inferred from actions and statements (Ceci and Liker, 1986). Furthermore, knowledge of this type is plainly described throughout the literature as learned through experience (Armstrong and Mahmud, 2008). A problem associated with capturing and relating tacit knowledge is that it is not in context for organizational members who are without the shared experience from which the knowledge originated.

Explicit knowledge can be formally articulated, communicated, repeated, and taught through cognitive and psychomotor exercises (Alavi and Leidner, 2001). Polanyi (1966) expressed that this type of knowledge could be codified and understood by members of a community through common language. This is knowledge that is observable, present, readily demonstrated, and measurable. Polanyi suggested that all knowledge is on a continuum between the tacit and explicit types.

Any recognized knowledge can never be at the extremes of the continuum (i.e. fully tacit or explicit).

6.3.2 Knowledge Processes

Knowledge management is primarily broken into at least four processes throughout the literature (Alavi and Leidner, 2001; Freeze and Kulkarni, 2008; Nonaka and Takeuchi, 1995; Turner and Makhija, 2006). The primary process is acquisition, which is recognition of value and the decision to transfer by a knowledge worker. Once knowledge is acquired, it must be stored in a manner consistent with organizational standards for cataloging. When the knowledge is needed, it must be presented through a straightforward system. Finally, the knowledge must be applied towards attainment of an outcome (Drucker, 1993).

Scholar-practitioners in the KM field have put various additional KPs forth. Davenport and Prusak (1998) used generation, codification, and transfer to describe the KM process. The KPs of creation, storage, retrieval, transfer, and application were used by Alavi and Leidner (2001) to provide a framework for developing IT solutions for KM. Creation, transfer, interpretation, and application was another set of KPs used for controlling organizational knowledge (Turner and Makhija, 2006). The KPs examined in the KMCA used by Freeze and Hodges' (2009) investigation were acquire, store, present, and apply. These are the KPs that are assessed in an educational setting.

The different KP views show the interrelatedness of the functions of processing knowledge for use. Each process previously described represents a formative nature; that knowledge cannot be stored until it is acquired. One reason for the differing theories is to myopically view a specific process with a function of an organization, as opposed to managing differing organizational processes to match the characteristics of the unique KMC areas. By applying a specific process to the KMC area that aligns with the type of knowledge the organization is trying to manage, there is potential for the process to be improved, while the knowledge attributes inherently do not change.

Three additional theories, whose views can also support a formative KMC, are absorptive capacity, tacit knowledge conversion, and professional practice. Absorptive capacity, put forth by Zarah and George (2002) is a static measurement that has two phases: potential and realized. In the potential stage, knowledge is acquired and assimilated, making it ready for use. In the realized stage, knowledge is transformed and exploited to meet organizational objectives. Tacit knowledge conversion, presented by Nonaka and Takeuchi (1995) is the socialization, externalization, combination, and internalization process. In this process knowledge is created, interpreted, and applied within the collective understanding of organizational members. Finally, the three levels of professional practice, knowing-in-action, reflection-in-action, and reflection-on-action suggested by Atkinson and Claxton (2000) represent an individual's cycle of acquiring, cataloging, and accessing knowledge. The knowledge is then used for future decisions related to the context in which the original knowledge was gained.

6.3.3 Knowledge Management Capability Constructs

Prior studies investigating causal links between KMC and individual organizational functions have been difficult for researchers to solidify. Tanriverdi (2005) discussed the synergistic effects of knowledge resource exploitation as an extension of applying the resource-based view (RBV) of the firm. This view suggests that proper delineation across KMC areas will extend benefits across constructs. Focusing on the development of multi-business firms, Tanriverdi approached operationalizing KMC as the degree of creating, transferring, integrating, and leveraging resources. This application was asserted to find a linkage among information technology (IT) relatedness, KMC, and firm performance across product, customer, and managerial sources. Viewing KMC from a RBV suggests that it affects the ability of an organization to effectively deploy and build resources (Makadok, 2001). The measurement of KMC in Tanriverdi's (2005) approach was cross-sectional and from an organizational perspective. The KMCA, in contrast, takes KMC measurement at an individual level. This individual perspective provides a more granular measurement in order to assess the impact of KM initiatives.

Freeze and Hodges (2009) presented the conceptualization of KMC as a formative construct through three knowledge areas: *Lessons Learned, Expertise, and Knowledge Documents*. These KMC areas each contain the generic KPs of *acquire*, *store*, *present*, and *apply*. Building upon that work, this study presents the evidence accumulated through the application of the KMCA in an educational setting. The following describes the uniqueness of how each KP is associated with a particular KMC area. Further, the uniqueness and distinction among the KMC areas are discussed and later will be shown through modeling.

Lessons Learned are specific and useful knowledge gained in the process of completing a project or a task, learned from past successes and failures, and are generated during social sessions designed to discuss results from previous organizational tasks. The Lessons Learned KPs are uniquely identified as *capture*, *repository*, *taxonomy*, and *usage*. The knowledge type is predominantly tacit, because it is developed through the shared experiences of members who comprise the organization. Lessons Learned are gained from experience and case studies of previously applied concepts and courses of action. In an educational setting this may be in the form of a course, an exercise, testing method, etc.

Expertise is knowledge available within the minds of organizational members, and hence, experts are individuals who have expertise to share. This area is also mostly tacit, as it is not necessarily easy to capture and share. One way to facilitate the transfer of knowledge is to profile the education and experience of faculty members within a database that will show who may be most qualified for new tasks. The expertise KPs are *expert profiling and registration*, *repository*, *taxonomy*, and *access*. Expertise is found among the faculty of the educational organization, in varying degrees, and is based on experience and education.

Knowledge Documents are those documents that contain codified, explicit, generated or gathered support material for the use of application to organizational tasks. The Knowledge Documents KPs are *categorization*, *repository*, *search and retrieval*, and *reference and use*. These specific documents are among the organization's internal library, reference material, shared files, databases, etc. External to the organization, publishers' textbooks, journals, and conference proceedings can also be identified for use. Knowledge Documents are used for codifying policy and process as well as resources for instruction within the educational organization.

For a description of the processes with each knowledge area used in this study, an example of each generic KP (acquire, store, present, and apply) in education can be describe through the task of generating and collecting knowledge when developing a new course. This example application will be associated directly with the three KMC areas: *lessons learned, expertise*, and *knowledge documents*. When a new course is developed at a university, a needs assessment is made of the potential students and possible course content. *Acquisition* of subject matter leads to *knowledge documents* that contain known scholarly literature and an existing framework for *presenting* the material to students according to university standards. A survey of the faculty yields which members have *expertise* in the area based on prior experience and education. After the faculty concludes an iteration of the course with a cohort of students, *lessons learned* are *stored* and shared to *apply* in the course during later sessions. This process crosses a variety of knowledge types and requires specific assessment to improve the KPs of each KMC area: *lessons learned*, *expertise*, and *knowledge documents*. Assessment and subsequent improvement is done through effective modeling and application of targeted KM initiatives.

6.3.4 Knowledge Management Capability Model

Because of the inherent tacit component of knowledge, the identification of metrics contributing to KMC growth are needed in order to better understand how to effectively manage knowledge. Previous efforts to assess KMC resulted in consolidation of knowledge and development of KM processes (Gold et al., 2001). During KMCA development and validation, Freeze and Kulkarni (2005) used structural equation modeling employing exploratory factor analysis followed by confirmatory factor analysis to identify loading values linking scale items to KPs, and KPs to KMC areas of KMC. This validation process established reliability of the instrument by assessing the variance in an item as attributable to the variance in a capability. Further KMCA validation by Freeze and Kulkarni (2008) was accomplished using second-order and general-specific reflective models. These models provided a conceptual framework of the overall KMC construct. Reflective correlation models and second-order reflective models verified the existence of KPs and KMC areas within three separate business units. While these models were useful in confirming KMC as a measurable construct, it did not show the formative nature of KMC. This oversight was due mostly to the heavy application of reflective models in similar studies (Jarvis et al., 2003). The studies proved that distinct KMC areas existed, and each one was measureable via its own set of KPs.

The research model in Fig. 6.1 represents the extended conceptual relationship investigated by Hodges (2009) between the scale items, processes, capabilities and KMC. Note that the first-order KPs are reflective constructs. The first-order KP representation is consistent with prior research (Freeze and Kulkarni, 2005; 2008; Freeze and Hodges, 2009). The investigation into the formative nature of KMC required the development of reflective scale items to measure the KMC areas and overall KMC. This is due to the proposal that changes in the extent of an existing

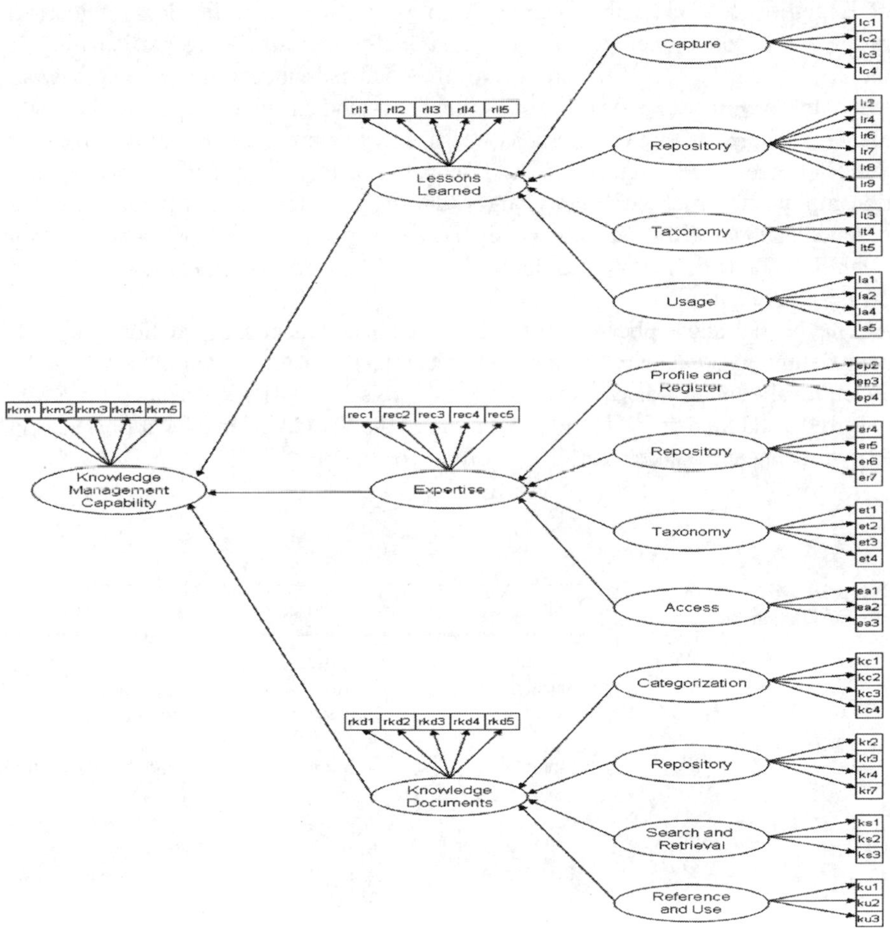

Fig. 6.1 Knowledge management capability conceptual model

first order KP would result in reflected changes in the scale item measurements. The first order scale items do not comprise the totality of each first order factor, but are a measurement that denotes the existence of the process and the extent to which it exists. As surmised by Jarvis et al. (2003), reflective scale items should be internally consistent, and because they are assumed to be equally valid they are each reliable and interchangeable. The construct validity is therefore unchanged if a single scale item is not found to be present.

An extension of prior work, the KMC areas are posited to be formed by the KPs. Each KMC area subsequently forms the total KMC. In this relationship, changes in the KMC areas individually translate into a change in the KMC of an organization. The formative depiction of KMC is theoretically dependent on the premise that a specific area can be improved independently of the other KMC areas. This can be demonstrated by analyzing the results of an organizational focus on improving the Lessons Learned area and the effect of those actions on the KMC area of Expertise. It is clear that the act of collecting and capturing lessons learned raises the organizational knowledge. Additionally, the individuals participating in the activities may become more aware of which individuals are experts in what area. However, that expertise is not codified and made available to the entire organization. The KMC area of Lessons Learned has improved while no changes, or minor changes, have occurred in the KMC area of Expertise. This formative relationship, posited by Freeze and Hodges (2009), indicates that direct improvement in organizational KMC can be made by targeting specific weak KMC areas or even weak KPs. Table 6.1 shows the relationship of KMC areas with specific KPs and the generic KP stages.

The theories and application of KMC, rooted in an accepted foundation of knowledge definitions, are the bedrock of this research. The need to examine KMC in the educational domain was established by multiple scholars. Refinement of the KMC constructs and models led to the application of the KMCA in an educational setting to investigate and confirm KMC as a formative construct.

Table 6.1 KMC factor and process relationship

KMC area	Generic stage	Specific factor
Lessons Learned	Acquire	Capture
	Store	Repository
	Present	Taxonomy
	Apply	Usage
Expertise	Acquire	Profile and register
	Store	Repository
	Present	Taxonomy
	Apply	Access
Knowledge Documents	Acquire	Categorization
	Store	Repository
	Present	Search and retrieval
	Apply	Reference and use

6.4 Expanding KMC into Educational Contexts

This section outlines the methodology of expanding KMC into educational contexts, and specifically shows how the KMC areas were found to be unique within the overall KMC construct. Reflective correlation models were used to show distinction among the three KMC areas, and Non-normed Fit Index (NNFI), Comparative Fit Index (CFI), and Standardized-Root Mean-Squared Residual (SRMR) indices were used to show the improvement of formative model fit over reflective models. The results are detailed in this section, followed by implications and conclusions.

Because of the importance of education and training, having the capability to manage knowledge is essential to achieving organizational objectives at all levels of operation. The problem being examined validates that improving the capability to manage knowledge within educational organizations can be done in a stepwise approach. The study identifies associated KPs and KMC areas within the education industry, in order to appropriately acquire, store, present, and apply knowledge, validating the use of the KMCA in a new organization type to better understand a new context. Understanding the unique educational organization's knowledge processes and how they form knowledge capabilities within a KMC setting would improve understanding of knowledge flows within those organizations.

The setting for this research was a Department of Defense educational organization. The purpose of the field study was to test the theory of organizational KMC that links areas of Lessons Learned, Expertise, and Knowledge Documents to KMC. The organization participating in the study employed approximately 110 active duty military members, USAF Reservists, government civilians, and contractors who educate approximately 2,000 students annually in a variety of professional continuing education and training courses. A counterpart of this organization type in the civilian sector would be a technical or trade school, designed for the advancement of a student who has chosen a particular career.

This research was focused on improving the understanding of how KMC is built and maintained in an educational organization. Understanding how KMC is structured within an educational organization provides administrators with a way to target improvements into weak areas of KM. With a theoretical foundation, knowing what KPs are associated with the different KMC areas and knowledge types enables specific infrastructure development of IT solutions to speed up knowledge transfer that meets the educator's needs. This in turn infuses the culture with an attitude of knowledge sharing inside the structure of the KMC model.

Consistent with the research approach of Freeze and Kulkarni (2008), a 90-question KMCA was administered to 109 personnel to assess the current KMC of the Department of Defense educational organization. The initial KMCA was designed to measure all of the latent variable constructs as reflective factors. Additional questions were developed to investigate overall KMC and KMC areas as formative latent variables. Reflective models presented in prior research (Freeze and Kulkarni, 2005; 2008) were revalidated prior to developing and validating formative construct models.

6.4.1 Department of Defense Field Study Results

Correlation, second-order and third-order reflective models, along with second-order and third-order formative models, were assessed to evaluate the formative nature of the construct. Significant results were gained that show KMC was a formative construct and a better fit over reflective models. Figure 6.2 provides the generic example of a correlation model used to validate that the KMC areas are unique and separate constructs. Figure 6.3 illustrates the generic reflective and generic formative models used to validate consistency with prior work (reflective model) and to provide a transportable formative model of each KMC area. Aspects of these measurement models are used to build and illustrate the nature of the educational organization's formative third-order overall KMC model.

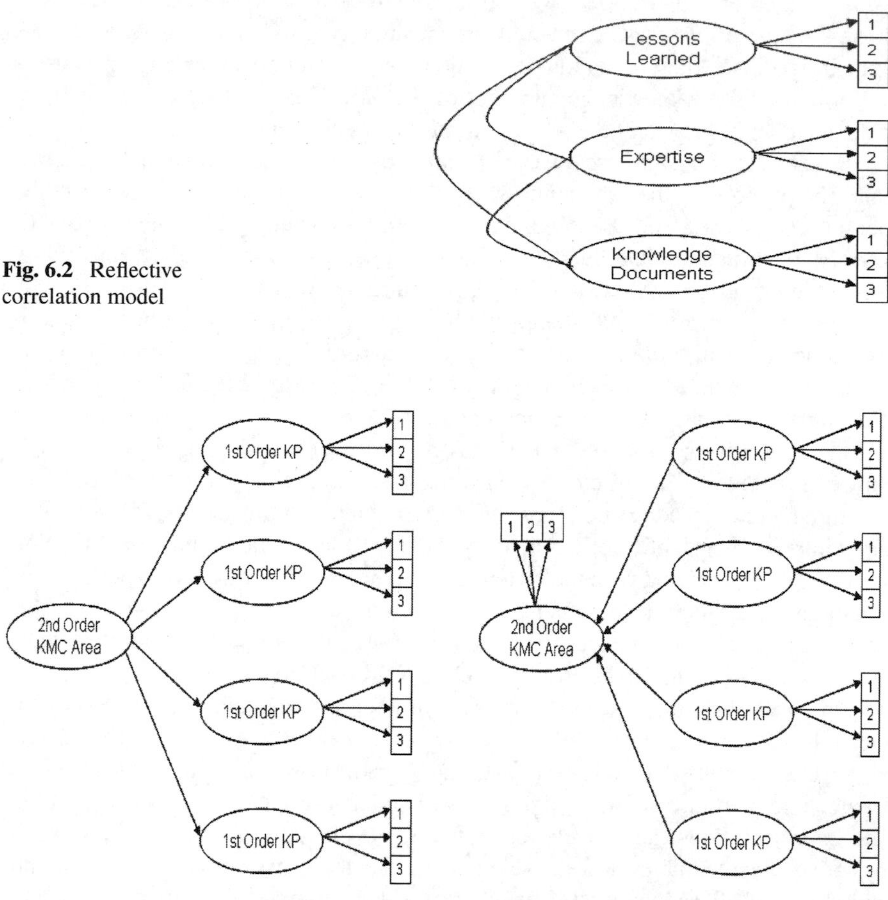

Fig. 6.2 Reflective correlation model

Fig. 6.3 Second-order reflective and formative model comparison

The reflective correlation model (Fig. 6.2) is used as an initial test to assess the uniqueness of the three KMC areas. This model was applied to the study outlined by Hodges (2009) to prove the distinct capability attributes of the knowledge associated with each KMC area. Reflective scale items were used to measure the existence of the three KMC areas. The correlation model provided both discriminant and convergent validity for the newly developed scale items. The resultant fit indices, NNFI, CFI, and SRMR, were 0.94, 0.95, and 0.057 respectively. These results demonstrate that the model was a good fit for the educational organization being studied. Furthermore, the suggested modification index function, provided by LISREL, indicated no cross-loading suggestions for the scale items of each KMC area. In addition, the correlation values between each KMC area were indicative of good construct validity. The correlations between each of the KMC areas were Lessons Learned – Expertise 0.63, Lessons Learned – Knowledge Documents 0.62, and Expertise – Knowledge Documents 0.64.

Second-order and third-order reflective models validated prior research models (Freeze and Kulkarni, 2008), and indicate the existence of each KP and KMC area, while also providing insight into the accuracy of the KMCA by indicating loading values for each KP's scale items. Thresholds of reflective constructs that were set by Comrey and Lee (1992) are generally accepted as good indicators to identify theoretical scale item candidates that could be removed due to a failure to load against a particular KP. Finally, second-order and third-order formative model fit are assessed using NNFI, CFI, and SRMR. Thresholds suggested by Hu and Bentler (1999) and Bagozzi and Yi (1988) have been used for model fit in similar KM studies (Freeze and Kulkarni, 2008; Lichtenthaler, 2009).

Figure 6.3 represents generic second-order reflective and formative models containing the generic first-order KPs, measured by reflective scale items, and one second-order KMC area. The reflective model example in Fig. 6.3 differs from the second-order formative model because the first-order factors in the formative model contribute to the second-order KMC area. The formative model is more complete because the second-order construct can be measured independently by reflective scale items as suggested by Jarvis et al. (2003). The formative model is a more accurate representation of KMC than the reflective model in the recent educational organization study as represented by the fit statistics in Table 6.2.

In the formative model, path significance can be studied to make improvements to a first-order KP factor, which will impact the second-order KMC area. This is important to note because it means that small KM initiatives can be targeted to a specific organizational KMC weakness with results that improve the overall construct. A more focused approach to improving KM within the organization is achieved through a deliberate process of measuring, implementing improvements, measuring again, and so on.

The formative model represented in Fig. 6.1 consistently indicated a better fit, with the exception of the KMC area of Expertise, than the reflective models. The KMC area of Expertise showed better fit with the SRMR and only slightly degraded fit with NNFI and CFI. Increasing scores for NNFI and CFI represent an

Table 6.2 KMC factor and process relationship

Fit index	Reflective	Formative	KMC model
NNFI	0.95	0.97	
CFI	0.96	0.97	Overall KMC
SRMR	0.13	0.09	3rd-order model
NNFI	0.96	0.98	
CFI	0.97	0.98	Lessons learned
SRMR	0.12	0.08	2nd-order model
NNFI	0.99	0.98	
CFI	0.99	0.98	Expertise
SRMR	0.10	0.07	2nd-order model
NNFI	0.94	0.96	
CFI	0.96	0.96	Knowledge documents
SRMR	0.11	0.10	2nd-order model

improvement, while decreasing SRMR results show one model's improvement over another.

6.5 Future Trends

The viability of the formative model was proven through the results of this research, and should be considered the litmus test for a complete KMC construct when examined in educational organizations. The formative model sets the stage for testing path significance to assess and improve weak areas of KMC. Utilizing this model reveals insight into the capability of an organization's ability to effectively acquire, store, present, and apply knowledge.

As organizations continue to position for strategic domain superiority within their respective industries, being able to allocate resources to specific KMC areas is critical to monitoring and adapting to a changing knowledge environment. Therefore, the use of the formative model should continue to be how managers assess, improve, and monitor KMC throughout an organization's operational processes. Continued use of the formative KMC model will also expand a standardized body of work from which more can be learned about KM.

The expansion of KMC research in one educational setting can be attributed to multiple educational settings (i.e. universities, trade schools, K-12 schools). Further studies in these types of educational firms would garner insight into further transferability of the instrument and research.

6.5.1 Implementation Issues

Several implementation issues are of concern for future practitioners studying and managing KMC at the organizational level. Lack of understanding KM terminology, lack of uniformity of job types and contributions among employees, and small sample sizes are among these difficulties. Each of these issues is examined to highlight trends problematic to the study of KMC with recommendations for overcoming them.

Lack of understanding KM terminology is a significant issue for employees completing an assessment to accurately represent the KMC of an organization. Some tools can be employed to overcome this problem. First, use organizational terminology that helps employees understand where KPs exist within their organization. This method must be done in a way that does not slant the respondent, but increases his or her ability to connect KM with related job duties. Second, providing definitions or help during the assessment to explain terminology would also increase the respondent's understanding. Finally, meeting with employees beforehand and explaining the concepts provides an orientation to KM that could enable employees to infer conclusions on their own about how their jobs relate to KPs.

Lack of uniformity of job types is another issue to consider when administering a KMCA. The lack of job uniformity is a significant issue between employee groups who consider themselves operations and those who consider themselves support. Those who support organizational processes may not see the need to capture Lessons Learned the same way as operations employees. For example, a group of instructors who teach a four-week course covering several disciplines may debrief at the end of the class to review the quality of their work. This may include student performance, sequencing, testing methods, teaching methods, and course objectives. The capturing of Lessons Learned in this respect is important to this group.

These are the operations personnel, who although from different disciplines, are all instructors who directly carry out the mission of educating the students. Support personnel on the other hand, may come from a variety of areas such as the registrar, records management, IT, facilities maintenance, etc. These disparate support personnel do not view Lessons Learned in the same way as the operations personnel. Responses from these different personnel could create a disconnection when trying to pinpoint results of a formative KMC model. Subsequent improvement recommendations would vary for these different groups if targeted improvement is required for any KMC area. If the Lessons Learned – capture results are low and indicate a need for improvement, it may only be because one group or the other has need of improvement. For this reason, groups with similar functions should be measured separately and combined for organizational results only if necessary. Freeze and Kulkarni (2008) followed this example by examining separate business units within the same company.

Finally, when possible, it is important to overcome sample sizes smaller than the total parameters of the model. Getting 100% participation may be difficult; however, through leadership within the company and a collective desire to improve KMC, a response rate as high as possible should be sought. The results of testing KMC when the number of cases is less that the number of parameters should be carefully considered before apportioning resources for KM initiatives. A culture of understanding the need for effective KM and anonymous participation leading to 100% involvement are the keys for receiving the most accurate results through KMC modeling.

6.5.2 Implications

Managers of educational organizations benefit from this KMC research by receiving a way to assess and target improvement areas for KM. Better understanding of KMC for managers of educational organizations allows them to direct changes at tactical and operational levels. This fine-tuning of the organization's KMC will enable the efficient use of resources. Additionally, future research can be focused on the organic nature of educational organizations, and how this structure and philosophy influences KMC. Further research into organizational culture, structure, use of teams, and teaching methods may also be necessary to encompass the scope of the implications.

The validation of the KMCA and KMC areas within a new organizational setting advances the external validity of the instrument and provides an indication that similar knowledge capabilities exist across multiple organizations. Further validation of the KMC areas was achieved through analysis of all four KPs for the three KMC areas. Possible future research then could include multi-organization testing, across universities and technical education and training centers. This application will further the base of research of KMC in the education industry with additional insight into specific organization types.

The confirmation of KMC as a formative construct has substantial implications for organizations. With KMC as a formative construct, each KP, as well as each KMC area, can be targeted for improvement in an organization. The initiatives will not need the larger funding of a general KM improvement project, but can target smaller projects that would produce larger gains on the overall strategic assets of the organization. This can be realized by targeting improvements in specific processes like Expertise – access.

Finally, managers throughout the organization can see the far-reaching effects of a better understanding of this important asset. Knowledge Management Capability touches on multiple areas of organizational management, to include resources, processes, and structures. Understanding KMC from a business unit perspective and coupling that with an organizational maturity model, may lead to future research about team composition for the best long term KMC. Managers may be able to glean efficiencies in processes of production, training, and staffing due to a better application of KMC. In addition, senior executives can incorporate KMC philosophy when creating new organizations, to decide on the appropriate structure for the optimal KMC. Applying KMC theories in this multi-tiered approach to management will pay dividends in the effective and efficient management and use of the organization's collective knowledge.

6.6 Conclusion

The study of KMC is important for managers in various industries, and an ongoing opportunity for examination by researchers. The potential for an organization to acquire, store, present, and apply knowledge is a critical component of strategically positioning a firm among competitors. Due to knowledge residing on a continuum between tacit and explicit, KPs should be independently managed with respect to their unique KMC areas. Lessons Learned, which result from a shared reflection upon the completion of an organizational task, are a combination of tacit inference and explicit data points. Expertise is housed in the minds of organizational members and is mostly tacit. In contrast, Knowledge Documents are mostly explicit and codified documents that are easily cataloged and accessed.

Further refinement and sustained validation in this study of the KMCA continues to allow efficient one-time measurements to be made of organizational KMC multiple organizations. Follow-up KMCA assessments can capture improvements resulting from organizational KM initiatives. A contribution of this research is that KMC is a formative construct with unique KMC areas and KPs. The application of the KMCA in manufacturing and educational domains indicates that additional domains can use this standardized instrument to evaluate organizational KMC using the third-order formative model for identifying and improving weak KMC factors and areas. Future KMC research should continue to use the formative model, with efforts to mitigate implementation issues. Reducing these issues will result in more precise measurements while honing the accuracy of the instrument and the model.

Like the capability of an organization to penetrate a new market or improve production or efficiency, KMC is an organizational capability with processes and products associated with the management of the organization's knowledge. On an organizational level, the influence of corporate culture impacts KMC by the habits and attitudes towards the effective and efficient use of knowledge. The knowledge capabilities of the organization are housed in the three KMC areas. On an individual level, organizational members are responsible for understanding and identifying their roles in managing knowledge using the KPs for each KMC area. The KPs are found to contribute differently to individual efficiency and effectiveness based upon the KMC area where the knowledge exists (Freeze and Kulkarni, 2008).

The expansion of KMC into the educational domain demonstrated the modeling of distinct KMC areas and that formative models were superior to reflective models for the third-order construct. Continued application of the KMC model should utilize the methodologies described herein to develop the understanding of educational KMC as well as further refine the work done to this point. Managers today should apply the KMC principles put forth to target improvement areas in the organization.

Acknowledgments This chapter is an extension of a paper accepted in the Proceedings of the Fifteenth Americas Conference on Information Systems (Freeze and Hodges, 2009) and part of the unpublished dissertation work of Hodges (2009).

References

Air Education and Training Command. (2008). *On Learning: The Future of Air Force Education and Training. Air Education and Training Command.* (White Paper). Maxwell AFB. Montgomery, AL: Air University Press.

Alavi, M., and Leidner, D. (2001). Review: Knowledge Management and Knowledge Management Systems: Conceptual Foundations and Research Issues. *MIS Quarterly*, 25, 107–136.

Armstrong, S., and Mahmud, A. (2008). Experiential Learning and the Acquisition of Managerial Tacit Knowledge. *Academy of Management Learning and Education*, 7, 189–208.

Atkinson, T., and Claxton, G. (2000). *The Intuitive Practitioner: On the Value of Not Always Knowing What One Is Doing*. Buckingham: Open University Press.

Bagozzi, R., and Yi, Y. (1988). On the Evaluation of Structural Equation Models. *Journal of the Academy of Marketing Science*, 52, 68–82.

Burke, L., and Sadler-Smith, E. (2006). Instructor Intuition in the Educational Setting. *Academy of Management Learning and Education*, 5, 169–181.

Ceci, S., and Liker, J. (1986). *Academic and Non-academic Intelligence: An Experimental Separation. Practical Intelligence: Nature and Origins of Competence in the Everyday World*. New York: Cambridge University Press.

Comrey, A., and Lee, H. (1992). *A First Course in Factor Analysis* (2nd ed.). Hillsdale, NJ: Erlbaum.

Davenport, T., and Prusak, L. (1998). *Working Knowledge: How Organizations Manage What They Know*. Cambridge, MA: Harvard Business School Press.

Drucker, P. (1993). *Post-capitalist Society*. Oxford: Butterworth/Heinemann.

Freeze, R., and Hodges, J. (2009). Building Knowledge Capabilities in Education. Fifteenth Americas Conference on Information Systems, San Francisco, CA, 2009, Paper 447.

Freeze, R., and Kulkarni, U. (2005). Knowledge Management Capability Assessment: Validating a Knowledge Assets Management Instrument. Thirty-Eighth Hawaii International Conference on System Sciences, Waikoloa, HI, pp. 1–10.

Freeze, R., and Kulkarni, U. (2008). Validating Distinct Knowledge Assets: A Capability Perspective. *International Journal of Knowledge Management*, 4, 40–61.

Gold, A., Malhotra, A., and Segars, A. (2001). Knowledge Management: An Organizational Capabilities Perspective. *Journal of Management Information Systems*, 18, 185–214.

Hodges, J. (2009). Examining Knowledge Management Capability: Verifying Knowledge Process Factors and Areas in an Educational Organization [Unpublished Dissertation].

Holsapple, C., and Wu, J. (2008). In Search of a Missing Link. *Knowledge Management Research and Practice*, 6, 31–40.

Hu, L., and Bentler, P. (1999). Cutoff Criteria for Fit Indexes in Covariance Structure Analysis: Conventional Criteria Versus New Alternatives. *Structural Equation Modeling*, 6, 1–55.

Jarvis, C., MacKenzie, S., and Podsakoff, P. (2003). A Critical Review of Construct Indicators and Measurement Model Misspecification in Marketing and Consumer Research. *Journal of Consumer Research*, 30, 199–218.

Kidwell, J., Vander Linder, K., and Johnson, L. (2000). Applying Corporate Knowledge Management Practices in Higher Education. *Educause Quarterly*, 4, 28–33.

Kulkarni, U., and Freeze, R. (2008). Measuring Knowledge Management Capabilities. *Journal of Knowledge Management*, 21, 1–20.

Lichtenthaler, U. (2009). Absorptive Capacity, Environmental Turbulence, and the Complementarity of Organizational Learning Processes. *Academy of Management Journal*, 52, 822–846.

Makadok, R. (2001). Toward a Synthesis of Resource-Based and Dynamic-Capability Views of Rent Creation. *Strategic Management Journal*, 22, 387–401.

Milam, J. (2001). Knowledge Management for Higher Education, *ERIC Digest*. Retrieved November 5, 2008, from http://www.ericdigests.org/2003-1/higher.htm

Nonaka, I., and Takeuchi, H. (1995). *The Knowledge-Creating Company*. Oxford: Oxford University Press.

Oltra, V. (2005). Impact of Team Demography on Knowledge Sharing in Software Project Teams. *South Asian Journal of Management*, 12, 67–78.

Polanyi, M. (1966). *The Tacit Dimension*. London: Routledge.

Tanriverdi, H. (2005). Information Technology Relatedness, Knowledge Management Capability, and Performance of Multi-Business Firms. *MIS Quarterly*, 29(2), 311–314.

Tsoukas, H. (2005). *Complex Knowledge: Studies in Organizational Epistemology*. Oxford: Oxford University Press.

Turner, K., and Makhija, M. (2006). The Role of Organizational Controls in Managing Knowledge. *Academy of Management Review*, 31, 197–217.

United States Bureau of Labor Statistics. (2008). Industries at a Glance: Educational Services NAICS 61. Retrieved November 3, 2008, from http://data.bls.gov/cgi-bin/print.pl/iag/tgs/iag61.htm

Zarah, S., and George, G. (2002). Absorptive Capacity: A Review, Reconceptualization, and Extension. *Academy of Management Review*, 27, 185–209.

Chapter 7
Knowledge Warehouse for Decision Support in Critical Business Processes: Conceptual Modeling and Requirements Elicitation

Meira Levy[1], Nava Pliskin[2], and Gilad Ravid[3]

[1] Department of Industrial Engineering and Management, Deutsche Telekom Laboratories, Ben-Gurion University of the Negev, Beer-Sheva, Israel, lmeira@bgu.ac.il
[2] Department of Industrial Engineering and Management, Ben-Gurion University of the Negev, Beer-Sheva, Israel, pliskinn@bgu.ac.il
[3] Department of Industrial Engineering and Management, Ben-Gurion University of the Negev, Beer-Sheva, Israel, rgilad@bgu.ac.il

7.1 Introduction

Dramatic events in the unpredictable global business environment make us all realize that harnessing knowledge for decision support of critical business processes is vital to success of organizations. A critical business process (CBP) refers to a business process, whose impact on the organization's performance is great, requiring decision making that incorporates various knowledge resources. Recent research (Bazerman, 2006; Kahneman, 2003; March, 1978; Stanovich and West, 2000; Levy et al., 2009), however, suggests that due to bounded rationality and limited cognitive capabilities, decision makers sometimes make poor CBP decisions, paying attention to neither the existing content embedded in information systems (IS) nor the opinions of various stakeholders. Yet, knowledge embedded in both is targeted by knowledge management (KM).

KM may allow CBP decision makers to learn from decentralized strategic decisions made by autonomous managers, as well as provide knowledge resources and decision-making structures (Nicolas, 2004). Under certain mission-critical scenarios (involving prevention, event recognition, early response, and recovery), KM may empower CBP decision makers who face time pressures, risks, contradictions, and information overflow. While the role of KM in CBP decision making is acknowledged in theory (Bolloju et al., 2002; Zhang et al., 2002; Nicolas, 2004) in the form of well-defined frameworks that embed KM components within decision support (DS), there exists a gap between existing KM theory and actual KM practice (Garrett, 2004).

Thus, a major challenge is to provide decision makers with a working environment that will enhance the rationality and transparency of CBP decision-making as well as facilitate the integration of knowledge into a collaborative space for communication and discussion amongst relevant stakeholders (Bolloju et al., 2002). Responding to this challenge requires knowledge integration similar to the

D. Schuff et al. (eds.), *Decision Support*, Annals of Information Systems 14,
DOI 10.1007/978-1-4419-6181-5_7, © Springer Science+Business Media, LLC 2011

integration of data enabled by data warehouse (DW) technology. While major theories about DW design methodologies are being developed by data management researchers (e.g. Adamson and Venerable, 1998; Giorgini et al., 2005; Guo et al., 2006; Holten, 2003; Kerschberg, 2001), KM research has yet to evolve sufficiently toward systematic and sustained design methodologies (Jongho et al., 2003).

To guide practical and systematic harnessing of KM for CBP decision support, we employed the design science research methodology (Hevner et al., 2004), proposing the knowledge warehouse (KW) conceptual model which integrates KM and DW aspects, while taking into account CBP, IS, and stakeholders. Our approach is based on the notion of arranging the organizational knowledge (often referred to as collective memory or organizational memory) as transactive memory (Wegner et al., 1991; Jennex and Olfman, 2003; Nevo and Wand, 2005; Jackson and Klobas, 2008). Extending the work of Levy (2009) and aimed at leveraging knowledge in support of CBP decision making, we also propose the KW4DS@CBP architecture which implements the KW concept within the DS and CBP perspectives. We qualitatively evaluate the proposed KW model and come up with critical success factors for implementing the KW4DS@CBP architecture based on interviews conducted with IS managers. Finally, we propose and illustrate a KW4DS@CBP requirements elicitation tool for an actual CBP. Our focus only on *critical* business processes, with a major influence on organizational outcomes, is practical as well as feasible, and thus most of the benefit from the proposed approach would be in the CBP context.

The following section is devoted to a description of the theoretical background about DW, KM, organizational and the linkage between KM and DW. Next, the research methodology is presented, highlighting the design science research paradigm. The four following sections describe the KW conceptual model, the KW4DS@CBP architecture, the KW4DS@CBP evaluation and requirements elicitation process, and the KW4DS@CBP requirements elicitation tool. Finally, we conclude and discuss future research directions.

7.2 Theoretical Background

The nature of knowledge and its representation have long been studied in the IS and AI (artificial intelligence) fields. Newell (1981), for example, realized that a structured symbolic form cannot solely represent knowledge since knowledge requires both structure and process representations. In addition, although knowledge is an abstract concept, a particular "piece" or "facet" of knowledge must be coupled with some formal level of representation to create a sufficiently viable view and to justify regarding it within a knowledge level. In this spirit, the proposed KW exhibits the knowledge level as an extended DW concept model with a knowledge perspective tier.

7.2.1 Data Warehouse

By selectively aggregating operational databases, DW technology makes it possible to support decision makers in, for instance, implementing OLAP practices. To enable OLAP efforts, the conceptual model of DWs is often multidimensional (Rizzi, 2007) with data represented in a cubic metaphor where the cubic dimensions represent analysis criteria, which consist of a hierarchy of attributes that further describe them. This conceptual model is often represented with a fact schema (see example in Fig. 7.1), including a fact table with aggregated data surrounded by source tables. In general, conceptual modeling and representation facilitate the design process by abstracting away implementation considerations, thus enabling designers and users to better understand the DW architecture and processes.

Researchers and practitioners (e.g., Malinowski and Zimányi, 2006; Rizzi, 2007) proposed several approaches for conceptually modeling DWs, including entity-relationship (E-R), unified modeling language (UML) and dimensional fact model (DFM). In addition, the MultiDimER hierarchy conceptual model (Malinowski and Zimányi, 2006) allows each dimension to be represented in hierarchy of attributes that represents any organizational, geographical, or other type of structure that is important for analysis. For instance, a spatial dimension might have a hierarchy with levels such as country, region, city and office. Hierarchies are also required for enabling roll-up and drill-down operations needed for OLAP. These modeling techniques address operationally-related concepts of the data, such as facts, dimensions, measures, hierarchies and cross-dimension attributes. While supporting OLAP processes, DW modeling techniques lack KM dimensions that may support integrating knowledge resources within decision making processes.

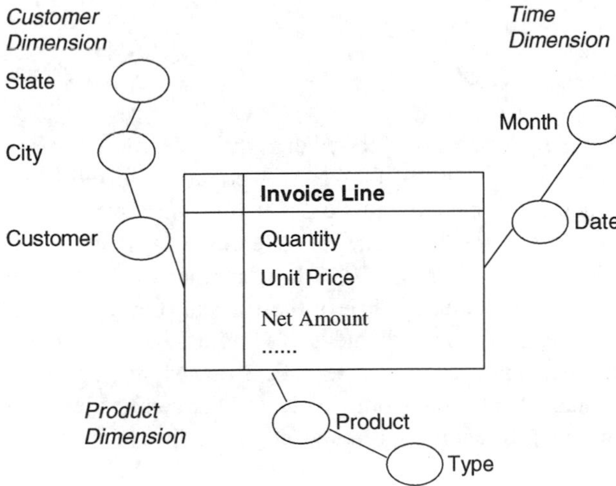

Fig. 7.1 An example of a partial basic fact schema for a DW (Rizzi, 2007)

7.2.2 Knowledge Management

Knowledge is considered as one of the main competitive assets of an organization, enabling the organization to be productive and deliver competitive products and services (Drucker, 1993), is embedded in people, systems, procedures and products. One of the cornerstones of KM is improving productivity by effectively sharing and transferring knowledge, activities which tend to be time-consuming and often impossible (Drucker, 1993; Davenport and Prusak, 2000).

Nonaka (1986) distinguishes between explicit knowledge, stored in textbooks, software products and documents; and tacit knowledge, stored in the mind in the form of memory, skills, experience, education, imagination and creativity. While manifestations of the mind are difficult to identify and manage, Alavi and Leidner (2001) claim that tacit knowledge processed in the mind of individuals can become information once it is articulated and presented in the form of a text, software product or other means.

Knowledge organizations face several KM challenges, especially with regard to tacit knowledge that their knowledge employees possess, such as knowledge transfer, knowledge extraction, and innovatively applying the right knowledge at the right place when needed (Nonaka, 1986; Holsapple and Joshi, 2003). Barriers to KM initiatives include separation between business processes and KM processes and time pressures that cause KM tasks to be avoided (Davenport and Prusak, 2000).

KM and decision-making are related and effective KM is considered essential for decision making (Bolloju et al., 2002; Nicolas, 2004; Raghu and Vinze, 2007; Levy et al., 2009). In this spirit, several DSSs incorporate the knowledge creation model (Nonaka, 1986; Nemati et al., 2002) that occurs through the synergy between tacit and explicit knowledge, based on a four-step process (SECI model) of socialization, externalization, combination, and internalization (Bolloju et al., 2002; Nemati et al., 2002; Raghu and Vinze, 2007).

7.2.3 Organizational Memory

Organizational knowledge is often referred to as the collective or organization memory (OM). Resides in various IS, OM can leverage organizational effectiveness and work coordination by enabling processes that acquire, retain, maintain, search and retrieve knowledge (Wegner et al., 1991; Jennex and Olfman, 2003; Nevo and Wand, 2005; Jackson and Klobas, 2008). In implementing these knowledge processes, employees are required to retrieve the relevant knowledge needed in their work context. However, Nevo and Wand (2005) point to several barriers to accessing OM. First, while knowledge can be understood in its creation context, it is often misinterpreted when it is de-contextualized. Another barrier relates to the difficulty in combining different types of knowledge residing in diverse locations (e.g. individuals; procedures, and rules; structure and roles; and physical settings of the workplace). Other barriers concern the management of tacit knowledge, as well as knowledge volatility and reliability.

To overcome these barriers, Nevo and Wand (2005) propose a conceptual model for managing and using OM. Their approach is based on examining, via transactive memory system concepts, the processes which support the sharing of collective knowledge assets within small groups that establish communities of practice. Extending their approach to the whole organizational memory context is possible with IS support.

The transactive memory approach is based on the three ways human beings encode knowledge: (1) internally in the mind; (2) externally in an external repository of some kind; or (3) through linkage to knowledge holder(s). This linkage resembles a meta-memory, hence memory on memory, consisting of a label of the knowledge and a pointer to its location. The meta-memory is managed with a directory which supports such operations as updating, allocation, and retrieval. Humans can naturally establish a transactive memory system within small groups, but this is impossible in an organizational context is because the required meta-memory is too large for the memory capacity of an individual and it is not always clear who holds certain knowledge.

To overcome these difficulties, Nevo and Wand (2005) suggest viewing the organization as a group of practice-based communities, where each community has established a transactive memory system that can be linked through an organizational IS which holds artificial directories containing transactive knowledge. In order to establish organization-wide memory, Nevo and Wand (2005) advocate constructing an organizational ontology that defines the domain of organizational knowledge concepts and their relationships, including generalized concepts (e.g. project plans) and concept instances (e.g. project A plan) as well as knowledge retainers, represented by roles (e.g. project manager) and role instances (e.g. project A's project manager, named "Linda"). In addition, the ontology includes a tacit knowledge representation, entitled meta-knowledge that defines the natural tacit perceptions possessed by members of communities of practice, addressing issues such as expertise, cognitive capabilities and source credibility.

7.2.4 Data Warehouses and Knowledge Management

As organizations move operations to the Internet (Kerschberg, 2001; Nemati et al., 2002; Ralaivao and Darmont, 2007), partnerships are established with external stakeholders (e.g., customers and suppliers), incorporating operational structured data generated by on-line transaction processing systems (OLTP) – e.g., enterprise resource planning (ERP) and customer relationship management (CRM) data – and unstructured data – e.g., emails and wikis – into organizational repositories. Thus, in order to facilitate business decision-making, there is a need for extending the DW role to a broader KM perspective that relates not only to operational transaction-oriented data, but also to knowledge created by knowledge workers within and outside the enterprise. Indeed, Kerschberg (2001) already discussed the need to aggregate heterogeneous data into the DW.

Several studies refer to the notion of integrating KM with DW. Jongho et al. (2003) propose a systematic conversion of knowledge into hypermedia artifacts and data warehouse components. Nemati et al. (2002) argue that there is a need for a new expanded DSS, which incorporates DW concepts, as well as a knowledge creation approach based on Nonaka's knowledge creation theory (1986). These studies, however, deal mainly with architecture and conceptual models for DSS that includes a DW but, as the above literature review showed, none of the existing approaches for conceptual modeling of DW addresses KM issues as part of the DW model.

Next we propose the KW conceptual model (KW-CM) which extends the DW conceptual modeling with a knowledge layer that addresses KM aspects and encompasses relevant stakeholders, CBP and IS. Then, we propose the KW4DS@CBP architecture, providing CBP decision makers with a comprehensive knowledge view with an environment which fosters collaboration amongst CBP stakeholders. Both the KW infrastructure and the KW4DS@CBP architecture rely on the organizational memory, seeking to improve knowledge transfer and to overcome the identified KM barriers by harnessing knowledge for decision support in critical business processes.

7.3 Research Methodology

In this research we employed the design science research methodology, which aims at understanding a problem domain and developing a solution that takes into account interactions among people, organizations, and technology (Hevner et al., 2004). Design science seeks to create innovative capabilities and products through which the optimal IS analysis, design, implementation, management, and use can be undertaken (Denning, 1997).

According to Hevner et al. (2004), design science research is fundamentally a problem solving paradigm, which relies on existing kernel theories that are applied, tested, modified, and extended through the experience, creativity, intuition, and problem-solving capabilities of the researcher. Conducting design science research includes:

- Creation of an innovative artifact in a rigorous and coherent manner to a certain relevant problem domain which yields utility for the specified problem
- Evaluation of the artifact with appropriate quality attributes (e.g. functionality, relevance) by using established methods; and
- Exploration of the effectiveness and efficiency of the proposed artifact.

However, the design artifacts must be evaluated with respect to what utility is provided in solving the identified problem, how feasible and suitable the artifacts are vis-à-vis the intended purpose are, and how users appropriate the design. In our research process we followed the guidelines:

> Fundamental questions on utility (what does it do?) and its demonstration (does it really do that?) are salient: "Contribution arises from utility. If existing artifacts are adequate, then

> design science research that creates a new artifact is unnecessary (it is irrelevant). If the new artifact does not map adequately to the real world (rigor), it cannot provide utility. If the artifact does not solve the problem (search, implementability), it has no utility. If utility is not demonstrated (evaluation), then there is no basis upon which to accept the claims that it provides any contribution (contribution). Furthermore, if the problem, the artifact, and its utility are not presented in a manner such that the implications for research and practice are clear, then publication in the IS literature is not appropriate (communication) (Hevner et al. (2004), pp. 25–26)

This paper defines the KW4DS@CBP architecture for CBP decision support, enhancing the interactions between organizational stakeholders and IS. Following the design research paradigm, we conducted a four stages research. In the first stage, the theoretical background (presented in the previous section) for developing the artifacts for the identified problem domain was established. In the second stage, the KW conceptual model and the KW4DS@CBP architecture were developed. In the third stage, the developed KW and KW4DS@CBP artifacts were evaluated by interviews with three IS managers from different organizations, also addressing requirements elicitation for implementing these artifacts. The qualitatively analyzed interviews allowed: final enhancement of the artifacts, identification of critical success factors for implementing the artifacts, and development of a new artifact for the KW4DS@CBP requirements elicitation. Finally, we further evaluated the thus developed KW4DS@CBP requirements elicitation tool via its illustration for an actual CBP.

7.4 Knowledge Warehouse Conceptual Model

Papers addressing decision support in DW design and implementation focused mainly on integrating patterns (Maddalena, 2004), management views (Holten, 2003) and quality factors (Tsoukas and Vladimirou, 2001). Yet, a DW is not directed toward CBP decision support (Tsoukas and Vladimirou, 2001; Holten, 2003; Maddalena, 2004). For harnessing knowledge in CBP decision making, we present the KW4DS@CBP architecture in the next section after presenting the KW conceptual model in this section.

Figure 7.2 depicts the KW concept as a central coordinator in a four-layer knowledge system. The first layer consists of the organizational OLTP systems that aggregate transactions. The second layer consists of the DW constructed based on OLTP data. The third layer consists of OLAP products (e.g., analytic reports). The fourth layer consists of the proposed KW infrastructure, aimed at providing decision makers with a comprehensive organizational view and understanding of each OLAP product vis-à-vis related CBP as well as relevant stakeholders and IS.

The conceptual model of the proposed KW layer (KW-CM) is an extension of the multidimensional DW conceptual modeling approach (Fig. 7.1 above, detailed in Rizzi, 2007). As can be seen in Fig. 7.3, the KW facts (events) are the OLAP products, and the KW dimensions consist of the CBP, the stakeholders, and the IS. These KW dimensions exhibit the meta-data of the OLAP products, implemented with an organizational ontology whose concepts are installed in the KW. For instance, for

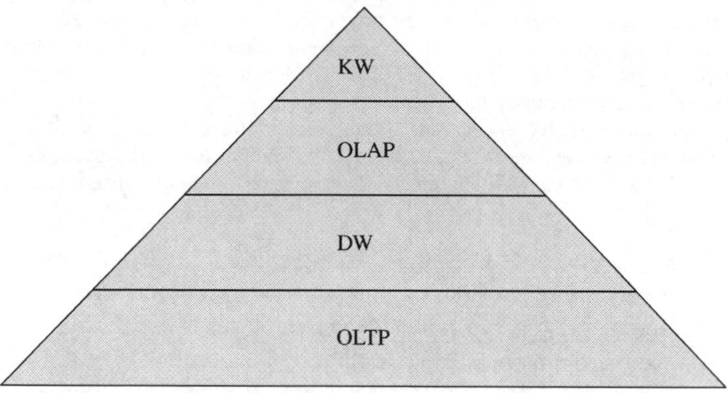

Fig. 7.2 KW – four-layer model

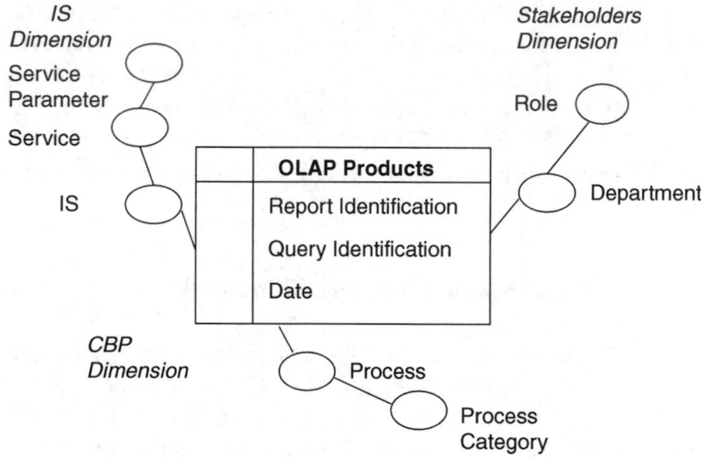

Fig. 7.3 A basic fact schema for a KW

each CBP the CBP meta-data may include title and category, for each stakeholder involved in the CBP the stakeholders meta-data may include the role and department, and for each CBP-relevant IS the IS meta-data may include the service (i.e., a software component which extracts the knowledge from an IS, or CBP-relevant information which resides in an organizational repository as presentation slides, reports that come from an outside source and any additional information required for decision makers in the context of a specific CBP) and the service parameters. It is beyond the scope of the current paper to fully develop the meta-data and suffice it to say that it is organization-dependent.

To illustrate KW-CM, consider for example a DW that handles information regarding customer product usage. If a manager gets an OLAP report showing insufficient usage of a certain feature of a new product, s/he needs more knowledge for making an intelligent decision within the CBP: Defining Product's New Features.

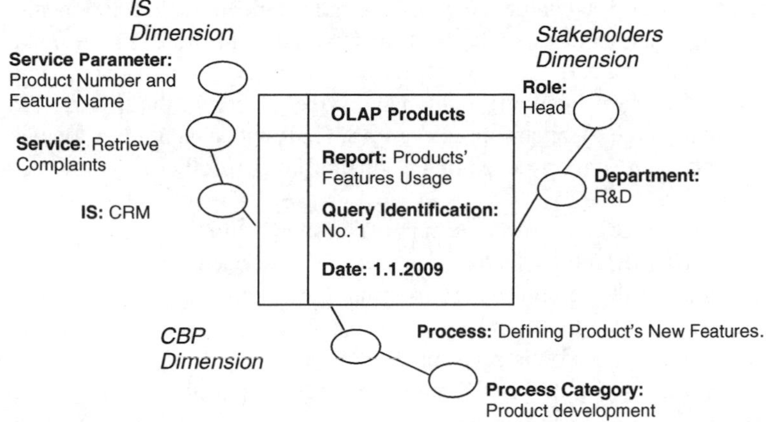

Fig. 7.4 An example of a basic KW fact schema

The KW layer (shown in Fig. 7.4) enables the manager to get a comprehensive knowledge view. In the IS dimension of the KW, data in the CRM application might reveal recurring complaints regarding a certain feature. The marketing IS application may provide information about campaign management processes addressing this feature. Presentation slides may provide the R&D department's roadmap regarding the product development. In the stakeholder dimension of the KW, a professional in the R&D department might help the manager by discussing the problems that were reported. Since all the mentioned resources are linked together with the Defining Product's New Features CBP dimension, these resources are presented to the manager in the context of this CBP.

To harness knowledge for CBP decision making which utilizes OLAP products, it makes sense to find out: Which critical business processes are involved in utilizing the OLAP products? Who are the stakeholders associated with these OLAP products? What other IS can contribute to getting a more comprehensive perspective of these OLAP products? Answering these questions should provide a systematic view on how to connect OLAP products with information regarding the CBP, stakeholders and IS, considering the original DW as a black box (Fig. 7.2) that remains unchanged (Adamson and Venerable, 1998; Kerschberg, 2001; Giorgini et al., 2005; Guo et al., 2006; Malinowski and Zimányi, 2006; Rizzi, 2007).

KW processes are different from the traditional DW processes. DW processes consist of extract, transform, and load (ETL) activities, aggregating data into the DW to which OLAP capabilities are applied. KW processes, on the other hand, utilize KW meta-data linkages for linking appropriate IS, stakeholders, and CBP to OLAP products. For each DW dimension (IS, CBP, and stakeholders), there is a specialized KW process entitled KW-Process. The KW-Process associated with the IS dimension, for instance, is implemented by the IS-services discussed above. When no IS-service can be provided, the decision-maker is presented with a reference to the IS so s/he may choose to further pursue information extraction. The KW-Process associated with the Stakeholders dimension enables identification of relevant stakeholders who relate to the specific CBP and with whom the decision maker may wish to consult. The KW-Process associated with the CBP dimension handles the integration of all the needed information and stakeholders for the specific CBP. The organizational ontology regarding relevant IS, CBP, and stakeholders together with KW-Processes can support development of interfaces to other applications across the organization.

Going back to the above example, a manager faced with the OLAP report regarding the under-used product feature can use a KW-service that aggregates all the information about the certain feature from the CRM application. Since the original OLAP report is based on certain fields, it is reasonable that some are used for aggregating information from other relevant IS. For example, the identification numbers of the product and the under-used feature are part of the OLAP report but also serve as parameters guiding further information extraction from the CRM application.

The three KW dimensions – IS, CBP and stakeholders – have many-to-many relations with the OLAP report. In the product feature example, for the purpose of aggregating customer information, the report can be linked to the CRM application as well as to the ERP application. At the same time, there can be a linkage connecting the report to another CBP or more, enabling development of new product features and review of product bugs. In addition, the stakeholders who relate to the report include the head of the R&D department, the product manager, and the head of the marketing department. For the sake of brevity and comprehensibility, the three bridge tables required for implementing these relations are not presented in Fig. 7.3. As explained next, KW-processes occur when observing a certain OLAP product via a collaborative environment within the KW4DS@CBP architecture.

7.5 KW4DS@CBP Architecture

In order to facilitate assimilation of the proposed KW-CM infrastructure, we propose the KW4DS@CBP architecture, incorporating the KW-CM infrastructure which utilizes the KW for aggregating the required information associated with a specific CBP. While the KW contains the links to the required information, the KW4DS@CBP actually presents the aggregated information to users. Figure 7.5 depicts the CBP focus when designing the KW4DS@CBP architecture. Within a specific CBP, the KW4DS@CBP architecture is capable of presenting users (decision-makers), via a comprehensive collaborative environment, with a certain OLAP product. Information aggregated by the KW-processes and consisting of relevant stakeholders and information gathered from various IS (i.e., reports produced by IS-services, slides presentations or documents that reside in organizational information repositories) are also included. The collaborative environment of the KW4DS@CBP architecture should also include utilities for tracking not only decisions and decision execution, but also performance indicators related to decision-execution outcomes. The collaborative environment would facilitate expression of unstructured information by stakeholders who provide insights or share experiences while discussing issues concerning a certain OLAP product.

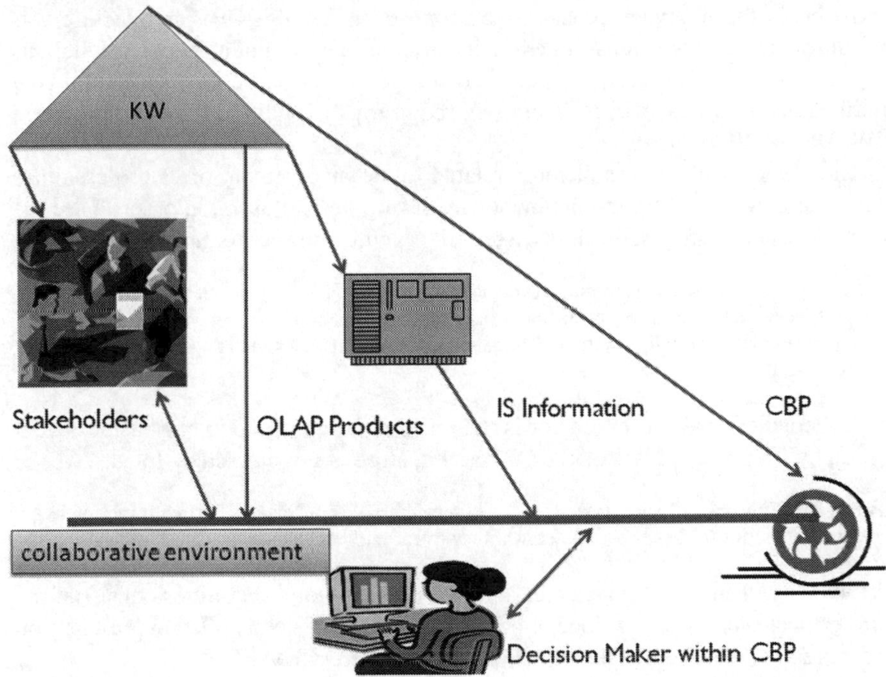

Fig. 7.5 KW4DS@CBP architecture

IS, CBP and stakeholders are thus depicted in both Figs. 7.3 and 7.5. However, Fig. 7.3 represents the KW concept, whereas Fig. 7.5 represents the KW4DS@CBP architecture, including the collaborative environment for the decision maker faced with a specific CBP, depicting how the KW provides aggregative knowledge within this environment. The proposed KW and KW4DS@CBP artifacts thus serve as an organizational transactive memory which links information from inside and outside the organization with relevant IS and stakeholders in the context of a specific CBP.

7.6 KW4DS@CBP Evaluation and Requirements Elicitation

Requirements elicitation is the first step in software development aimed at discovering and understanding system requirements based on interviews, brainstorming, and joint application design (Raghavan et al., 1994). However, system failure is quite prevalent when requirements elicitation is not done well (Davey and Cope, 2008). Keeping this in mind, we carefully conducted semi-structured interviews with three IS managers (denoted hereinafter Interviewee 1, Interviewee 2, and Interviewee 3) for the purpose of evaluating and proposing (in the next section) a requirements elicitation tool for the proposed KW4DS@CBP architecture. The interviewees belong to different small, medium and large organizations from the public and private sectors.

To begin the interview process, the proposed KW4DS@CBP architecture was presented, asking questions aimed at its evaluation and finding how to elicit its requirements. Analyzing the responses of the interviewees revealed the following findings about critical success factors in requirements elicitation for the proposed KW4DS@CBP *architecture.*

The first critical success factor is related to the involvement of IS professionals and managers, in addition to the involvement of potential users, in order to see the big picture and share responsibility regarding eventual usage. As Interviewee 1 said:

> In order to develop such environment you need to provide the managers not only the requirements they state, but also understand what other information you can provide from the organizational information systems. The IS manager should understand the decision making process.

A second critical success factor is the understanding of the major business goal served by the proposed KW4DS@CBP architecture. As expressed by Interviewee 3:

> The main purpose of such system is to present the decision makers, in real-time, plans versus activities for better planning toward next year budgets.

Diversity of information sources and rich presentation capabilities consist of the third critical success factor since important information is embedded in presentation slides, reports, dashboards and more, as noted by Interviewee 2:

> We need to get information from Excel, DW and other IS for enabling us to arrive at an intelligent decision.

Decision support by the KW4DS@CBP architecture is the fourth critical success factor at three levels: historical operational information (e.g., report generators), data analysis (e.g., what-if scenarios), and managerial presentations (e.g., dashboards). As stated by Interview 3:

> For understanding future decisions we must realize how divisions spent in the past, what they are spending today and how our decisions may impact their expenses in the future and what will be the impact on their cash-flow.

Fifth, it is critical to success of the KW4DS@CBP architecture that it combines on-line (e.g., data mining or analysis processes) and off-line capabilities (Anderson-Lehman et al., 2004). As indicated by Interviewee 3:

> We need capabilities to realize decisions' changes that took place in a certain quarter.

Decision tracking in a collaborative decision making environment is the sixth critical success factor, to insure continuity from the baseline upon which decisions are made via follow-up of decision execution processes and evaluation of key performance indicators. Interviewee 3 emphasized:

> We need to communicate with all the divisions as well with suppliers and customers. The information should be accessed through a collaborative environment and not kept in private PCs.

Finally, the seventh critical success factor in requirements elicitation for the KW4DS@CBP architecture is that a decision taken at a certain level may be decomposed to several lower-level decisions and follow-ups. Interviewee 2 explained:

> There are high-level decisions that should be decomposed to several low-level decisions. For example if we realize that the support service is not conducted professionally, the training division should further design training materials and courses to support people. The follow-up procedures should be handled in both levels.

Based on our literature review and findings from the three interviews, we propose next a requirements elicitation tool and demonstrate it based on information extracted in an interview with Interviewee 3.

7.7 Requirements Elicitation Tool

The KW4DS@CBP requirements elicitation tool (Table 7.1) is a semi-structured interview focusing on decision support for a specific CBP. Applying the first CSF, CBP owners (managers, decision makers), as interviewees, and IS developers, as interviewers, share during the interview views regarding KW4DS@CBP needs. Specifically, applying the second, third, fourth and fifth CSFs, information is sought regarding the goal and description of the specific CBP, CBP decisions supported, and OLAP products used for CBP decision support. Also sought for each OLAP product are the title, production process, duration, analysis capabilities, update frequencies, and inside/outside resource indication. The additional information required for filling the bottom two rows of Table 7.1 concerns CBP-relevant IS, as well as CBP-relevant stakeholders.

Table 7.2 demonstrates application of the proposed requirements elicitation tool for the budget-planning CBP at a large organization to which the third and last interviewee belonged. This is an illustration of the KW4DS@CBP requirements elicitation tool and should not be considered a full-scale analysis. Since the iterative design process is a common design science practice when suggesting a new solution

Table 7.1 Requirements elicitation tool

CBP title						
CBP goal and description						
Decisions supported during CBP						
CBP decision support OLAP products	Product title	Production process	Production duration	Analysis capabilities	Update frequency	Inside/ outside
CBP-relevant IS						
CBP-relevant stakeholders						

Table 7.2 Illustration of the requirements elicitation tool

CBP title	Budget planning					
CBP goal and description	Analyzing budget expenses against budget plan along the year					
Decisions supported during CBP	Budget allocation along the current year, in accordance with performance measurements, and budget allocations for the following year					
CBP decision support OLAP products	Product title	Production process	Production duration	Analysis capabilities	Update frequency	Inside/outside
	G	B, D, F	Flexible time frame	Drill-down capabilities; risk analysis	On-line	Inside
	H	B, D, F	Flexible time frame	What-if scenarios	Off-line	Inside
	I	B, D, F	Flexible time frame	Drill-down and additional analysis capabilities	Off-line	Inside
CBP-relevant IS	Reports A/C/E from IS B/D/F; meeting reports, organizational standards and decision tracking system					
CBP-relevant stakeholders	Project and unit managers, purchasing departments					

to a defined problem (Hevner et al., 2004), we present here only the first iteration of the proposed model implementation.

Budget planning involves two decisions: budget allocation for the current year, in accordance with performance measurements, and budget allocation for the following year. In this case, three OLAP products (reports) are used for decision support. OLAP Report G which aims at studying inappropriate budget allocations allows historical analysis, learning development of expenses including fluctuations during the year. There is also an option for on-line queries and additional risk analysis tools. OLAP Report G provides insights such as whether to approve a budget request by a certain unit and budget requests for the following year as well as what budget to allocate for different goals. OLAP Product H consists of what-if scenarios and special purpose DW views. OLAP Report I includes dashboards and graphical presentations (i.e., clock) about managerial perspectives (i.e., how much of the budget was used), which are defined in advance possibly allowing drill-down and additional analysis capabilities. OLAP Reports G, H, and I are based on data aggregated into the DW from IS B, D and F.

Additional relevant information for the budget planning process consists of three reports. Report A, extracted from IS B, pertains to management of the operational expenses within the total budget. Report C, extracted from IS D, pertains to management of purchases from various vendors. Report E, extracted from IS F, pertains to management of the expenses plan. Additional information requirements include meeting reports, organizational standards and decision-tracking system. The various stakeholders involved in the budget-planning process include project and unit managers, able to follow expenses, as well as the purchasing departments.

The requirement elicitation tool should be discussed separately for every CBP, aligned with the relevant stakeholders and IS. Once a user is engaged with a specific CBP, the appropriate knowledge will be presented through the collaborative environment for facilitating the decision-making process, applying the sixth CSF and seventh CSF.

7.8 Conclusion and Future Work

The need for leveraging OLTP, DW and OLAP during decision-making processes is well acknowledged (Tsoukas and Vladimirou, 2001; Stenmark, 2002; Holten, 2003; Maddalena, 2004). Yet, employing the design science research paradigm, this paper proposes and demonstrates the need for adding a knowledge layer – KW – on top of the existing OLAP, DW and OLAP applications (Fig. 7.1 above). The rationale behind the proposed knowledge layer stems from the value of harnessing knowledge for CBP decision support. The proposed KW4DS@CBP architecture, including its collaborative environment, addresses the management of structured and unstructured information, supporting CBP decisions associated aided by relevant IS and stakeholders.

Encompassing the stakeholder view in the KW4DS@CBP architecture, based on the KW conceptual modeling, responds to Nevu and Wade's (2007) claim that there is a need to align system performance with stakeholder expectations, thus enhancing usability and user satisfaction. Since in the KW4DS@CBP architecture the DW is a separate layer, it is applicable for existing DW without DW redesign and can also help in analysis of DW usage.

The proposed KW4DS@CBP architecture is based on the notion of arranging the organizational knowledge as transactive memory (Wegner et al., 1991; Jennex and Olfman, 2003; Nevo and Wand, 2005; Jackson and Klobas, 2008). To establish transactive memory intended for sharing, it is necessary to formalize explicit organization-wide knowledge into a perceptional common ground by constructing an organizational ontology which defines knowledge concepts and their relationships. We propose to define an organizational ontology which includes critical business processes, stakeholders, and information systems. In addition to representing the explicit knowledge embedded for CBP decision support within an organizational ontology, we also propose to handle the tacit knowledge relevant to CBP decision making that is embedded in unstructured information (e.g., emails and discussion forums) by means of a collaborative environment that enables open communication and fosters natural shared practices.

The work presented in this paper, including the KW concept, KW4DS@CBP architecture, and requirements elicitation tool, can open new directions in DW research and implementation as well as enhance knowledge assimilation for decision support in critical business processes. Following the design science research paradigm (Hevner, et al., 2004), the presented artifacts open the way for additional research. While these artifacts were qualitatively evaluated in this work, further research is needed regarding application and use issues associated with the proposed knowledge infrastructure and architecture, including IS services and products, organizational ontology, KW and analytic processes, human-computer interaction, and computer supported collaborative work.

References

Adamson, C., and Venerable, M. (1998). *Data Warehouse Design Solutions*. Danvers, MA: Wiley.

Alavi, M., and Leidner, D. E. (2001). Review: Knowledge Management and Knowledge Management Systems: Conceptual Foundations and Research Issues. *The Mississippi Quarterly*, 25(1), 107–136.

Anderson-Lehman, R., Watson, H. J., Wixom, B. H., and Hoffer, J. A. (2004). Continental Airlines Flies High with Real-Time Business Intelligence. *The Mississippi Quarterly Executive*, 3(4), 163–176.

Bazerman, M. H. (2006). *Judgment in Managerial Decision Making*. Hoboken, NJ: Wiley.

Bolloju, N., Khalifa, M., and Turban, E. (2002). Integrating Knowledge Management into Enterprise Environments for the Next Generation Decision Support. *Decision Support Systems*, 33, 163–176.

Davenport, T. H., and Prusak, L. (2000). *Working Knowledge*. Boston, MA: Harvard Business School Press.

Davey, B., and Cope, C. (2008). Requirements Elicitation – What's Missing? *Issues in Informing Science and Information Technology*, 5, 543–551.

Denning, P. J. (1997). A New Social Contract for Research. *Communications of the ACM*, 40(2), 132–134.

Drucker, P. (1993). *Post-Capitalism Society*. Oxford: Butherworth-Heinemann.

Garrett, T. M. (2004). Whither Challenger, Wither Columbia: Management Decision Making and the Knowledge Analytic. *The American Review of Public Administration*, 34, 389–402.

Giorgini, P., Rizzi, S., and Garzetti, M. (2005). Goal-Oriented Requirement Analysis for Data Warehouse Design. In *Proceedings of DOLAP*, 47–56.

Guo, Y., Tang, S., Tong, Y., and Yang, D. (2006). Triple-Driven Data Modeling Methodology in Data Warehousing: A Case Study. *Proceedings of ACM 9th International Workshop on Data Warehousing and OLAP (DOLAP)*, Arlington, Virginia, USA, pp. 59–66.

Hevner, A. R., March, S. T., Park, J., and Ram, S. (2004). Design Science in Information Systems Research. *The Mississippi Quarterly*, 28(1), 75–105.

Holsapple, C. W., and Joshi, K. D. (2003). A Knowledge Management Ontology. In C. W. Holsapple (Ed.), *Handbook on Knowledge Management* (Vol. 1, pp. 89–124). Lexington, KY: Springer.

Holten, R. (2003). Specification of Management Views in Information Warehouse Projects. *Information Systems*, 12, 709–751.

Jackson, P., and Klobas, J. (2008). Transactive Memory Systems in Organizations: Implications for Knowledge Directories. *Decisions Support Systems*, 44, 409–424.

Jennex, M. E., and Olfman, L. (2003). Organizational Memory. In C. W. Holsapple (Ed.), *Handbook on Knowledge Management* (Vol. 1, pp. 207–234). Lexington, KY: Springer.

Jongho, K., Woojong, S., and Heeseok, L. (2003). Hypermedia Modeling for Linking Knowledge to Data Warehousing System. *Expert Systems with Applications*, 24, 103–114.

Kahneman, D. (2003). A Perspective on Judgment and Choice: Mapping Bounded Rationality. *American Psychologist*, 58, 697–720.

Kerschberg, L. (2001). Knowledge Management in Heterogeneous Data Warehouse Environments. In *3rd International Conference on Data Warehousing and Knowledge Discovery (DaWaK 01), volume 2114 of LNCS*, Munich, Germany pp. 1–10.

Levy, M. (2009). The Knowledge Perspective of Data Warehouse: Knowledge Warehouse Conceptual Model. *Proceedings of the Conference on ENTERprise Information Systems (CENTERIS'2009),* Ofir, Portugal.

Levy, M., Pliskin, N., and Ravid, G. (2009). Studying Decision Processes via a Knowledge Management Lens: The Colombia Space Shuttle Case. *Decision Support Systems (DSS)*, 48, 559–567. Available online: http://dx.doi.org/10.1016/j.dss.2009.11.006

Maddalena, A. (2004). Pattern Based Management: Data Models and Architectural Aspects. In W. Lindner, et al. (Eds.), *Edbt 2004 Workshops, LNCS 3268* (pp. 54–65). Berlin Heidelberg: Springer.

Malinowski, E., and Zimányi, E. (2006). Hierarchies in a Multidimensional Model: From Conceptual Modeling to Logical Representation. *Data and Knowledge Engineering*, 59, 348–377.

March, G. (1978). Bounded Rationality, Ambiguity, and the Engineering of Choice. *Bell Journal of Economics*, 9, 2.

Nemati, H. R., Steiger, D. M., Iyer, L. S., and Herschel, R. T. (2002). Knowledge Warehouse: An Architectural Integration of Knowledge Management, Decision Support, Artifical Intelligence and Data Warehousing. *Decision Support Systems*, 33(2), 143–161.

Nevo, D., and Wade, M. R. (2007). How to Avoid Disappointment by Design. *Communications of the ACM*, 50, 4.

Nevo, D., and Wand, Y. (2005). Organizational Memory Information Systems: A Transactive Memory Approach. *Decision Support Systems*, 39, 549–562.

Newell, A. (1981). The Knowledge Level. *AI Magazine*, 2, 1–20.

Nicolas, R. (2004). Knowledge Management Impacts on Decision Making Process. *Journal of Knowledge Management*, 8(1), 20–31.

Nonaka, I. (1986). A Dynamic Theory of Organizational Knowledge Creation. *Organization Sciences*, 5(1), 14–37.

Raghavan, S., Zelesnik, G., and Ford, G. (1994). *Lecture Notes on Requirements Elicitation, Software Engineering Institute*, Carnegie Mellon University http://www.sei.cmu.edu/library/abstracts/reports/94em010.cfm

Raghu, T. S., and Vinze, A. (2007). A Business Process Context for Knowledge Management. *Decision Support Systems*, 43, 1062–1079.

Ralaivao, J., and Darmont, J. (2007). Knowledge and Metadata Integration for Warehousing Complex Data. *6th International Conference on Information Systems Technology and Its Applications (ISTA 07),* Kharkiv: Ukraine.

Rizzi, S. (2007). Conceptual Modeling Solutions for the Data Warehouse. In R. Wrembel, and C. Koncilia, (Eds.), *Data Warehouses and OLAP: Concepts, Architectures and Solutions* Ch 1. Hershey, PA: IGI Global, IRM Press.

Stanovich, K. E., and West, R. F. (2000). Individual Differences in Reasoning: Implications for the Rationality Debate. *Behavioral and Brain Sciences*, 23, 645–665.

Stenmark, D. (2002). Information vs. Knowledge: The Role of Intranets in Knowledge Management. *Proceedings of the 35th Hawaii International Conference on System Sciences*.

Tsoukas, H., and Vladimirou, E. (2001). What is Organizational Knowledge? *Journal of Management Studies*, 38(7), 972–993.

Wegner, D. M., Erber, R., and Raymond, P. (1991). Transactive Memory in Close Relationships. *Journal of Personality and Social Psychology*, 61(6), 923–929.

Zhang, D., Zhou, L., and Nunamaker, J. F., Jr. (2002). A Knowledge Management Framework for the Support of Decision Making in Humanitarian Assistance/Disaster Relief. *Knowledge and Information Systems*, 4, 370–385.

Chapter 8
Agent-Based Modeling and Simulation as a Tool for Decision Support for Managing Patient Falls in a Dynamic Hospital Setting

Gokul Bhandari[1], Ziad Kobti[2], Anne W. Snowdon[3], Ashish Nakhwal[4], Shamual Rahaman[5], and Carol A. Kolga[6]

[1] Odette School of Business, University of Windsor, Windsor, ON, Canada N9B3P4, gokul@uwindsor.ca
[2] Department of Computer Science, University of Windsor, Windsor, ON, Canada N9B3P4, kobti@uwindsor.ca
[3] Odette School of Business, University of Windsor, Windsor, ON, Canada N9B3P4, snowdon@uwindsor.ca
[4] Department of Computer Science, University of Windsor, Windsor, ON, Canada N9B3P4, nakhwal@uwindsor.ca
[5] Department of Computer Science, University of Windsor, Windsor, ON, Canada N9B3P4, rahaman@uwindsor.ca
[6] Kingston General Hospital, Kingston, ON, Canada, ckolga@kos.net

8.1 Introduction

A falls incident is said to occur when an individual accidentally comes to rest at a lower level of their body (Vu et al., 2004). Patient falls are one of the most reported patient safety events in hospitals. It has been found that about 50% of all nursing home residents succumb to falls each year (American Geriatrics Society, 2001) and that the number of falls in hospital in-patients range from 3 to 14 per 1,000 bed days in observational and intervention studies (Mahoney, 1998). Management of patient falls is a critical healthcare priority because it has direct impact on patients, their relatives, healthcare professionals and administrators with various physiological, psychological, legal, economic, and medical ramifications. For example, falls in hospitals can lead to complications such as fractures, anxiety and reduced strength, power and confidence and many other physical injuries (Mahoney, 1998). Falls are also associated with impaired rehabilitation and increased duration of hospital stay (Murray et al., 2007). Oliver (2007) finds that patient falls can lead to potential litigation by patients and their relatives if they believe that such falls could have been prevented.

Prior studies have documented several factors that lead to patient falls. For example, Myers (2003) outlines the following patient characteristics that can contribute to falls: mental state, changes in gait/mobility, prior fall history, medications, vision, continence, age, hearing, mood, dizziness/blackouts, weakness, blood pressure, ambulatory devices, personality factors, postoperative factors, seizures, physical disabilities, length of stay, unsafe footwear, environment changes, drugs,

D. Schuff et al. (eds.), *Decision Support*, Annals of Information Systems 14,
DOI 10.1007/978-1-4419-6181-5_8,

gender, sleeplessness, protective factors, knowledge level, type of admission, temperature, and restraints. Vu et al. (2004) divide risk factors for potential falls into two categories: intrinsic and extrinsic. Intrinsic risk factors include cognitive impairment, visual impairment, muscle weakness, neurologic impairment, balance impairment, and cardiovascular condition whereas extrinsic risk factors are primarily environmental variables and medications. They underscore that it is very difficult to design and implement effective fall prevention programs because of the complexity of interactions among the risk factors outlined above. American Geriatrics Society (2001) provides comprehensive best practice guidelines and systematic reviews related to falls prevention in the elderly population.

In order to reduce error and improve prevention of these adverse incidents electronic information systems are increasingly being used in health care settings for decision support (Dixon, 2002; Wald and Shojania, 2001). Such systems are found to offer several other advantages such as reduction in documentation time, increase in the quality of data collected and the significant improvement in data analysis capabilities (Aspden et al., 2004). While the benefits of adopting electronic information systems for falls incident reporting is widely documented, several researchers emphasize the need for more comprehensive and integrated system-wide understanding (such as complex adaptive systems view) of falls incidents so that improvement in patient outcomes can be achieved (Rutledge et al., 1998; Tsilimingras et al., 2003). Many services in the healthcare sector can be examined from the complex adaptive systems (CAS) perspective because CAS are dynamic systems consisting of non-linear interactions among actors such as humans, processes, and environment (Holland and Miller, 1991).

Due to non-linear and adaptive interactions among actors, CAS are too complex to be modelled by analytical techniques such as regressions and differential equations and therefore, researchers are increasingly turning to software agents to study such systems (Wang et al., 2009). Maes (1995) defines software agents as computational systems that populate some complex dynamic environment, perceive and act autonomously in this environment, and by doing so accomplish a set of objectives for which they are designed. According to Kalakota and Whinston (1996), agents should exhibit the following properties: independence, learning, cooperation, reasoning, and intelligence. Casti (1997) divides rules associated with agents into two categories: base-level rules, and higher-level rules. Base-level rules determine an agent's responses to its environment whereas the higher-level rules, which are essentially rules to change its base-level rules, provide it the capability for adaptation. Agent-based modeling and simulation (ABMS) refers to a computational framework in which agents' dynamic interactions are simulated repeatedly over time.

ABMS has been used in several diverse disciplines such as economics, archeology, sociology and healthcare. For example, a distinct field called Agent-based Computational Economics (ACE) has emerged around the application of ABMS to economic systems (Tesfatsion, 2002). Kohler et al. (2005) applied ABMS to explore the economic status of ancient cities in Mesopotamia and to understand the environmental factors that led to the extinction of Anasazi in the southwestern United States. Subsequently, Kobti et al. (2006) introduced social organization by means of hierarchical networks into the simulation. Similarly, ABMS has also been widely used in the study of social and organizational behavior and individual decision-making because of its descriptive power (Bonabeau, 2001) and in fact, computational social science, which primarily relies on agent simulation, is becoming a subfield in social sciences (Sallach and Macal, 2001). In such systems, agents represent people, and agent relationships represent social interactions among the people. In healthcare, ABMS has been used for several decades to reduce errors and medical costs and to improve service quality and efficiency of operations (Brailsford, 2007). Lanzola et al. (1999) proposed a generic computational model for building cooperative software agents for medical applications. Agent-based systems have also been used to provide the best possible treatment for patients and to remind them about their follow-up tests (Miksch et al., 1997).

In this research, we use an ABMS toolkit called Repast (Recursive Porous Agent Simulation Toolkit) to study patient falls incidents in a dynamic hospital setting in order to more fully examine the dynamic nature of patient falls in hospitals. Repast is one of the most powerful repository of agent tools and libraries useful for modeling and simulating complex multi-agent systems using programming languages such as Java, .Net and Python (Tobias and Hofmann, 2004). We contend that the ABMS framework is appropriate for studying patient falls incidents because of its richness and power to model complex interactions which are intrinsic to real world healthcare settings. In this sense, the ABMS encapsulates both the web of causation and the Person-Place-Time model which have been widely used in delivering patient care. The web of causation (MacMahon and Pugh, 1970) views a health condition as a result of a complex interactions among various factors which can be at the macro (societal) level, meso (familial, local) level, or micro (individual) level. Another framework that is applicable to the patient care is the Person-Place-Time model (Mausner and Kramer, 1985) in which the investigators examine the characteristics of the party affected (Person), the associated environment (Place) and the time period involved. In the next section, the use of Repast as a tool for analyzing patient falls in hospitals is illustrated in our simulation study described in detail in the following sections.

8.2 Prior Research

Simulation as a modeling and forecasting tool has been widely used in several disciplines. According to Naseer et al. (2009), top five simulation techniques used in healthcare sector are discrete event simulation, Monte Carlo simulation, system dynamics, agent-based simulation, and distributed simulation. In healthcare, simulation has been instrumental in coping with the complexity of decision making that evolves from the intricate interactions between various stakeholders, healthcare governance policy, and resource constraints. Prior works have demonstrated the usefulness and feasibility of simulation in several areas of healthcare such as hospital performance improvement (Gunal and Pidd, 2008), resource management (Ballard and Kuhl, 2006), staff scheduling and optimization (Guo et al., 2004; Spry and Lawley, 2005; Takakuwa and Wijewickrama, 2008), patient overcrowding minimization (Kolb et al., 2008), patient experience enhancement (Khurma et al., 2008) and forecasting their arrivals (Channouf et al., 2007) in emergency departments. For a comprehensive survey and review of simulation in health sector, refer to

Jacobson et al. (2006); Jun et al. (1999); White (2005). However, none of these studies examines the impact of shift types and duration, and patient acuity level on the percentage of patients served in time which has direct impact on potential patient falls. Our study is also unique in that it uses real world parameters in the simulation models thereby increasing the practical significance of this work for stakeholders.

8.3 Background

Leamington District Memorial Hospital (LDMH) is an 88-bed acute care hospital located in southern Ontario. This hospital serves a rural population of 45,000 people and typically admits elderly patients experiencing acute medication conditions. Hospitalized elderly are at risk for functional decline due to changes in their mobility, placing the person at high risk for falls while in the hospital. The impetus for this simulation study began in 2005, when LDMH participated in the Canadian Council on Health Services Accreditation Patient Safety Cultural Assessment project (Tiessen, 2008). This project was designed to assist healthcare institutions to examine their individual patient safety cultures. The findings from this project revealed the need to change the culture at LDMH from one that was focused on blame, to one that focuses on hospital system factors to ensure patients are safe and receive quality patient care. The leadership at LDMH created a Patient Safety Action Plan, with the goal of improving safety culture at LDMH. Part of this plan was a comprehensive Falls Management Plan that focused on creating safe environments for elderly patients with minimal use of restraints. Minimal restraint use respects the elder's autonomy and protects their right to make decisions about their care and hospital experience. At the onset of the Falls Management Program, the Chief Nursing Executive engaged an interdisciplinary university research team to collaborate with LDMH to examine patient falls and management strategies from a system perspective. The overall goal of the project was to develop system level strategies to manage falls and prevent falls related injury throughout the hospital, thus creating a culture of patient safety. The model examined the influence of the extrinsic factors that contribute to patient falls, namely features of the physical environment of the hospital. One of the key factors in patient falls is a nurse's ability to observe and monitor patients for the risk falls. The model and simulation accounts for the actual layout of the hospital floor plan in order to account for the distance nurses walk and the time required for the nurse to arrive at the patient's room. The physical layout and how it is built into the model is described in the following sections.

8.3.1 Description of the Hospital Floor Plan

Figure 8.1 of the second floor illustrates the hospital floor plan. The floor plan shows the hallways, staircases, elevators, waiting areas, cafeterias, doctor/staff offices, patient rooms, nurse stations, and patient/public washrooms. The physical

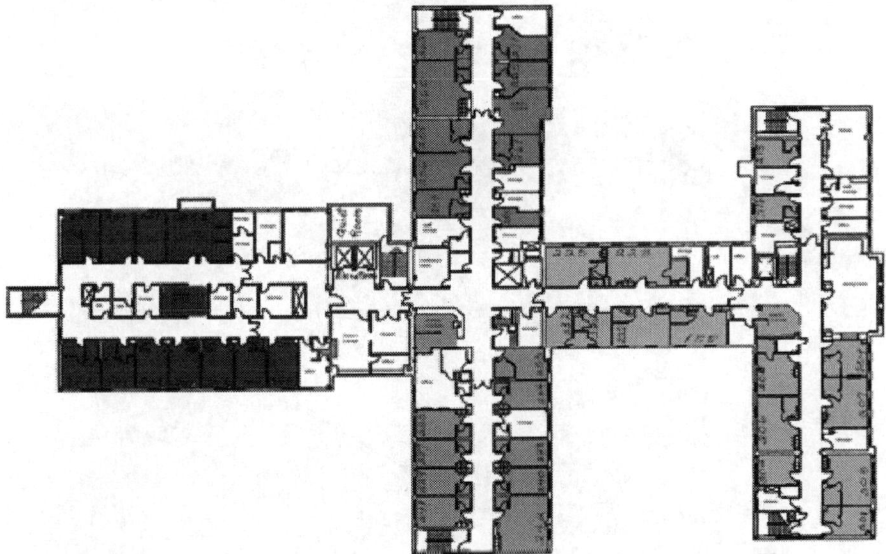

Fig. 8.1 Second level floor plan of LDMH

layout depicted in Fig. 8.1 was converted into a connected graph to be used in the simulation with nomenclature outlined in Table 8.1.

A sample graph representation is shown in Fig. 8.2 which depicts that the hall (H1) is connected to the patient room (PR250), storage room (SR2, SR1), rooms (R251, R252), washroom (WR1), nurse station (NS1), and other halls (H16, H3). The graph also shows that the hall (H2) is connected to nurse station (NS1), storage room (SR1) and patient rooms (PR246, PR247, PR248) which are connected to their respective washrooms (WR246, WR247, WR248).

While running the simulation, the physical connection in the floor plan is represented as a weighted directed graph where the vertex v represents a particular area and each edge e represents the ability to travel between two adjacent areas (i.e., out-vertex vo and in-vertex vi). Thus, edge e establishes a connection between vo and vi (Fig. 8.3). The weight of each edge represents the travel time from vo to vi

Table 8.1 Nomenclature for the floor plan used in the simulation graph

Name of node	Abbr.	Name of node	Abbr.	Name of Edge	Abbr.
Patient room	PR	Visitor lounge	VL	Hall	H
Room	R	Chapel	CH	Stairs	ST
Storage room	SR	Conference Room	CR	Elevators	EL
Wash room	WR	Staff lounge	SL		
Office	OF	Shower	SH		
Nurse station	NS	Dining room	DR		
Kitchen	KIT				

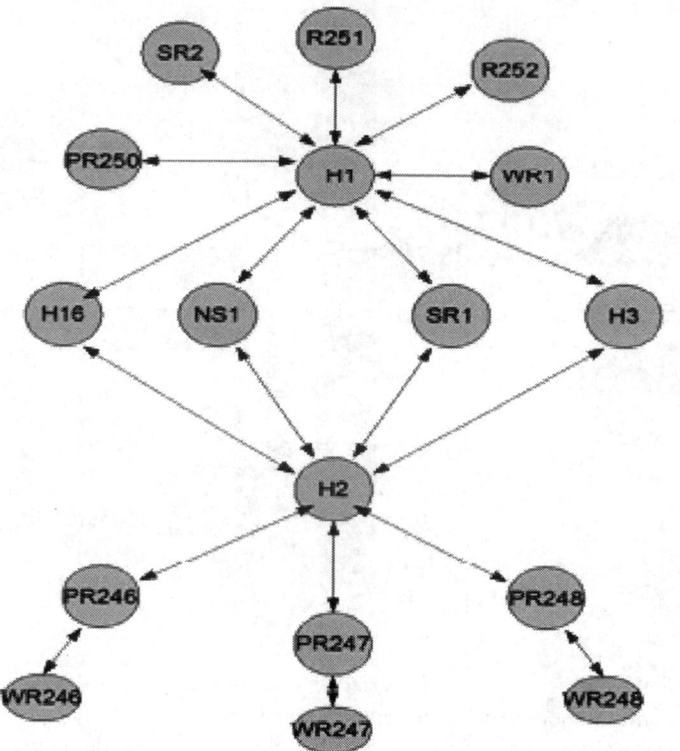

Fig. 8.2 A sample graph showing the connection of the halls H1 and H2

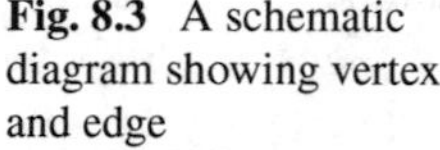

Fig. 8.3 A schematic diagram showing vertex and edge

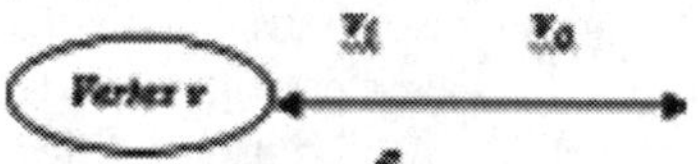

for nurse agents. Graph representation as shown in Fig. 8.2 is necessary to compute the shortest path nurses can take to reach their patients to respond to their calls for help. Let us consider an example to illustrate this. Suppose a nurse is going to check on a patient admitted to room PR250 and is taking this path: NS1 → H1→ PR250. Further suppose that the nurse meets another nurse on the way and realizes that a patient in room PR248 needs to be attended quickly. She now has the following options to travel to PR248:

PR250 → H1 → NS1 → PR248; PR250 → H1 → SR1 → PR248;
PR250 → H1 → H16 → PR248; PR250 → H1 → H3 → PR248.

As a general rule, the nurse takes the shortest path to go to the patient room destination. Along the way she/he looks for other nurses in patient rooms or hallways. If she/he finds other nurses, then there is a probability for interaction with them for a random interval of time, and consequently may change the nurse's initial path to the patient at PR248. The nature of the interactions is not specified in the model, but typical of a realistic behaviour that encapsulates: consultation and socialization, modeling and simulation of patient falls incidents, and how nurses respond to those situations are described in the following section.

8.4 Modeling and Simulation of Patient Falls Incident

As explained in the Introduction, agents are autonomous, active, persistent software components that perceive, reason, act, and communicate with other agents. In a simulated hospital setting, there are several agents such as doctor agents, nurse agents, patient agents, visitor agents, cleaning staff agents etc. However, in our base model we consider only patient agents and nurse agents. In order to establish a base simulation model, we have excluded several environmental variables and complex interactions found in a realistic setting. However, the base model allows us to progressively introduce such attributes in future iterations to mimic the characteristics of the real world hospital setting.

Patient Agent (PA): PAs are confined to their beds and need nurses' assistance to move out of their beds. The majority of patients at LDMH were elderly and required assistance to safely get out of bed without falling. Each patient is assigned an interaction time with a nurse and during this interaction the patient can get assistance to move from the nurse. Each patient has a maximum waiting period (based on their acuity and patience) for a nurse to arrive and provide care. If a nurse does not arrive within the waiting time period, the patient tries to move by him or herself and thereby becomes susceptible to a potential fall that the simulation probe promptly measures. It is worth noting that the nurse is not made aware of the patient's waiting period duration.

Nurse Agent (NA): All NAs are initially located at the Nurse Stations. They possess knowledge about the hospital floor plan and routinely check on each patient every hour. However, they are not cognisant of their patients' maximum waiting periods as they are latent by virtue of being intrinsic characteristics of the patients. Nurses can also compute the shortest path from their current location to the patient scheduled for a next visit. While NAs generally follow the shortest path to their patients, they may alter their path if they meet and communicate with other nurses on their path in order to update and share patient information among themselves. Such interaction, while important and necessary, causes delay in the nurses' intended interaction with their patients, thereby increasing the likelihood of the patients' unguarded movement and consequently, potential risk of falling.

The following assumptions have been made in the base model for the initial iteration:

(a) Environmental variables such as area temperature, humidity, floor friction and lighting of the hospital are constant.

(b) Patients are initially located to their rooms and there is only one patient in a room.
(c) All nurses are initially located at the Nurse Station (NS).
(d) Nurses are familiar with the floor plan and pathway of the hospital. Such knowledge constitutes the domain knowledge of the Nurse Agent.
(e) Nurse Agents may interact with other Nurse Agents when they meet them on the hospital pathway.
(f) Nurse agents have an average walking speed of 2.9-km/h (Chiu and Wang, 2007).

8.4.1 Simulation Setup

At the beginning of the simulation (with time = 0), all NAs and PAs are located in their respective rooms. They can be randomly assigned, or instantiated into specific locations (wings) in the hospital based on the user option. Then, NAs start moving on the pathways to meet with the patients based on practice routines of checking patients hourly. Each NA chooses the shortest path to reach their patients. However, they may alter their path if they interact with other NAs on their way. If a PA is reached by the nurse within its waiting time, it is considered successful. Otherwise, the PA runs out of patience and decides to move without assistance thereby becoming susceptible to a potential fall. Following is the list of the parameters used in this simulation.

- *Num Of Nurse Agent*: Total number of nurse agents available for serving the patients.
- *Num Of Patient Agent*: Total number of patient agents in the hospital inpatient units.
- *Max Patient Wait Time*: Maximum time a patient waits for a nurse to arrive
- *Interaction Time*: A nurse's interaction period with other nurses.
- *Prob Of Interaction*: Probability of a nurse interacting with other nurses.
- *Percent Of Acute Patient*: An acute patient is one who needs immediate nursing attention with a high frequency. This parameter gives the percentage of acute patients in the hospital at any given time. Acuity level of a patient may change (increase or decrease) after meeting with the nurse. The nurses are made aware of the acuity level of their patients.
- *Shift Type*: Indicates whether it is a day or a night shift. In a day shift, there will be 12 nurses available whereas there will be only eight nurses in a night shift. This data reflects the current nurse-patient ratio at LDMH under optimal circumstances. In reality, the staff ratio may be often reduced due to sick calls, or shortage of nursing staff that may occur on occasion.

The objective of this simulation study is to observe the impact of critical parameters such as interaction time delay, number of nursing staff available for work, shift duration (8 h vs. 12 h), and patient acuity on the percentage of patients successfully served in a timely manner by the nurses. The next section describes these results. Ultimately, the guiding motivation of the nurse agent is to service as many patients as possible on time, as dictated by their acuity levels, while gaining the most time in interacting with other nurses.

8.5 Results

The simulation results are illustrated in Figs. 8.4 through 8.6. The standard or base model has the following parameter values: shift duration (8 h), shift type (day), patient acuity level (a normal distribution with the range of 0–1; a patient with an acuity level of 0.8 or more is considered very ill and needs service within 3 min), percent of patients with high acuity of illness (40%), maximum waiting period of a patient (20 min), nurses' interaction time (between 1 and 3 min), number of patients (50), and number of nurses (12 in a day shift and 8 in a night shift). These values are based on the aggregate historical data from the hospital. We now discuss our findings (Figs. 8.4, 8.5, and 8.6) regarding the impact of critical parameters such as nursing staff available for work, shift duration, and patient acuity level on the percentage of success nurses are able to achieve with patient interactions in a timely manner (termed average success rate in the following graphs).

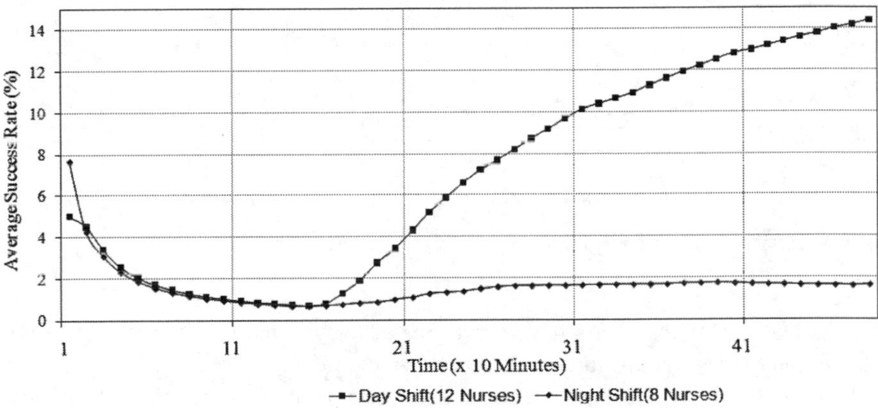

Fig. 8.4 Impact of shift type on percentage of patients served in time

In Fig. 8.4, we vary the number of nurses to simulate day and night shifts. The outcome confirms that reduced number of nurses decreases the number of patients that were served on time. It is worth noting that the first few time steps are typically ignored from any interpretation and used to allow the simulation to calibrate itself after it was initialized with random values. It is not surprising that in Fig. 8.5 the impact of a longer shift has on the physical abilities of the nurse. The success rate starts dipping following the eighth hour, thereby reflecting the impact of the stress on the nurse on patient service response time. Figure 8.6 examines the case where

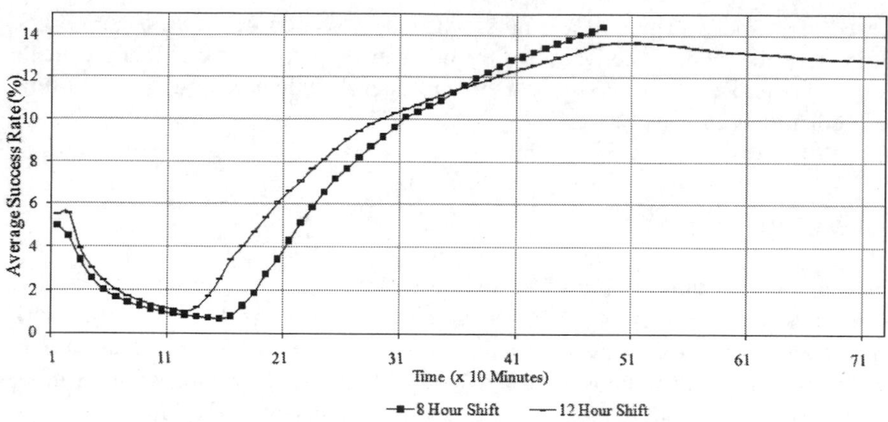

Fig. 8.5 Impact of shift hours on percentage of patients served in time

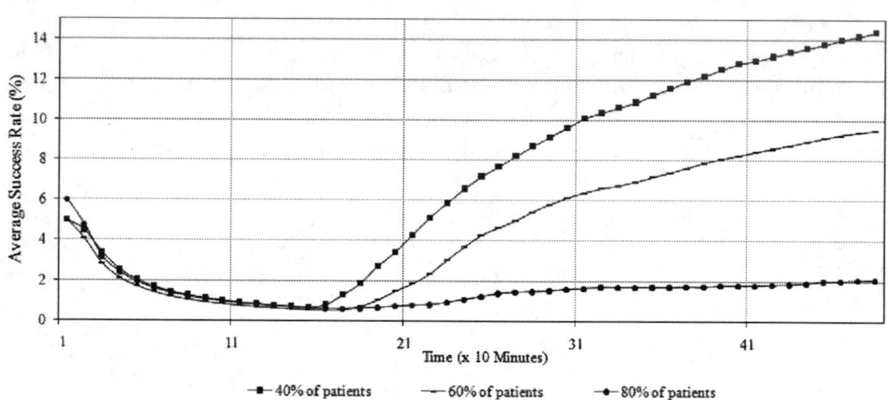

Fig. 8.6 Impact of patient acuity on percentage of patients served in time

patients had varied acuity. As the severity increases we find significant impact on the average success rate for timely patient service.

The validation of the base model against comparable expectations from the LDMH ensures correct calibration of the simulation. The parameters are fully driven by a graphical user interface that enables the user to setup the model based on his/her preferences and examines the outcome in terms of the effect of the parameters on the quality of patient timely service. Missing a patient's time window for service introduces a risk potential for a fall. If an administrator is to cut a nurse from the shift for instance he/she can see the impact in the simulation. The simulation becomes the test bed for countless executive decisions.

Figure 8.4 illustrates the impact of reduced number of nurses providing patient care on night shifts compared to day shifts. The majority of hospitals in Canada schedule fewer nurses on nights based on the assumption that patients are sleeping and require fewer interactions with nurses. However, hospitalized elderly patients often require frequent interactions with the nurse throughout the night, particularly when the patient is very ill. The simulation identifies the limitation of nurses being able to meet patient's need for attention when the number of available nurses is reduced on night shifts.

The length of the nurses' shift in the simulation model is found to alter the nurse's ability to respond successfully to the needs of patients. Figure 8.5 illustrates the decline in the nurse's success in responding to patient needs over the final 4 h of a 12 h shift. This finding may suggest that there is a "fatigue" factor for nurses who work prolonged shifts in hospital settings. As a nurse reaches the last 4 h of the shift, fatigue may reduce the speed and ability of the nurse to successfully interact with patients when they are in need of assistance.

The impact of a patient's acuity level (severity of illness) is illustrated in Fig. 8.6. The greater the acuity level of patients' on the hospital unit, the less likelihood of success of nurses in being able to interact with patients in a timely manner. This finding in the model identifies the importance of severity of illness has on the effectiveness of nurses' responses to meeting patient needs.

8.6 Conclusions and Future Work

This study describes the design and implementation of an agent based simulation model to examine patient falls in the dynamic environment of a hospital. The use of a custom Repast simulation offers researchers and clinicians a tool for examining systems level dynamics that contribute to patient falls in the complex hospital environment in a realistic manner. The advantage of this approach is the ability to examine how system level factors interact to either contribute to patient falls, or serve as protective functions in preventing falls. This preliminary model focuses only on the Nurse Agents and Patient Agents without any specific details of the hospital environment. In the future, the model will be further developed to include multiple types of agents, such as, Doctor Agents, Visitor Agents, Maintenance and Administrative Staff Agents, and Other Staff Doctor agents etc. In future, the environment effects like temperature, humidity, day and night, dark and brightness, friction of floor, wet floor and hindrances in hallways or in patient rooms will be built into the model. In this simulation, Patient Agents cannot move, but in future the model will include specific patient care tasks and care giving routines that more adequately capture the reality of hospital environments and the wide range of interactions that are typical of health care environments. Thus, how Nurse and Patient agents interact will be examined in more detail in the next model. In this simulation, Nurse Agents only perform single tasks while interacting with the patient by going from nurse station to patient room. In the next iteration of the model, Nurse Agents will have several tasks to carry out and there will be more interaction among agents in order to more adequately simulate real hospital environments. Reputation of agents will also be included in the model that will have an impact on nurse agents' strategy for interaction.

The present work can be extended by providing various probability distributions (e.g., Poisson) for the arrival of patients, acuity level, and time delays in the simulation model. Another major extension of this work would be to incorporate the current simulation toolkit in a managerial decision support system so that routine as well as ad-hoc reports can be generated to assist hospital managers in formulating effective falls prevention strategies.

Agent based modeling and simulation offers an innovative new approach to examine complex health system issues such as patient falls in hospital settings. As this tool is further refined and validated with real world patient falls data, modeling of innovative interventions and practice routines will be done to examine the effectiveness of new intervention approaches on the frequency and severity of patient falls. Agent based modeling may offer a new approach to "virtual testing" of practice initiatives using simulation models to improve the quality and cost effectiveness of quality patient care initiatives in the Canadian health care system.

Acknowledgment We thank CIHR/Auto21 and NSERC Discovery Grant for their generous financial support. We also appreciate the assistance provided by Paul Preney in the earlier work on this project and the nurses from the Leamington District Memorial Hospital without whose support this study would not have been possible.

References

American Geriatrics Society, The British Geriatrics Society, The American Academy of Orthopaedic Surgeons. (2001). Guideline for the Prevention of Falls in Older Persons. *Journal of the American Geriatrics Society*, 49, 664–672.

Aspden, P., Corrigan, J. M., Wolcott, J., and Erickson S. M. (2004). *Patient Safety: Achieving a New Standard for Care*. Washington, DC: The National Academies Press.

Ballard, S. M., and Kuhl, M. E. (2006). The Use of Simulation to Determine Maximum Capacity in the Surgical Suite Operating Room. Proceedings of the 2006 Winter Simulation Conference, 433–438.

Bonabeau, E. (2001). Agent-Based Modeling: Methods and Techniques for Simulating Human Systems. Proceedings of National Academy of Sciences, 99, 7280–7287.

Brailsford, S. C. (2007). Tutorial: Advances and Challenges in Healthcare Simulation Modeling, Proceedings of the 2007 Winter Simulation Conference, Southampton: United Kingdom.

Casti, J. (1997). *Would-be Worlds: How Simulation is Changing the World of Science*. New York, NY: Wiley.

Channouf, N., Lécuyer, P., Ingolfsson, A., and Avramidis, A. N. (2007). The Application of Forecasting Techniques to Modeling Emergency Medical System Calls in Calgary, Alberta. *Health Care Management Science*, 10, 25–45.

Chiu, M.-C., and Wang, M.-J. J. (2007). Professional Footwear Evaluation for Clinical Nurses. *Applied Ergonomics*, 38, 133–141.

Dixon, J. F. (2002). Going Paperless with Custom-Built Web-Based Patient Occurrence Reporting. *Journal on Quality Improvement*, 28, 387–395.

Gunal, M. M., and Pidd, M. (2008). DGHPSim: Supporting Smart Thinking to Improve Hospital Performance. Proceedings of the 2008 Winter Simulation Conference, 1484–1489.

Guo, M., Wagner, M., and West, C. (2004). Outpatient Clinic Scheduling – A Simulation Approach. Proceedings of the 2004 Winter Simulation Conference, 1981–1987.

Holland, J. H., and Miller, J. H. (1991). Artificial Adaptive Agents in Economic Theory. *American Economic Review*, 81, 365–370.

Jacobson, S. H., Hall, S., and Swisher, S. R. (2006). Discrete-Event Simulation of Health Care Systems. In R. W. Hall (Ed.), *Patient Flow: Reducing Delay in Healthcare Delivery* 211–252. New York, NY: Springer.

Jun, J. B., Jacobson, S. H., and Swisher, J. R. (1999). Application of Discrete-Event Simulation in Health Care Clinics: A Survey. *Journal of the Operational Research Society*, 50, 109–123.

Kalakota, R., and Whinston A. (1996). *The Frontiers of Electronic Commerce*. Redwood City, CA: Addison-Wesley.

Khurma, N., Bacioiu, G. M., and Pasek, Z. J. (2008). Simulation-Based Verification of Lean Improvement for Emergency Room Process. Proceedings of the 2008 Winter Simulation Conference, 1490–1499.

Kobti, Z., Reynolds, R., and Kohler, T. (2006). The Emergence of Social Network Hierarchy Using Cultural Algorithms. *International Journal on Artificial Intelligence Tools*, 15(6), 963–978.

Kohler, T., Gumerman, G., and Reynolds, R. (2005). Simulating Ancient Societies. *Scientific American*, 293(1), 76–84.

Kolb, E. M. W., Peck, J., Schoening, S., and Lee, T. (2008). Reducing Emergency Department Overcrowding – Five Patient Buffer Concepts in Comparison. Proceedings of the 2008 Winter Simulation Conference, 1516–1525.

Lanzola, G., Gatti, L., Falasconi, S., and Stefanelli, M. (1999). A Framework for Building Cooperative Software Agents in Medical Applications. *Artificial Intelligence in Medicine*, 16, 223–249.

MacMahon, B., and Pugh, T. F. (1970). *Epidemiology: Principles and Methods*. Boston, MA: Little, Brown.

Maes, P. (1995). Artificial Life Meets Entertainment: Life-Like Autonomous Agents. *Communications of the ACM*, 38, 108–114.

Mahoney, J. (1998). Immobility and Falls in the Acute Care Setting. *Clinical Geriatrics Medicine*, 14, 699–726.

Mausner, J. S., and Kramer, S. (1985). *Epidemiology: An Introductory Text*. Philadelphia, PA: Saunders.

Miksch, S., Cheng, K., and Hayes-Roth, B. (1997). An Intelligent Assistant for Patient Health Care, Proceedings of Agents '97. 458–465. New York, NY: ACM Press.

Murray, G., Cameron, I., and Cumming, R. G. (2007). The Consequences of Falls in Acute and Subacute Hospitals in Australia. *Journal of American Geriatrics Society*, 55, 577–582.

Myers, H. (2003). Hospital Fall Risk Assessment Tools: A Critique of the Literature. *International Journal of Nursing Practice*, 9, 223–235.

Naseer, A., Eldabi, T., and Jahangirian, M. (2009). Cross-Sector Analysis of Simulation Methods: A Survey of Defense and Health-Care. *Transforming Government: People, Process and Policy*, 3, 81–189.

Oliver, D. (2007). Preventing Falls and Falls Injuries in Hospital. A Major Risk Management Challenge. *Clinical Risk*, 13, 173–178.

Rutledge, D. N., Donaldson, N. E., and Parvikoff, D. S. (1998). Fall Risk Assessment and Prevention in Healthcare Facilities. *Online Journal of Clinical Innovations*, 1, 1–33.

Sallach, D., and Macal, C. (2001). The Simulation of Social Agents: An Introduction. *Social Science Computer Review*, 19, 245–248.

Spry, C. W., and Lawley, M. A. (2005). Evaluating Hospital Pharmacy Staffing and Work Scheduling Using Simulation. Proceedings of the 2005 Winter Simulation Conference, 2256–2263.

Takakuwa, S., and Wijewickrama, A. (2008). Optimizing Staffing Schedule in Light of Patient Satisfaction for the Whole Outpatient Hospital Ward. Proceedings of the 2008 Winter Simulation Conference, 1500–1508.

Tesfatsion, L. (2002). Agent-Based Computational Economics: Growing Economies from the Bottom Up. *Artificial Life*, 8, 55–82.

Tiessen, B. (2008). On the Journey to a Culture of Patient Safety. *Healthcare Quarterly*, 11, 58–63.

Tobias, R., and Hofmann, C. (2004). Evaluation of Free Java Libraries for Social-Scientific Agent-Based Simulation. *Journal of Artificial Societies and Social Simulation*, 7(1), http://jasss.soc.surrey.ac.uk/7/1/6.html

Tsilimingras D., Rosen, A. K., and Berlowitz, D. R. (2003). Patient Safety in Geriatrics: A Call for Action Journal of Gerontology. *Medical Sciences*, 58A, 813–819.

Vu, M. Q., Weintraub, N., and Rubenstein, L. Z. (2004). Falls in the Nursing Home: Are They Preventable? *Journal of American Medical Directors Association*, 5, 401–406.

Wald, H., and Shojania, K. G. (2001). Chapter 4: Incident Reporting. In K. G. Shojania, B. W. Duncan,, and K. M. McDonald (Eds.), *Making Health Care Safer: A Critical Analysis of Patient Safety Practices* (Evidence Rep/Technological Assessment No 43). Rockville, MD: Agency for Healthcare Research and Quality.

Wang, J., Gwebu, K., Shanker, M., and Troutt, M. D. (2009). An Application of Agent-Based Simulation to Knowledge Sharing. *Decision Support Systems*, 46, 532–541.

White, K. P. (2005). A Survey of Data Resources for Simulating Patient Flows in Healthcare Delivery Systems. Proceedings of the 2005 Winter Simulation Conference, 926–935.

Chapter 9
Context-Aware Mobile Medical Emergency Management Decision Support System for Safe Transportation

Frada Burstein[1], Pari Delir Haghighi[2], and Arkady Zaslavsky[3]

[1] Centre for Organisational and Social Informatics, Monash University, Caulfield, VIC, Australia, frada.burstein@infotech.monash.edu.au
[2] Centre for Organisational and Social Informatics, Monash University, Caulfield, VIC, Australia, pari.delirhaghighi@infotech.monash.edu.au
[3] Lulea University of Technology, Lulea, Sweden, arkady.zaslavsky@ltu.se

9.1 Introduction

Decision Support Systems (DSS) are computer-based information systems that are used in a wide range of application domains such as weather predication, climate change science and financial planning to assist decision makers to solve the problems and generate possible solutions (Beynon et al., 2002). Importance of DSS has been particularly recognized in emergency management and its associated activities such as medical emergency management, hazard mitigation and rescue and recovery operations (Gaynor et al., 2005; Sujanto et al., 2008; Thompson et al., 2006).

Context-awareness refers to up-to-date knowledge and run-time understanding of the surrounding environment within which a decision support system has to operate as well as run-time understanding of internal states of a decision support system. For instance, the parameters of the available technical infrastructure such as bandwidth and device profile, and a history of completed transaction form are the context attributes that should be taken into consideration when it comes to efficiency of DSS operation in mobile environments. On the other hand, some user-defined parameters, e.g. geographical location of the decision maker, his or her specific level of expertise may lead to differences in knowledge and information requirements towards the decision support system. While the notion of context is interpreted by computer science researchers somewhat differently, we subscribe here to the definition of context as adopted by the pervasive computing research community. Namely, context is defined as "the set of environmental states and settings that either determines an application's behaviour or in which an application event occurs and is interesting to the user" (Chen and Kotz, 2000). Within the context of emergency management decision support, it is imperative to equip the decision maker with full information based on the best possible context model (Sujanto et al., 2008; Brézillon, 2007). For instance, awareness of the user's confidence in making a decision (context attribute), currency of available information measured on the basis of

D. Schuff et al. (eds.), *Decision Support*, Annals of Information Systems 14,
DOI 10.1007/978-1-4419-6181-5_9,

the last synchronization when using a mobile device, or the approximate time to take a patient to a hospital where he/she will get the best care, are all context attributes, which need to be obtained at the time of calculating decision alternatives (Burstein et al., 2005). In the time-critical decision situations accuracy of the data and information considered in the decision model is crucial for overall quality of the decision outcome. Hence, utilizing context modelling approaches within the decision support architecture provide an opportunity to better cater the decision-maker with the decision choices relevant to his or her specific requirements, taking into account special dynamically updated situation parameters, as well as specific technical settings.

This chapter brings together context awareness and domain ontology modeling by proposing a real-time DSS for the highly dynamic and variable healthcare emergency domain. In particular, we consider one of the potential subfields of emergency management that could benefit from context-aware decision support is medical emergency transportation management in mass gatherings. Mass gathering events typically attract large numbers of people and are potentially hazardous (Arbon, 2004). Due to the crowd size, density and mood as well as other environmental factors, emergency situations in mass gatherings are typically associated with uncertainty and complexity. In such situations, medical emergency officers need to make critical and split-second decisions with regard to the provision of the necessary on-scene medical care as well as transportation of critically ill people to the nearby hospitals (Gaynor et al., 2005).

In this chapter, we propose an original architecture for context-aware decision support for medical emergency management in mass gathering that aims specifically to improve transportation safety. We describe an illustration of the proposed decision support architecture, which is according to the specific technical and user-specific application requirements set out based on thorough analysis of the literature and our previous research in real-time and context-aware decision support (Burstein et al., 2005; Cowie and Burstein, 2006; Padmanabhan et al., 2006). We present an emergency scenario to demonstrate the validity and feasibility of our proposed model. In this model, a domain ontology is applied as the key enabling technology because they offer a uniform, generic framework in which distributed real-time emergency decision support applications can be implemented more efficiently capitalizing on the pre-defined parameters and the relationships between them.

In the next section we discuss challenges of decision support in medical emergency transportation management and present an illustrative scenario to highlight these challenges. Section 9.3 describes the importance of including context-awareness in the decision support systems for effective management interventions. In Section 9.4, we discuss the need for a domain ontology that can present a standardized and formal conceptual model for emergency transportation management decision support. 9.5. presents the proposed architecture for context-aware medical emergency management decision support system for safe transportation. This section is followed by the description of the main components of this architecture. In Section 9.6 we discuss the implementation of the proposed architecture. Finally, Section 9.7 concludes the chapter and discusses the future work.

9.2 Challenges of Decision Support in Medical Emergency Transportation Management

Safety hazards on the road are faced by every driver in the world. Road tragedy is one of the highest causes of death universally (Jones, 2002). As the traffic volume increases in urban areas, emergency transportation services face a growing risk to the safety of their personnel while responding to or returning from an incident (Borri and Cera, 2006, FEMA, 2004). Computer science and wireless sensor technologies play major parts in the developments of tools and techniques for improving road safety. Using Intelligent Transportation Systems (ITS) enable access to contextual information on traffic and current location collected from sensors installed in vehicles/ambulances or on the road, and hence they can assist drivers to avoid collisions and reduces the fatalities (Kargupta et al., 2004). The ITS systems apply information and communication technologies and sensor networks to the vehicles and transportation services in order to improve the efficiency and safety of transport systems (FEMA, 2004). These systems basically rely on context-awareness for maintaining road safety (Meier et al., 2005, Santa and Gomez-Skarmeta, 2009).

To achieve context-awareness, there is a need for building an appropriate and relevant model of the surrounding environment (Zaslavsky, 2002). Road system, traffic accidents, congestion and knowledge of individual and emergency vehicles need to be included as part of such a model. Leveraging this model for decision support in medical emergency management can provide considerable assistance to emergency response departments for controlling the traffic, managing optimal navigation of their vehicles and ensuring safety of the personnel (FEMA, 2004).

Medical emergency management environments are typically very dynamic and uncertain where time-critical decisions are made. Planning, organizing and coordination of medical emergency transportation services in mass gathering events are complex and challenging tasks. One of these challenges is the lack of standardization. Medical emergency decisions (including transportation decisions) include inputs and the feedback from a wide range of relevant emergency stakeholders such as emergency agencies, medical emergency services, government, experts and communities. It is also important to realize that the domain is very information-intensive (Grimson et al., 2000). Decision making in such situations requires a standardized information structure to aggregate the unstructured data and information from various sources and platforms. The lack of standardization across different institutions prevents from using a single common solution to support a co-operative working environment (Bilykh et al., 2003).

Another challenge is that there is a risk of making incorrect emergency decisions based on incomplete or outdated information. Hence, it is important to provide the decision-maker with real-time and fresh contextual information for better understanding of decision parameters and implications of selecting particular decision alternatives. Incorporating emergency transportation decision support with a rich and unified knowledge model that represents common concepts and characteristics of this domain and supports dynamic data and real-time context (i.e. sensory originated data) can considerably improve effectiveness and accuracy of decision making process in dynamic and uncertain environments. Such approach enables sharing the knowledge model across various agencies and organizations and it can considerably assist decision makers with complex decisions and maintaining safe transportation.

In the following subsection, we present an illustrative scenario of medical emergency transportation management in a mass gathering event and highlight the arising challenges and specific technical application requirements.

9.2.1 Illustrative Scenario

Consider a mass gathering event (i.e. a sporting event with approximate 5,000 attendees) which was held between the hours of 12:00 and 18:00 during a hot summer day in Melbourne. Among the attendees, there was a crowd of 32 seniors.

Technical challenges: identifying, locating and tracking seniors with the use of sensors – understanding different types of mass gatherings and hazardous factors

As part of emergency response plan, a medical team that included volunteer nurse practitioners, internist, and physicians was located at the venue

Technical challenge: mutual awareness of seniors and medical support personnel using personalized location technology – understanding of the emergency response plan team and activities

Clinical facilities included the basic first aid and splinting and suturing equipment, and common oral pharmaceuticals

Technical challenge: awareness of available medications through RFID tags

Paramedics were also situated at the venue and supported with two ambulances. The medical team and resources were not equipped to treat critically ill or injured patients

Technical challenge: awareness of availability of medical facilities and resources, via a distributed, possibly web-based, and inclusive of mobile components and computing system – coordination between different emergency services/sections

At 15:00, the temperature rose up to 42°C (108°F), and several people were treated for dehydration and sunburn

Technical challenge: system level awareness of external localized environmental conditions with sensors

However, the crisis occurred when 14 seniors were identified as critically ill. Three of these patients needed immediate cardiac care due to heart problems. The medical team, paramedics and event organizers had to make instant and critical decisions with regard to transportation of these patients to the hospital that had the cardiac care, and whether to request extra ambulances in case of further incidents

Technical challenge: awareness of transportation facilities, hospital facilities and availability, awareness of patient's conditions and transportation constraints, optimisation of utilisation of available ambulances for transporting multiple patients with real-time routing and traffic support – coordination between transportation services, hospitals and other emergency services

Ambulance drivers also needed to make decisions about selection of the nearest hospital and the appropriate route considering the traffic flow and school zone programs at that time of day (i.e. the speed limit of 40 km/h during 14:30–16:00)

Technical challenge: safe and efficient transportation of multiple patients in presence of internal and external actors supported by different technologies – understanding and conceptualization of emergency transportation concepts

The above-described scenario illustrates the decision making challenges and technical needs that the medical emergency management face with regard to transportation of the ill or injured patients to hospitals and highlights the traffic-related hazards and issues that threatens the safety of transportation service personnel and patients they carry as well as the safety of the pedestrians or other vehicles in urban areas.

The proposed decision support architecture aims to address the above-mentioned challenges and provide the decision makers with real-time context and useful information regarding emergency transportation that enables generation of more effective recommendations and alternatives. The proposed DSS can run on both the onboard computers of ambulances and the computer/laptops of the medical emergency team and organizers. Ambulances today have a GPS system that helps to provide awareness to the driver of the current location, speed, direction, and angle of the vehicle. These data are useful when collected and analysed for the purpose of improving safety. Context-aware decision support system is able to collect the useful information about the traffic and road status and use this information for better-informed recommendations. On the other hand, application of domain ontology for medical emergency management and transportation in DSS enables decision support to take into account the major and common concepts and parameters that applies to a mass gathering emergency situation and leverage this knowledge to generate more effective alternatives.

9.3 The Need for Context-Awareness and Its Role in Decision Support

Context is a powerful and multi-faceted concept. It can be related to a network, application, environment, process, user or device. Contextual information can be sensed, derived, reasoned, computed, calculated or explicitly entered by users. Context is a very broad term that encompasses different aspects and characteristics (Delir Haghighi et al., 2006). For instance, context can be static such as hospital name and address and can be dynamic like traffic flow and condition. Context-awareness is a key to enabling intelligent adaptation in pervasive computing applications that need to cope with dynamic and uncertain environments. It enables applications to perform their tasks in an efficient and intelligent manner and enhance the user experience by increasing productivity and satisfaction.

One of the main sources of contextual information is sensors. Sensors are small computational devices that can be deployed or tagged almost on any object and provide the means to monitor the physical environment. Today's vehicles and on-road infrastructures are equipped with a large number of sophisticated sensory devices. These sensory devices are capable of monitoring and providing data pertaining to vehicle status, real-time traffic conditions, traffic incidents, and road crashes. By including and analysing the sensory data, there is a potential to determine contextual knowledge about situations that can lead to crashes. Such knowledge can have a significant positive impact on the key issue of improving decision making regarding road safety. In the context of transportation, we can categorize sensors into two types: (i) in-vehicle; and (ii) environmental sensors. Examples of the in-vehicle sensors include mechanical sensors like engine condition sensors or tire pressure sensors (Strobel et al., 2004). Environmental sensors can provide awareness of environmental changes related to the road safety, e.g. detecting wet or snowy roads (Jones, 2002). Access to the real-time contextual information about vehicle, traffic and road conditions enables drivers and traffic authorities to make better informed and more accurate decisions and avoid possible incidents or delays.

A major factor in measuring the success and efficiency of emergency transportation is the time. The other proposed factors include the ratio between the number of casualties and the number of interventions, and the percentage of interventions per unit (Adenso-Diaz and Rodriguez, 1997). Alternatively, Transport-to-Hospital Rate (TTHR) proposed by Arbon et al. (2001) shows the transport rate by ambulance from the on-scene medical service to hospitals. Selecting an appropriate route by considering the road and traffic status is a key issue to improve efficiency of emergency transportation (Borri and Cera, 2006). Recent advances in technology have considerably facilitated this process. Most of the commercially available systems are static route guidance systems that provide users with a turn-by-turn plan for reaching a destination using a digital map. These systems often use estimation of speed limits, road classification, and the number of intersections to compute a recommended route (Kantowitz and Leblanc, 2006). On the other hand, dynamic route guidance technologies are able to select a route by using real-time information about traffic, weather and road conditions, such as congestion-related measurements (Kantowitz and Leblanc, 2006).

9.4 Importance of Applying Domain Ontology to DSS for Medical Emergency Transportation Management

Medical emergency management involves multiple activities/operations, different organizations and various concepts. Developing medical emergency management decision support systems for safe transportation largely depend on a rich and standardized knowledge structure/model that can be shared between various emergency medical stakeholders and event planners. Ontologies are conceptual models that provide a formal representation of concepts and their relationships within a certain domain that can be used for knowledge sharing. Using a domain ontology enables representation of a general conceptual model of medical emergency management (including emergency transportation) concepts, their characteristics and relationships. Applying such domain ontology to decision support not only improves effectiveness of the decision-making process but it can avoid delays in the emergency medical care responses and ensure road safety during emergency transportation.

Figure 9.1 illustrates how decision making in emergency transportation management in mass gathering can be improved by inclusion of the real-time context about traffic and road conditions and application of a domain ontology. The figure shows that gathering of large numbers of people at mass gathering events have a potential for a wide variety of illnesses and injuries that will require an immediate medical emergency response. During providing medical care and treatment, the critically ill/injured patients are identified and transported to the nearby hospitals.

The coordination and decision making regarding providing necessary emergency transportation services during mass gathering events can be complex and challenging. In the model that we propose, the emergency vehicles (ambulances) are equipped with onboard computers running the context-aware and ontology-driven DSS that facilitates and improves the decision making process. These intelligent

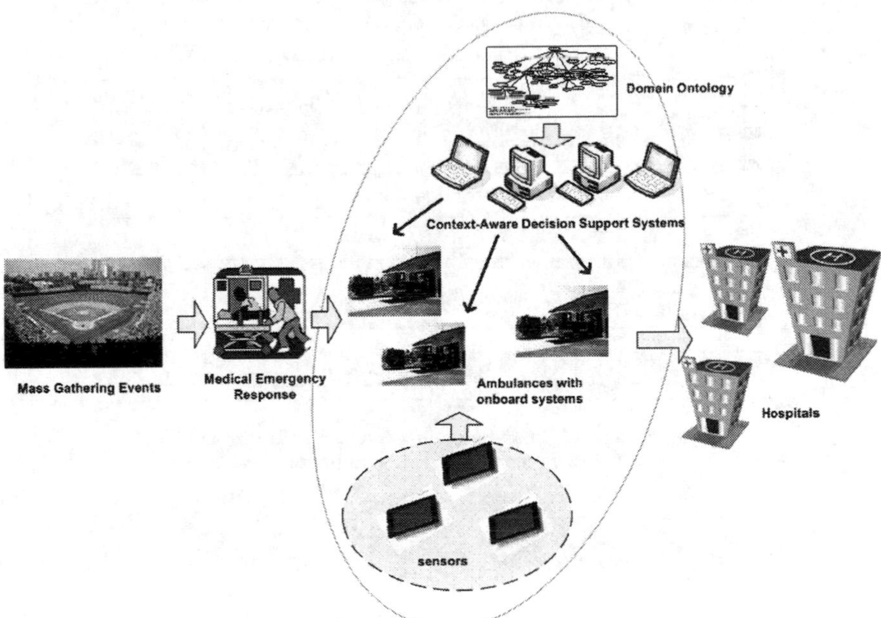

Fig. 9.1 The context-aware DSS model for emergency transportation

decision support systems are able to receive and process sensory originated data and leverage this knowledge for better-informed and real-time decisions to achieve safe transportation.

9.5 The Architecture of a Context-Aware Decision Support Model for Safe Transportation in Medical Emergency Management

The architecture of context-aware medical emergency management DSS (shown in Fig. 9.2) consists of two main parts: (1) knowledge base; and (2) decision support model. We have enhanced the knowledge base with including context-awareness and domain ontology. Contextual information is collected from in-vehicle and environmental sensors and Traffic Control Centres and used to infer and reason about current context by applying appropriate reasoning techniques (discussed in 9.5.1).

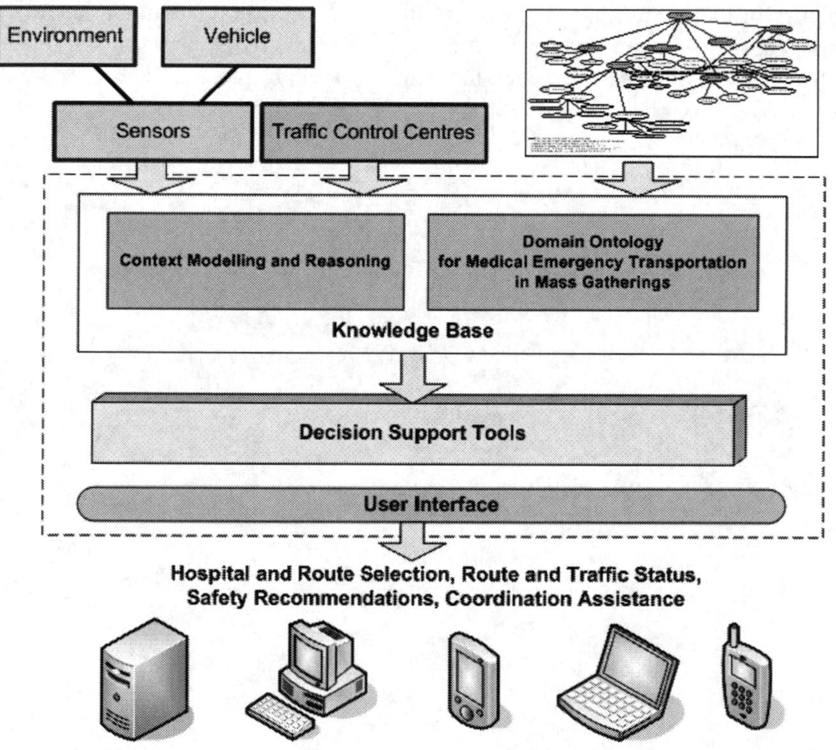

Fig. 9.2 The architecture for CA decision support

The domain ontology component is an extension of DOEM (Sujanto et al., 2008) for medical emergency transportation (discussed in 9.5.1). The combination of real-time context and domain ontology comprises the input fed into the decision support tools.

The architecture includes a user-friendly interface that support heterogeneous environments including mobile devices (such a PDA) and desktop computers. The output of the system include recommendations about the road and safety status, guidance with selecting the appropriate route, awareness of incoming traffic hazards as well as assistance with coordination and management of emergency response and transportation operations. The following subsections discuss the architecture components in further detail.

9.5.1 Knowledge Base

In the proposed architecture, the key role is devoted to a knowledge base which contains various mechanisms for representing and reasoning about the specific context in which the decision maker is situated and obliged to make decision about efficient transportation of mass gathering participants, especially in the situations of emergency management. Such mechanisms include the domain ontology and context modeling and reasoning that we described here.

9.5.1.1 Context-Awareness

With regard to the medical emergency transportation situations, context would include information about the onboard patient, the driver, the vehicle, the destination hospital, the environment in which the car is situated, and the road and traffic related elements/features. Real-time context is mainly collected from in-vehicle and environment sensors as well as Traffic Control Centres. The proposed onboard decision support system uses this low-level information to reason about current context/situation by using reasoning methods. There is an abundance of approaches in the literature proposed for modeling and reasoning about sensory data. These approaches apply well-known concepts and principles such as Bayesian reasoning methods (Castro and Munz, 2000; Fox et al., 2003), Dempster-Shafer theory (Jian et al., 2007; Wu et al., 2002), fuzzy logic (Anagnostopoulos et al. 2008, Mäntyjärvi and Seppanen 2002), ontology-based modeling approaches (Ranganathan and Campbell, 2003; Truong et al., 2005) and Graphical modeling (Buchholz et al., 2004; Henricksen et al., 2002).

While the current context modeling approaches are able to represent various types of contextual information, they have limited capabilities in dealing with different characteristics of context that are important for reasoning over sensory data. Among these approaches, the Context Spaces (CS) (Padovitz et al., 2004; 2006) is specifically designed for pervasive computing environments and is able to represent multi-dimensional nature of context under uncertainty (in terms of accuracy and reliability of sensor readings). The extension of this model has been proposed in

(Delir Haghighi et al., 2008), termed as Fuzzy Situation Inference (FSI) that enhances CS with fuzzy logic principles to represent real-world situations and uncertainty associated with them when these situation evolve from one to another. The CS and FSI offer powerful and sophisticated techniques to model sensory data as well as other sources of context. They are also able to reason about uncertain situations such as medical emergency transportation scenarios. Awareness of current context/situation enables decision makers (including driver) to understand the situation they (and their vehicle) are in and the risks involved. Feeding the information about current context/situation to DSS enables time-critical decisions to aid the driver to avoid dangers such as vehicle situations (e.g. nearby "dangerous" cars, lane-change, and road-departure, and intersections) and road conditions (such as vehicle traffic, wet or dry, and so on) (Krishnaswamy et al., 2005). The proposed context reasoning methods enable recognizing these situations in the timely and reliable manner. Augmenting DSS with such awareness in real-time results in more effective decision making that reduces risks that driver and passengers are being exposed and leads to safer transportation.

9.5.1.2 Domain Ontology

Ontologies as the formal and shared conceptualization play a key role in the development of Knowledge Based Systems. They reduce the workloads of the system builders from "building from scratch to 'extending and augmenting an existing structure'" (Swartout et al., 1996). The use of ontologies in DSS enables sharing common knowledge about the application domains and facilitates knowledge modeling and reuse (Ceccaroni et al., 2004). There are a number of decision support systems that have recognized the importance of ontologies to provide better support and results for complex problem-solving and decision-making situations. Examples of such systems include EON (Musen et al., 1996), OntoWEDSS (Ceccaroni et al., 2004), and EUEDE.

Emergency transportation in mass gathering as a part of the medical emergency management can considerably benefit from the use of ontologies in DSS. The transportation of patients to and from hospitals in a timely, efficient and safe manner during emergency requires careful planning and complex decision making. A domain ontology that provides a rich knowledge structure of emergency transportation concepts, the related elements and their relationships can be shared between different services and agencies, and facilitate management and coordination of transportation tasks during emergencies.

One of the major contributions towards building a domain ontology for emergency management is DOEM (Sujanto et al., 2008). Due to the scalable and extendable nature of this ontology for different subfields of EM, DOEM provides a potential knowledge structure for building ontology for emergency transportation in mass gatherings. The DOEM is built based on IFCCEM (Sujanto et al., 2008) that is a framework to incorporate and structure various dimensions of emergency management. DOEM covers major generic concepts in the emergency management domain that are applicable for all hazards situation. Figure 9.3 depicts parts of the DOEM

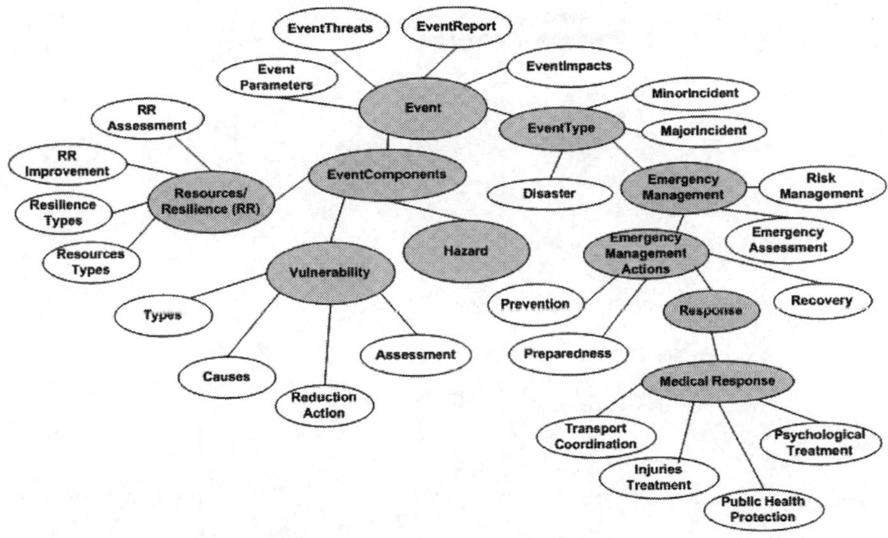

Fig. 9.3 Fragments of DOEM (adapted from Sujanto et al., 2008)

with relevant concepts highlighted. For further details of the complete ontology and the process of its construction, we refer the reader to Sujanto et al. (2008).

DOEM is built on modularization and therefore it enables reuse of the portions of the ontology that are more relevant and applicable to emergency transportation. We propose context-specific instantiation and qualitative extension of DOEM for emergency transportation in Mass Gathering sub-domain. To develop this ontology we have collected information from internal organization reports; public reports; research journals and papers; and emergency best practices and standards such as FEMA, EMA and ADPC, and intend to extend the ontology further by arranging focus groups with the mass gathering's emergency domain experts. Figure 9.4 presents our proposed ontology.

One the main strengths of the proposed domain ontology is supporting both static and dynamic data. Those concepts that relate to dynamic data are populated at run-time by real-time contextual information obtained from sensors. Static and dynamic information are combined and consolidated and then fed into the decision support tools to enable generation of better-informed solutions.

9.5.2 Decision Support Tools and User Interface

The Decision Support tools module would allow the users to analyse the parameters of the decision situation, which are important for making a transportation decision in a systematic and "just in time" mode. This will become possible as a result of the emergency transportation ontology providing the basis for making

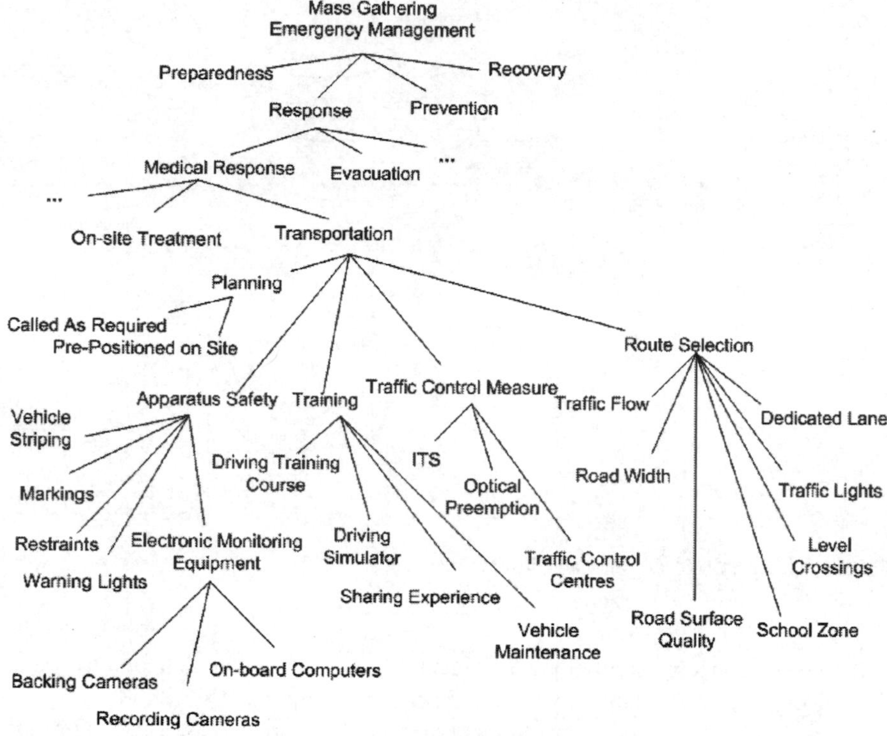

Fig. 9.4 The domain ontology for emergency transportation

sure all important factors are presented to the users in a consistent and comprehensive way. In addition a multi-attribute analytical model could be applied to allow the user to differentiate parameters by their utility or importance for the current context. For example, depending on the level of injury of the patience the choices of parameters for Route Selection line could be different. The role of the tool is to aggregate the information sourced from the ontology and instantiate real-time parameters provided from sensors in the most appropriate format and allow the user to navigate through the concepts and relationships of the specific part of the ontology thus equipping the user with necessary information for making better decisions.

The information representation is an issue of particular importance for the success of decision support tool (Zhu and Chen, 2008). It can be envisaged that graphical interface or a "dashboard" type representation could be beneficial for such decision support tools (Adam and Pomerol, 2008). Some further consideration is necessary for the most necessary and sufficient information provision as a mobile platform would be most suitable for such decision support tools to be available in real-time and on the move. The restrictions of the screen of the device and speed of the information download will be given appropriate consideration.

9.6 Implementation of the Proposed Architecture

The implementation of the context-aware decision support architecture for medical emergency transportation in mass gathering is an extension to our previous work developed for context-aware mobile agents for healthcare emergency DSS (Burstein et al., 2005). This work uses mobile software agents to support the deployment of an ambulance service in a real-time. Mobile agents are autonomous programs that have the ability to transport themselves between the nodes of a network entirely under its own control, carrying with them the data and execution state required to resume execution at the destination host from the point it ceased on the original host (Lange, 1998). In this work, agents are responsible for collecting and processing the required information from various Hospital Information Systems (HIS) and involved in coordination activities and decision support.

9.6.1 An Overview of the Prototype of Context-Aware Agents for Healthcare Emergency Decision Support

The architecture of context-aware mobile agents for healthcare emergency DSS involves a mix of stationary and mobile nodes supported by a combination of static and wireless networks (Burstein et al., 2005). The nodes includes: (1) ambulance node; (2) hospital node; (3) medical archives mode; (4) road authority website; and (5) mobile hospital assistant. These nodes communicate and share information using mobile agents. The developed application gets initiated when the paramedic selects a list of hospitals based on the accident location, keys in the patient ID and clicks on the "Launch Agent" button on the user interface component of the ambulance node. This deploys the two mobile assistants associated with the application – "hospital assistant" and "data assistant". Figure 9.5 shows the DSS user interface based on the information entered.

The hospital assistant is programmed to visit a list of hospitals identified by the paramedic. Once launched, it migrates to the various hospital nodes, interacts with the stationary hospital agent and retrieves the latest resource utilization details. Then the mobile agent moves to the next hospital on its list, repeating the series of requests. It keeps doing this till it arrives at the last hospital on the list, following which the mobile assistant moves back to the ambulance node. Based on the obtained results, the short-listed hospitals are ranked in their order of suitability. This ranked list of hospitals is then published to the user interface and is shown to the paramedics as illustrated in Fig. 9.6. While the hospital assistant retrieves the resource utilization details, another mobile agent referred to as the data assistant simultaneously gathers the relevant medical history of the current patient.

It starts off migrating to the medical archives node in the network and obtains the relevant database connection details by interacting with the stationary archives agent. It then uses these connection details to retrieve the medical history associated

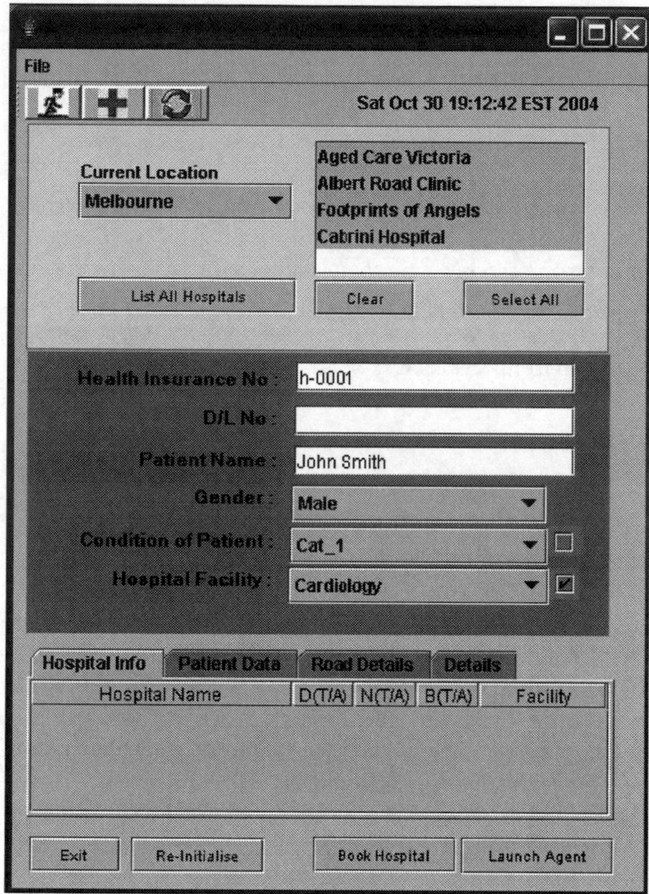

Fig. 9.5 The DSS interface for a healthcare emergency

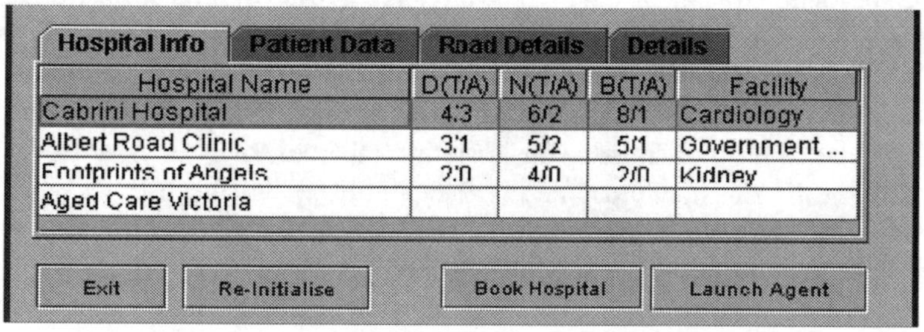

Hospital Info | Patient Data | Road Details | Details

Hospital Name	D(T/A)	N(T/A)	B(T/A)	Facility
Cabrini Hospital	4/3	6/2	8/1	Cardiology
Albert Road Clinic	3/1	5/2	5/1	Government ...
Footprints of Angels	2/0	4/0	2/0	Kidney
Aged Care Victoria				

Exit | Re-Initialise | Book Hospital | Launch Agent

Fig. 9.6 Hospitals ranked in terms of suitability

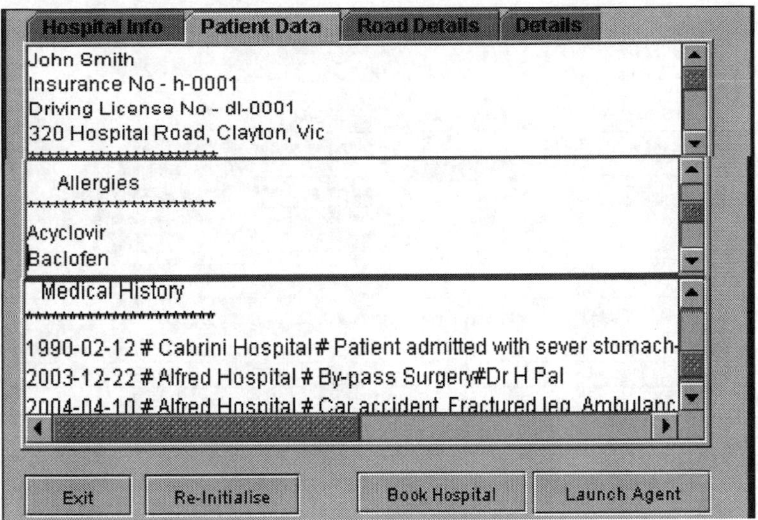

Fig. 9.7 The medical history information retrieved by data assistant agent

with the current patient based on the identification details specified (i.e. his ID). Figure 9.7 illustrates the retrieved patient's medical history.

In the prototype developed in (Burstein et al., 2005), the data assistant agent also travels to the "road authority web site" and gets the latest updates on road status information for each of the selected hospital. This approach provides very limited assistance to ambulance drivers and does not focus on safe transportation. The implementation of our proposed architecture (shown in Fig. 9.8) incorporates context-awareness and domain ontology for medical emergency transportation and improves effectiveness of DSS by assisting the driver to select the most appropriate and shortest route while avoiding traffic and road hazards.

According to the scenario that we described in 9.2.1, in mass gathering events, the critically ill or injured patients need to be transported into nearby hospitals by emergency vehicles (i.e. ambulances). The DSS shown in Fig. 9.8 allows the driver to enter their location and then it displays the nearby hospitals and routes from which one or all can be chosen. Then according to the selected routes, the road conditions are displayed and estimated travel time is computed.

9.7 Conclusions and Future Directions

The provision of emergency medical care and transportation in mass gatherings requires careful and standardized planning and synchronized management. When the crisis occurs, the organizers and emergency medical team need to make split-second and complex decisions. Providing the emergency medical and transportation personnel with context-aware decision support can facilitate time-critical decision

Fig. 9.8 Assistance with route selection based on domain ontology

making in this dynamic and uncertain environment and ensure safe emergency transportation.

Incorporating context-awareness into DSS improves decision making process and enables making better-informed and real-time decisions. In this chapter, we proposed a context-aware DSS architecture for medical emergency transportation in mass gathering that leverages mobile communication technologies and sensor networks. Context includes information about road infrastructure, data gathered from sensor networks, and other sources of context. For instance, route selection requires contextual information such as the width of the roads, road surface conditions and presence of traffic lights, priority lanes, schools or level crossings (Borri and Cera, 2006). The proposed architecture is underpinned by a domain ontology that is extended from DOEM (Sujanto et al., 2008) to provide a unified and standardized knowledge structure to represent emergency transportation concepts. The application of ontology will result in gaining a clearer understanding of the nature and requirements of road safety in medical emergency during mass gathering events.

In future we intend to extend this work by utilizing the state-of-the-art Intelligent Transportation Systems used in modern vehicles for providing the ambulance driver with rich information about the vehicle and environment. We aim to use visualization techniques to display the results of decision support and navigation recommendations graphically. Future work will also require extending implementation of the mobile real time decision support tool and testing its impact on improving efficiency of transportation decisions. It can be expected at least that such tools will strengthen ability to manage potential health-related hazards in real-time and on the move.

Acknowledgment This research is funded by Australian Research Council funding (LP0774834 and LP0453745).

References

Adam, F., and Pomerol, J. C. (2008). Developing Practical Support Tools Using Dashboards of Information. In F. Burstein, and C. Holsapple (Eds.), *Handbook on Decision Support Systems* (pp. 151–174). International Handbook on Information Systems Series. London: Springer.

Adenso-Diaz, B., and Rodriguez, F. (1997). A Simple Heuristic for the MCLP: Application to the Location of Ambulance Bases in Rural Region, Omega. *International Journal of Management Science*, 25(2), 181–187.

Anagnostopoulos C. B., and Hadjiefthymiades, S. (2008). Enhancing Situation-Aware Systems Through Imprecise Reasoning. *IEEE Transactions on Mobile Computing*, 7(10), 1153–1168.

Arbon, P. (2004). The Development of Conceptual Models for Mass Gathering Health. *Journal of Pre-hospital and Disaster Medicine*, 19, 208–212.

Arbon, P., Bridgewater, H. G., and Smith, C. (2001). Mass Gathering Medicine: A Predictive Model for Patient Presentation and Transport Rates. *Prehospital & Disaster Medicine*, 16(3), 109–116.

Beynon, M., Rasmequan, S., and Russ, S. (2002). A New Paradigm for Computer-Based Decision Support. *Decision Support Systems*, 33, 127–142.

Bilykh I., Bychkov, Y., Dahlem, D., Jahnke, J. H., McCallum, G., Obry, C., Onabajo, A., and Kuziemsky, C. (2003). Can GRID Services Provide Answers to the Challenges of National Health Information Sharing? In *Proceedings of the Centre for Advanced Studies Conference on Collaborative Research*, Toronto, 39–53.

Borri, D., and Cera, M. (2006). An Intelligent Hybrid Agent for Medical Emergency Vehicles Navigation in Urban Spaces. *Geo-Information for Disaster Management* (pp. 951–963). Berlin: Springer.

Brézillon, P. (2007). Context Modeling: Task Model and Model of Practices. In B. Kokinov et al. (Eds.), *Modeling and Using Context* (pp. 122–135). Heidelberg: Springer (CONTEXT 07), LNAI 4635.

Buchholz, T., Krause, M., Linnhoff-Popien, C., Schiffers, M. (2004). CoCo: dynamic composition of context information, In *Proceedings of the First Annual International Conference on Mobile and Ubiquitous Systems: Networking and Services*, Boston, Massachusetts, 335–343.

Burstein, F., Zaslavsky, A., and Arora, N. (2005). Context-Aware Mobile Agents for Decision-Making Support in Healthcare Emergency Applications, in T. Bui and A. Gachet (Eds.), *Proceedings of the Workshop on Contextual Modeling and Decision Support, at the Fifth International Conference on Modeling and Using Context,* Paris, France, 1-16, Aachen, Denmark: URL http://ceur-ws.org/Vol-144/07_burstein.pdf.

Castro, P., and Munz, R. (2000). Managing Context Data for Smart Spaces. *IEEE Personal Communications*, 7(5), 4–46.

Ceccaroni, L., Cortes, U., and Sanchez-Marre, M. (2004). Ontowedss: Augmenting Environmental Decision-Support Systems with Ontologies. *Environmental Modeling & Software*, 19, 785–797.

Chen, G., and Kotz, D. (2000). *A Survey of Context-Aware Mobile Computing Research* Technical Report TR2000-381. Dartmouth College: Department of Computer Science.

Cowie, J., and Burstein, F. (2006). Quality of Data Model for Supporting Mobile Decision Making. *Decision Support Systems*, 43(4), 1675–1683.

Delir Haghighi, P., Krishnaswamy, S., Zaslavsky, A., and Gaber, M. M. (2008). Reasoning About Context in Uncertain Pervasive Computing Environments, In *Proceedings of the 3rd European Conference on Smart Sensing and Context (EuroCSS 2008), Zurich*, Switzerland, October 29–31, Lecture Notes in Computer Science (LNCS) 5279, Berlin: Springer, 112–125.

Delir Haghighi, P., Zaslavsky, A., and Krishnaswamy, S. (2006). An Evaluation of Query Languages for Context-Aware Computing, In *Proceedings of the 17th International Conference on Database and Expert Systems Applications (DEXA'06)*, Crakow, Poland, September 4–8, IEEE Computer Society Press, 455–462.

FEMA. (2004). Emergency Vehicle Safety Initiative, FEMA, FA-272, Retrieved August 2004 from: http://www.usfa.dhs.gov/downloads/pdf/publications/fa-272.pdf.

Fox, D., Hightower, J., Liao, L., Schulz, D., and Borriello, G. (2003). Bayesian Filtering for Location Estimation. *IEEE Pervasive Computing*, 2(3), 24–33.

Gaynor, M., Seltzer, M., Moulton, S., and Freedman, J. (2005). A Dynamic, Data-Driven, Decision Support System for Emergency Medical Services. *International Conference on Computational Science*, 2, 703–711.

Grimson, J., Grimson, W., and Hasselbring, W. (2000). The SI Challenge in Health Care. *Communications of the ACM*, 43(6), 48–55.

Henricksen, K., Indulska, J., and Rankotonirainy, A. (2002). Modeling Context Information in Pervasive Computing Systems. *Lecture Notes in Computer Science* (pp. 79–117). (LNCS) 2414. Berlin/Heidelberg: Springer.

Jian, Z., Yinong, L., Yang, J., and Ping, Z. (2007). A Context-Aware Infrastructure with Reasoning Mechanism and Aggregating Mechanism for Pervasive Computing Application, In *Proceedings of the 65th IEEE Vehicular Technology Conference (VTC Spring 2007)*, Dublin, Ireland, April 22–25, 257–261.

Jones, W. D. (2002). Building Safer Cars. *IEEE Spectrum*, 39(1), 82–85.

Kantowitz, B. H., and LeBlanc, D. J. (2006). Emerging Technologies for Vehicle-Infrastructure Cooperation to Support Emergency Transportation Operations, University of Michigan, Transportation Research Institute, Retrieved from: http://deepblue.lib.umich.edu/bitstream/2027.42/55212/1/99812.pdf.

Kargupta, H., Bhargava, R., Liu, K., Powers, M., Blair, P., Bushra, S., Dull, J., Sarkar, K., Klein, M., Vasa, M., and Handy, D. (2004). VEDAS: A Mobile and Distributed Data Stream Mining System for Real-Time Vehicle Monitoring, In *Proceedings of the SIAM International Data Mining Conference*, Lake Buena Vista, Florida, 300–311.

Krishnaswamy, S., Loke, S. W., Rakotonirainy, A., Horovitz, O., and Gaber, M. M. (2005). Towards Situation-awareness and Ubiquitous Data Mining for Road Safety: Rationale and Architecture for a Compelling Application, In *Proceedings of Conference on Intelligent Vehicles and Road Infrastructure*, Melbourne, Australia, February 16–17, 1–6, URL http://www.csse.monash.edu.au/~mgaber/CameraReadyIVRI05.pdf.

Lange, D. B. (1998). Mobile Objects and Mobile Agents: The Future of Distributed Computing? In *Proceedings of European Conference on Object-Oriented Programming*, LNCS, Vol. 1445, pp. 1–12.

Meier, R., Harrington, A., and Cahill, V. A. (2005). A Framework for Integrating Existing and Novel Intelligent Transportation Systems, In *International IEEE Conference on Intelligent Transportation Systems (ITSC'05)*, Vienna, Austria, 8th, September 2005, IEEE Computer Society, 154–159.

Musen, M. A., Tu, S. W., Das, A., and Shahar, Y. (1996). Eon: A Component-Based Approach to Automation of Protocol-Directed Therapy. *Journal of the American Medical Informatics Association*, 3, 367–388.

Mäntyjärvi, J., and Seppänen, T. (2002). Adapting Applications in Mobile Terminals Using Fuzzy Context Information, In *Proceedings of the 4th International Symposium (Mobile HCI 2002)*, Pisa, Italy. Springer, 95–107.

Padmanabhan, N., Burstein, F., Churilov, L., Wassertheil, J., Hornblower, B.,, and Parker, N. (2006). A Mobile Emergency Triage Decision Support, In *Proceedings of the 39th Annual Hawaii International Conference on System Sciences*, 5, 96b.

Padovitz, A., Loke, S., and Zaslavsky, A. (2004). Towards a Theory of Context Spaces, In *Proceedings of the Second IEEE Annual Conference on Pervasive Computing and Communications Workshops*, Orlando, Florida, 38–42.

Padovitz, A., Zaslavsky, A., and Loke, S. W. (2006). A Unifying Model for Representing and Reasoning About Context under Uncertainty, The 11th International Conference on Information Processing and Management of Uncertainty in Knowledge-Based Systems (IPMU), Paris, France, 1983–1989.

Ranganathan, A., and Campbell, R. H. (2003). An Infrastructure for Context-Awareness Based on First Order Logic. *Personal Ubiquitous Computing*, 7(6), 353–364.

Santa, J., Gómez-Skarmeta, A. F. (July-Sept 2009). Sharing Context-Aware Road and Safety Information, *IEEE Pervasive Computing*, 8(3), 58–65.

Strobel, T., Servel, A., Coue, C., and Tatschke, T. (2004). Compendium on Sensors – State-of-the-art of Sensors and Sensor Data Fusion for Automotive Preventive Safety Applications, *ProFusion IP Deliverable*, PReVENT IP, European Commission, Retrieved 4 February 2010 from: http://www.prevent-ip.org/download/deliverables/ProFusion/PR-13400-IPD-040531-v10-Compendium_on_Sensors.pdf.

Sujanto, F., Burstein, F., Ceglowski, A., and Churilov, L. (2008). Application of domain ontology for decision support in medical emergency coordination, In *Proceedings of the 14th Americas Conference on Information Systems (AMCIS 2008)*, Toronto, Ontario, August 14–17, 1–10.

Swartout, W., Patil, R., Knight, K., and Russ, T. (1996). Toward Distributed Use of Large Scale Ontologies, In *Proceedings of the 10th Banff Knowledge Acquisition Workshop*, Banff, Alberta, Canada. URL: http://ksi.cpsc.ucalgary.ca/KAW/KAW96/swartout/Banff_96_final_2.html

Thompson, S., Altay, N., Green, W. G. III, and Lapetina, J. (2006). Improving Disaster Response Efforts with Decision Support Systems. *International Journal of Emergency Management*, 3(4), 250–263.

Truong, B. A., Lee, Y., and Lee, S. (2005). Modeling Uncertainty in Context-Aware Computing, In *Proceedings of the Fourth Annual ACIS International Conference on Computer and Information Science (ICIS'05)*, Jeju Island, South Korea, 676–681.

Wu, H., Siegel, M., Stiefelhagen, R., and Yang, J. (2002). Sensor Fusion Using Dempster-Shafer Theory, In *Proceedings of the 19th IEEE Instrumentation and Measurement Technology Conference (IMTC'02)*, Anchorage, Alaska, 7–12.

Zaslavsky, A. (2002). Adaptability and Interfaces: Key to Efficient Pervasive Computing, *NSF Workshop series on Context-Aware Mobile Database Management*, Brown University, Providence, 1-3, Retrieved 12 July 2010 from: http://www.cs.brown.edu/nsfmobile/wshop.html/zaslavsky.pdf.

Zhu, B., and Chen, H. (2008). Information Visualization for Decision Support. In F. Burstein, and C. Holsapple (Eds.), *Handbook on Decision Support Systems* (pp. 699–722). International Handbook on Information Systems Series. London: Springer.

Chapter 10
General Motors Bailout Problem: A Teaching Case Using the Planners Lab™ Software

Jim Courtney[1], Kristen Brewer[2], Randy Kuhn[3], and Gerald R. Wagner[4]

[1] Louisiana Tech University, Ruston, LA, USA, courtney@latech.edu
[2] Louisiana Tech University, Ruston, LA, USA, klb046@latech.edu
[3] University of Louisville, Louisville, KY, USA, jrkuhn01@louisville.edu
[4] Bellevue University, Bellevue, NE, USA, grwagner@mail.unomaha.edu

10.1 Introduction

In the fall of 2008 the "Big 3" US automakers – General Motors, Ford and Chrysler – approached the US Congress to seek transition loans, commonly referred to as "bailouts", to survive the economic downturn of the time. Ford was not seeking financial assistance, but said that if the others went into bankruptcy that they too would be in trouble, since so many suppliers would also be likely to fail. Congress refused to support the bailouts, but the Bush administration did, providing approximately \$9.4B to GM and \$4B to Chrysler with funds from the Toxic Asset Relief Program (TARP). Terms of the loan included, among other things, that the firms produce restructuring plans by March of 2009 that would produce a positive net present value over an unspecified time period.

What follows is a classroom handout for a case study developed to illustrate use of the Planners Lab (PL) software as a tool for analyzing the loan repayment and stability plan for GM through the year 2014. Instructors may hand this out as given, or modify it as desired. This case was first introduced as an assignment in a Master's level Information Systems course early in 2009; the response was very positive and the students were able to successfully model, forecast and form opinions regarding the financial viability and future stability of GM. The handout assumes knowledge of the Planners Lab. The model with solutions to the problems and an introductory PL tutorial is included in the Appendix.

10.2 The Assignment

10.2.1 Analysis of the GM Bailout Loan Agreement Using the Planners Lab

For this assignment, you are to modify and use a Planners Lab model of the "bailout" loan between the United States federal government and General Motors (GM) in late 2008. One of the provisions of the loan agreement was that GM must produce a plan

D. Schuff et al. (eds.), *Decision Support*, Annals of Information Systems 14,
DOI 10.1007/978-1-4419-6181-5_10, © Springer Science+Business Media, LLC 2011

by March 2009 showing a positive net present value using "reasonable" assumptions, or it may be required to repay the loans immediately. The time frame for the NPV calculation was not given, but GM was required to provide pro forma financial statements out to 2014, so that is the time horizon we will use. This is actually a very real problem and GM analysts were required to do the kind of analyses that you will be doing in this problem. This problem is an on-going one and terms of the agreement undoubtedly will have changed before you get this assignment, but you can understand how such analyses are conducted by using the terms of the original agreement.

A summary of GM's income and cash flow statements for 2006 through 2008 were downloaded from the Internet into an Excel spreadsheet and imported into the Planners Lab to start the development of the model. All the data is in millions of dollars, so a figure of $500 is actually $500 million and $13,400 is $13.4 billion.

GM was awarded loans totaling $13.4 billion at 5% per year, and these were to be repaid by December 29, 2011. Loans are actually to be repaid quarterly, but we are going to assume annual payments in the amount of $4.921 billion per year from 2009 through 2011. GM must also reduce executive compensation and eliminate perks such as corporate jets. Furthermore, it cannot declare new dividends as long as money is owed to the government.

In addition to these requirements, the prior Bush administration suggested several other "targets" that GM should attempt to achieve, but these are not strict requirements. These targets are summarized in Table 10.1 below; along with the way they are treated in the Planners Lab model. To get started, read the Wikipedia entry for the American auto industry and the NPR story in the inset on the next page about the terms for the loans.

Wikipedia Auto Industry Entry: http://en.wikipedia.org/wiki/Automotive_industry_crisis_of_2008

Here is a link to the actual agreement between the government and GM: http://www.ustreas.gov/press/releases/reports/gm%20final%20term%20&%20appendix.pdf. Much of it is in legal terms that are difficult to understand, but the NPR story (and others on the Web) have interpreted it for you.

10.3 Instructions for Analyzing the Problem

1. Open the model and go to the Playground and perform the operations described below. Put your answers to the questions below in Sticky Notes beside the required tables and charts.

   a. Under one tab labeled "1.a Sales and Expenses" create a table with all the variables from the Sales and Revenue node and the Cost and Expenses node.
   b. Create a second tab labeled "1.b Cash Flow & NPV" and add all the variables in each of the three Cash Flow nodes, plus the variables in the Net Cash Flow & Net Present Value node.
   c. Create a third tab labeled "1.c Bailout Activities" and add the variables from the Net Cash Flow & Net Present Value and the Bailout Activities node.

Q and A: A bailout for GM and Chrysler

by Joshua Brockman
NPR.org, December 19, 2008
http://www.npr.org/templates/story/story.php?storyId=98522778

President Bush on Friday sent a clear signal that US automakers are an essential part of the economy by saying the government would make $17.4 billion in loans to General Motors and Chrysler. The loans, which Congress had failed to approve, are an effort to keep these companies afloat in the near-term and to give them a stepping stone to achieving long-term viability.

The car companies have until March 31, 2009, to come up with viable plans for their survival. Here, a look at whether this will be enough time and whether consumers will be any more interested in purchasing cars 3 months down the road.

Will the loans make a difference?

"The economy couldn't take the failure of these companies in a disorderly way," says Dennis Jacobe, chief economist for Gallup, echoing the president. Jacobe says the loans will give the automakers a fighting shot at survival. All of the debate about whether to rescue the industry has had a somewhat negative impact on the perception of these companies. "But our polling has shown that most Americans will buy an American-made auto," he says.

Where will the loans come from?

The loans will come from the bailout funds administered by the Department of Treasury known as the Troubled Asset Relief Program (TARP). A Treasury official said that of the first $350 billion set aside under TARP, only $15 billion has yet to be allocated. Much of that money was already spoken for, but since it has yet to leave the Treasury's coffers, it's still available to tap for other purposes. On Friday, Treasury Secretary Henry Paulson also called on Congress to release the second $350 billion from the bailout package to "support financial market stability."

What are the terms of the loans for each automaker?

General Motors Corp. will receive a loan of up to $13.4 billion. Part of that, $4 billion, will be available to the company on Dec. 29 and the next installment of $5.4 billion will be available on January 16, 2009. The remaining $4 billion is contingent on Congress taking action.

Chrysler will receive a $4 billion loan on Dec. 29. There are no loans being made to Ford at this time as the company has previously said that it doesn't need immediate financial assistance.

The loans to GM and Chrysler are for a term of three years. However, if the companies fail to meet the loan terms, the president's designee can accelerate the loan so that the companies must repay it within 30 days, according to the Treasury official. If things don't go well for the automakers, the Treasury will have first priority over any assets that could be sold.

Both GM and Chrysler will also have to provide the government with warrants, or guarantees, that will give the government the ability to buy the companies' stock at a specified price. The loans will also require the companies to limit executive compensation, including no bonuses or incentives for their 25 highest-paid employees.

President Bush said he hopes the loans will help give the automakers time to put plans in place to restructure into viable companies. If that isn't possible without filing for bankruptcy, he said, the loans will give them time to set up "an orderly Chapter 11 process that offers a better prospect of long-term success."

What concessions will automakers have to make and will their present executives stay on board?

The conditions of the loan have some historical precedents. Brian Johnson, senior equity analyst who watches the auto industry for Barclays Capital, says it resembles the help the government

Q and A: A bailout for GM and Chrysler

extended in 1979 to Chrysler, which came with "hard targets imposed by Congress." (In 1979, Chrysler engaged in a 5-month battle to get government loans to prevent filing for bankruptcy. Congress passed the Chrysler Corporation Loan Guarantee Act of 1979, which ultimately provided the company with $1.5 billion in loan guarantees.)

By March, the automakers will have to show a plan for long-term viability. That plan must include cutting their outstanding debt by two-thirds of their outstanding debt; they'll have to cut half of the contribution they make to an independent health care trust fund; they'll have to alter wages and benefits by the end of 2009 to fall into closer alignment with those offered by foreign automakers, such as Toyota and Honda, that operate in the US; and they must eliminate their jobs-bank programs, which help autoworkers who are laid off to find new jobs.

Will consumers have a stronger appetite for car purchases 3 months from now?

It seems unlikely, especially based on recent polls conducted by Gallup. "I think it's going to take probably longer than that but it's all a matter of how much of a shock all of the financial crisis has been to the average consumer," Jacobe says. "Our most recent consumer surveys show consumer confidence remains very negative, particularly upper-income consumers are pessimistic."

How much time will it take for the automakers to be deemed viable?

The loans are an effort to help the companies create long-term viability, but it's not clear how much time the car companies will have to prove that they can survive. President Bush said the loans would "give the auto companies an incentive to restructure outside of bankruptcy." But he also made it clear that by March 31, both GM and Chrysler's restructuring plans would have to address three major issues: creating sustainable retirement plans; convincing bondholders to transfer debt into capital that the companies can use now; and bringing wages more into line with foreign automakers operating in the US.

Where does this leave the United Auto Workers?

While the automakers welcomed the loans, the terms of the deal are not so appealing to the United Auto Workers. "While we appreciate that President Bush has taken the emergency action needed to help America's auto companies weather the current financial crisis, we are disappointed that he has added unfair conditions singling out workers," says UAW President Ron Gettelfinger.

Johnson of Barclay's Capital says the "new terms set up a new round of brinksmanship" between the government, the union and automakers. The enforcement of the terms will fall to the Obama administration. The Obama designee could be less demanding than Secretary Paulson. Johnson expects the UAW to lobby Congress and the Obama administration to "loosen the strings," on some of the conditions of the deal – including the call for autoworker compensation to fall in line with what foreign automakers pay US workers.

2. Create another tab labeled "2. Target NPV" and add a target variable chart with Net Present Value as the target and Automotive Cost of Sales Rate as the What If variable.

    a. Is the Net Present Value positive in 2014 with the current assumptions?
    b. Create a What If chart with Automotive Cost of Sales Rate as the variable so you can see how it behaves when you change the target value for Net Present Value. For 2011 and beyond, shift the points for the Net Present Value line in the target chart so that it rises gradually and ends just above zero in 2014.

Table 10.1 GM targets and planners lab assumptions

GM must:	Assumption in PL model
• Be financially viable, which means GM must be able to show a positive net present value using reasonable assumptions	• Net present value will be based on net cash flows projected out to 2014 Variable name: net present value Node: net cash flow and present value
• Repay loans totaling $13.4 billion with an interest rate of 5% payable quarterly and a maturity date of December 29, 2011	• Assume annual payments, not quarterly. The annual payments will be $4.921 billion per year from 2009 to 2011 Variable name: bailout loan payment Node: bailout activities
• Accept limits on executive compensation and eliminate perks such as corporate jets	• Assume this reduces expenses by $25 million per year, starting in 2009 Variable name: reduction in perks Node: bailout activities
• Issue no new dividends while it owes government debt	• Starting in 2009 dividends will be zero, saving about $300 million per year until the debt is repaid in December 29, 2011 Variable name: reduction in dividends Node: bailout activities
GM should attempt to:	*Assumption in PL model*
• Reduce debts by 2/3 via a debt for equity exchange. That is, get bondholders to trade bonds for stock	• Reduce interest expense by 2/3, not including the bailout loan. This will be modeled by reducing expenses by $500 million a year Variable name: reduction in interest expense Node: bailout activities
• Make one-half of the Voluntary Employees Beneficiary Association ("VEBA") payments in the form of stock. VEBA is the retirement fund which will be administered by the UAW. Payments start in 2010	• GM's payments are expected to be about $600 million per year, so this will still result in a net increase in expenses of about $300 million starting in 2010 instead of the $600 million it would have been otherwise Variable name: reduction in VEBA payments Node: bailout activities
• Eliminate the jobs bank	• This is likely to happen. Assume this will save about $400 million per year Variable name: elimination of jobs bank Node: bailout activities
• Work rules and wages that are competitive with transplant auto manufacturers (US operations of Toyota, and Honda) by 12/31/09	• This is perhaps the key variable as it affects the cost of vehicles sold. We will want to see how much the Automotive Cost of Sales Rate has to be reduced to get to a positive NPV by 2014, given the other savings. In the past, this was running about 90%, but in 2008 it was 101%. The model currently assumes that it stays at 101% in 2009, but declines to 95% in 2010 and then stabilizes at 90% in 2011 and afterwards Variable name: automotive cost of sales rate Node: cost and expenses

About what value does Automotive Cost of Sales Rate have to be by 2014 to achieve a positive NPV? Do you think this is feasible?

3. For the remaining analyses, set the Automotive Cost of Sales Rate to 85% in 2012 through 2014.
4. For 2009, assume that Automotive sales will be the previous year's sales times a triangularly distributed growth rate with a minimum of 75%, expected value of 78% and maximum value of 80%.
5. Also, for 2010 through 2012, assume that the economy recovers and sales improve considerably and are triangularly distributed with a minimum of 5%, expected value of 10%, and maximum of 13% (use 1.04, 1.08, 1.10 in the TRIRAND statement).
6. Assume sales level off in 2013 and 2014 and have a triangular distribution with a minimum of 2%, expected value of 4% and a maximum of 5%.
7. Create a Risk Analysis chart and a Confidence Analysis chart for Net Present Value and run simulations (500 iterations each) to answer the following questions with discount rates (in the Net Cash Flow & Present Value node) of 9.5, 10.5 and 11.5% (this is roughly what GM did). You will have 3 different simulation runs with the different discount rates.

   a. With these assumptions, in what year can you be 90% certain that net present value will be positive?
   b. What is the 90% confidence interval range of values for NPV in 2014?
   c. As of the end of March 2009, GM had been unsuccessful in getting bondholders to accept an exchange for stock. Thus, it appears that GM may be unable to reduce its interest expense. Rerun the risk analysis above with a discount rate of 10.5% only and a Reduction in Interest Expense in Bailout Activities of 0 (zero) for the entire time horizon. In what year can you be 90% certain that NPV will be positive?

8. Do you think GM will survive? Why or why not? Your answer may be based on reasons not included in this analysis, such as political factors or other things not considered here.

10.4 The Model

10.4.1 Sales and Revenue

Automotive sales = 171179, 178199, 147732, PREVIOUS*TRIRAND(0.75, 0.78, 0.80), PREVIOUS*TRIRAND(1.04,1.08,1.10) FOR 2, PREVIOUS*TRIRAND(1.02, 1.04, 1.07)
Financial services revenue = 34422, 2923, 1247, Automotive sales* 1%
Total revenue = SUM(Automotive sales THRU Financial services revenue)

10.4.2 Costs and Expenses

Automotive cost of sales = 163742, 166259, 149311, Automotive sales IN Sales and revenue* Automotive cost of sales rate
Selling and general and administrative expense = 13650, 14412, 14253, Automotive sales IN Sales and revenue* 0.10
Financial services and insurance expense = 29794, 2742, 1292, Financial services revenue IN Sales and revenue* Financial services and insurance expense rate
Other expenses = 4238, 2099, 5407, Automotive sales IN Sales and revenue* Other expenses rate
Total costs and expenses = SUM(Automotive cost of sales THRU Other expenses)
Operating gain or loss = Total revenue IN Sales and revenue – Total costs and expenses
Equity in gain or loss of GMAC LLC = –5, –1245, –6183, 0
Automotive and other interest expense = –2642, –2902, –2345, PREVIOUS
Automotive interest income and other nonoperating income = 2812, 2284, 424
VEBA payments = 0 FOR 4, 600
Gain or loss from operations before taxes and adjustments = Operating gain or loss + SUM(Equity in gain or loss of GMAC LLC THRU Automotive interest income and other nonoperating income)
Income tax expense or benefit = –3046, 37162, 1766, IF Gain or loss from operations before taxes and adjustments <= 0 THEN 0 ELSE 0.35* Gain or loss from operations before taxes and adjustments
Equity income net of tax = 513, 524, 186
Minority interests net of tax = –324, –406, 108
Gain or loss from continuing operations = Gain or loss from operations before taxes and adjustments – Income tax expense or benefit + Minority interests net of tax + Equity income net of tax
Income from discontinued operations = 445, 256, 0
Gain on sale of discontinued operations = 0, 4309, 0
Net income = Gain or loss from continuing operations + SUM(Income from discontinued operations THRU Gain on sale of discontinued operations)
Automotive cost of sales rate = 0.97, 0.95, 1.01, 1.01, 0.95, 0.90
Financial services and insurance expense rate = 1.0 FOR 3, PREVIOUS –.02 FOR 2, PREVIOUS
Other expenses rate = 1.0 FOR 3, 0.03

10.4.3 Cash from Operating Activities

Depreciation = 10885, 9513, 10014
Amortization = 1021, 0
Deferred Taxes = – 4241, 35666, 2207, 0
NonCash Items = –3837, –2052, 15764, 0
Changes in Working Capital = –24746, 3336, –9190, 0

Cash from Operating Activities = Net income IN Costs and expenses + SUM(Depreciation THRU Changes in Working Capital)

10.4.4 Cash from Investing Activities

Capital Expenditures = –7902, –7542, –7530
Other Investing Cash Flow Items = 27597, 5782, 5766
Cash from Investing Activities = SUM(Capital Expenditures THRU Other Investing Cash Flow Items)

10.4.5 Cash from Financing Activities

Financing Cash Flow Items = 2490, –5, 0
Cash Dividends Paid = –563, –567, –283 FOR 3, –600
Net Issuance of Stock = 0 FOR 2, 0
Net Issuance of Debt = –5694, –5021, 4126, 0
Cash from Financing Activities = SUM(Financing Cash Flow Items THRU Net Issuance of Debt)

10.4.6 Net Cash Flow and Present Value

Foreign Exchange Effects = 365, 316, –778
Net Change in Cash = Cash from Operating Activities IN Cash from operating activities + Cash from Investing Activities IN Cash from investing activities + Cash from Financing Activities IN Cash from financing activities + Foreign Exchange Effects + Net cash from bailout activities IN Bailout Activities
Net present value = 0 FOR 3, NPV(Net Change in Cash, Discount rate)
Discount rate = 0.105

10.4.7 Bailout Activities

Bailout loan amount = 0 FOR 3, 13400 FOR 3, 0
Bailout loan interest = 0 FOR 3, AMORTINTEREST(Bailout loan amount, 0.05, 3) FOR 3, 0
Bailout loan payment = 0 FOR 3, AMORTPAYMENT(Bailout loan amount, 0.05, 3) FOR 3, 0
Bailout loan net = 0 FOR 3, Bailout loan amount – Bailout loan payment, – 1.0* Bailout loan payment
Reduction in executive compensation = 0 FOR 3, 25 FOR 3, 0COMMENT Reduction in executive comp is –25 for 2009–2011
Reduction in perks = 0 FOR 3, 1 FOR 3, 0COMMENT Reduced –1 in 2009 thru 2011

Reduction in interest expense = 0 FOR 3, 500COMMENT Equal to Automotive and other interest expense IN Costs and expenses
Reduction in VEBA payments = 0 FOR 4, 300COMMENT –300 in 2010 and after
Reduction in dividends = 0 FOR 3, 300 FOR 3, 0
Elimination of jobs bank = 0 FOR 3, 4COMMENT –400 2010 and after
Net cash from bailout activities = SUM(Bailout loan net THRU Elimination of jobs bank)

10.4.8 Market Capitalization

Shares outstanding = 610.5
Earnings per share = Net income IN Costs and expenses/Shares outstanding
Share price Dec 31 = 30.72, 24.89, 3.20, IF Net income IN Costs and expenses >= 0.0 THEN TRIRAND(4.25, 4.50, 4.75)* Earnings per share ELSE TRIRAND(1.50, 2.00, 2.50)
Market value = Share price Dec 31* Shares outstanding

10.5 Appendix A: Introduction to the Planners Lab™

Jim Courtney
Kristen Brewer

Successful financial planning is a core critical success factor for every organization. The Planners Lab (PL) is not solely for financial planning, but that is its primary focus. Example applications include strategic planning, financial planning, capital budgeting, balanced scorecards, project investment analysis, merger and acquisition analysis and sales forecasting. This document provides an introduction to the basic features of the Planners Lab and assumes no prior knowledge of this software.

The basic components of the Planners Lab (PL) are (1) an algebraically-oriented model-building language and (2) easy to use options for visualizing model output and answers to what-if and goal-seek questions; that is, to analyze results of changes in assumptions. The combination of these components allows business managers and analysts to build, review and manipulate the assumptions that underlie a decision-making scenario.

To illustrate, let's keep things simple and assume that the company is a small store that sells only one kind of notebook computer. The price in 2007 was $1350.00 and 300 units were sold. We will build a PL model to make financial plans for this company through 2012.

When you launch the Planners Lab, you get a screen like that in Fig. 10.1. Models are written in an algebraic-like language and may be written in the native language of the user. Models are arranged into hierarchically organized nodes shown in the left window. Node names are defined by the user and are initially blank. The model we will use will have three nodes: Revenue, Expenses and Profit. To create the Revenue node in the leftmost window, single click new node 1, then double click

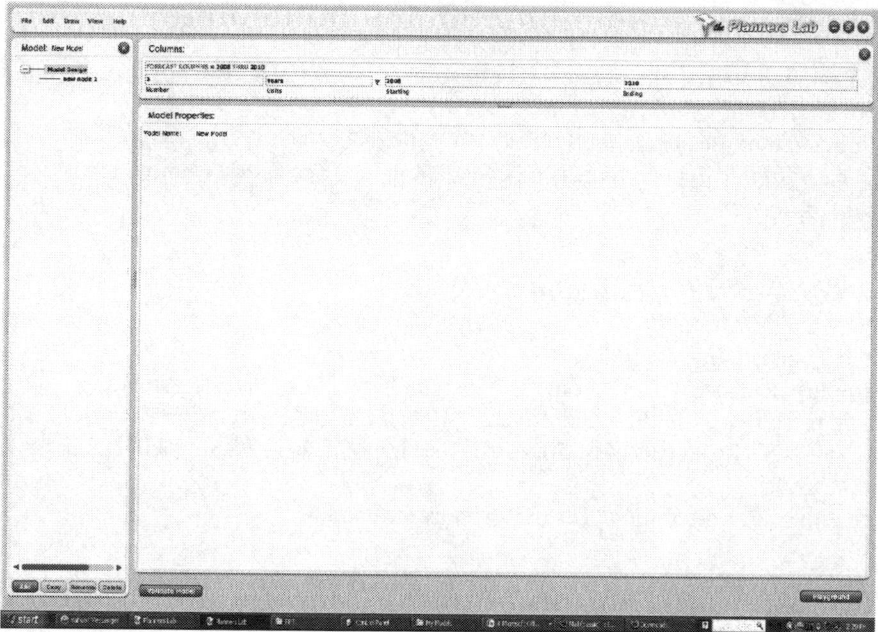

Fig. 10.1 Initial screen for entering a new planners lab model

and type Revenue to name the node. To add a node, click Model Design so the node goes under its level (the same level as the Revenue node) and click the Add button at the bottom of the screen. Then name this node Expenses as before. Repeat to add the Profit node.

Nodes are initially blank, like the cells in a new Excel spreadsheet would be. The user must define the equations in the model. The equations for Revenue are shown below and in the large window on the right of the screen shot in Fig. 10.2. These have been typed in directly by the user, although you can copy them from a word processing document and paste them into a PL node. The narrow window at the top right indicates that the columns are to cover years 2007 through 2012. The default is 2008–2010, but these have been changed by the user. Line 1 in the model indicates that Sales Price starts out at 1350 in 2007 and the phrase PREVIOUS* Inflation Rate means that prices in subsequent years will be the previous year's price times the inflation rate.

1 Sales Price = 1350, PREVIOUS* (1.0 + Inflation Rate)
2 Units Sold = 300, PREVIOUS* (1.0 + Sales Growth Rate)
3 Total Revenue = Units Sold* Sales Price
4 Sales Growth Rate = TRIRAND (–0.05, 0.10, 0.15)
5 Inflation Rate = 0.05

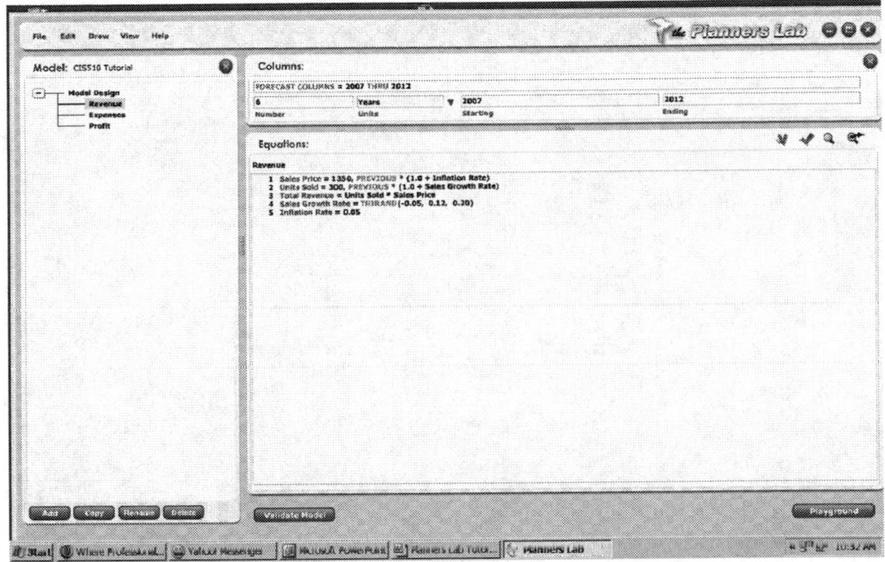

Fig. 10.2 Equations in the revenue node

The inflation rate is set to 0.05 in line 5. It is assumed to be that for all the years in the model. Similarly, Units Sold starts at 300 and increases by the Sales Growth Rate. In line 4, Sales Growth Rate is defined to be a random variable with a triangular distribution with values ranging from –5.0% to +15% with an expected value of 10%. Normally distributed variables are also supported.

Here are the equations in the Expense node (which is not shown):

1 Unit Sales Expense = 100, PREVIOUS* 1.10
2 Unit Cost = 1000, PREVIOUS* (1.0 + Inflation Rate IN Revenue)
3 Total Cost = (Unit Sales Expense + Unit Cost)* Units Sold IN Revenue

The only thing new here is use of the IN keyword in line 2 to indicate that the variable Inflation Rate is found IN the Revenue node. Planners Lab keywords are always in all capital letters. Variable names *are* case sensitive so, for example, Unit Cost is not the same as Unit cost. To complete the model, here are the equations that go in the Profit node:

1 Net Profit = Total Revenue IN Revenue – Total Cost IN Expenses
2 Net Profit After Taxes = 0.80* Net Profit

For visualizing model output, the PL provides a ready ability for managers to "play" with assumptions that reflect alternative views of the future in an engaging, visual manner. To view output and perform what If analysis, the user clicks on the Playground button in the bottom right of the screen. Output can be viewed in tabular form similar to that of spreadsheets (Fig. 10.3). The table is originally blank and is

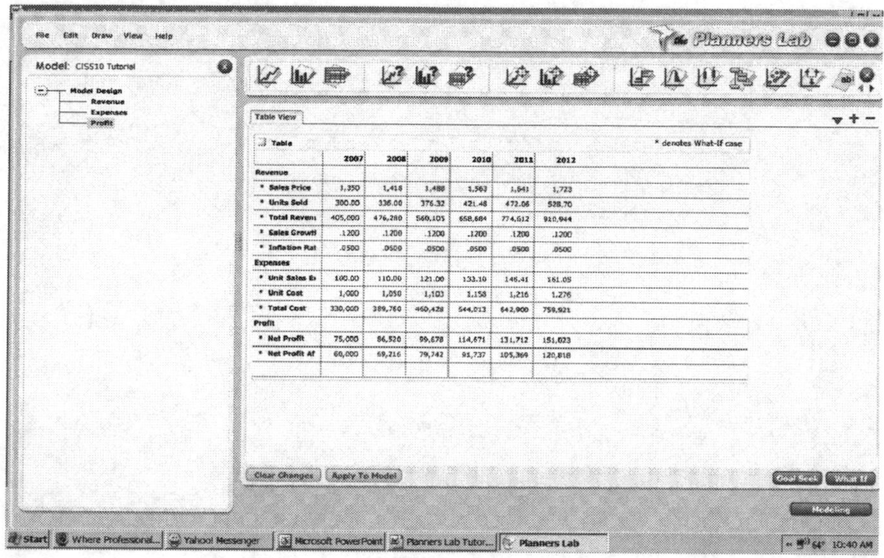

Fig. 10.3 Tabular display of all the variables in the model

populated by clicking on a node in the left window, a list of the variables in the node appears in a pop-up window and some or all of the variables may be selected and dragged onto the table. All the variables in the model have been dragged to the table in Fig. 10.3.

A more engaging, "imagistic" view with trend lines for Net Profit After Taxes, Sales Growth Rate and Unit Sales Expense is shown in Fig. 10.4. Net profit is a goal variable in this scenario and Sales Growth Rate and Unit Sales Expense are What If variables. Goal variables do NOT appear on the right hand side of any equation in the model; What If variables do. Notice that the expected value is used for the random variable Sales Growth Rate. Randomness is treated with risk analysis as described later.

It's a trivial matter to create line charts and other graphs. The window above the line charts in Fig. 10.4 shows icons for the various charts that are currently available in the Planners Lab. From left to right, the icons represent charts for goal variable trend lines, goal variable bar charts, tables (which may contain either goals or What If variables), then 3 icons with question marks (?) on them for What If trend lines, bar charts and tables, respectively.

To create a chart simply drag the icon onto the display window (stage) and a blank chart pops up. Then click the desired node on the Model Tree (which has been closed in Figures 10.4 to make room for the display), and a list of variables pops up from which you select the variables desired and drag them to the chart. The system automatically chooses scales for the charts.

To perform a sensitivity analysis, you may grab a What If trend line with the pointer and drag it to a desired point, and the lines for the Goal variables will change

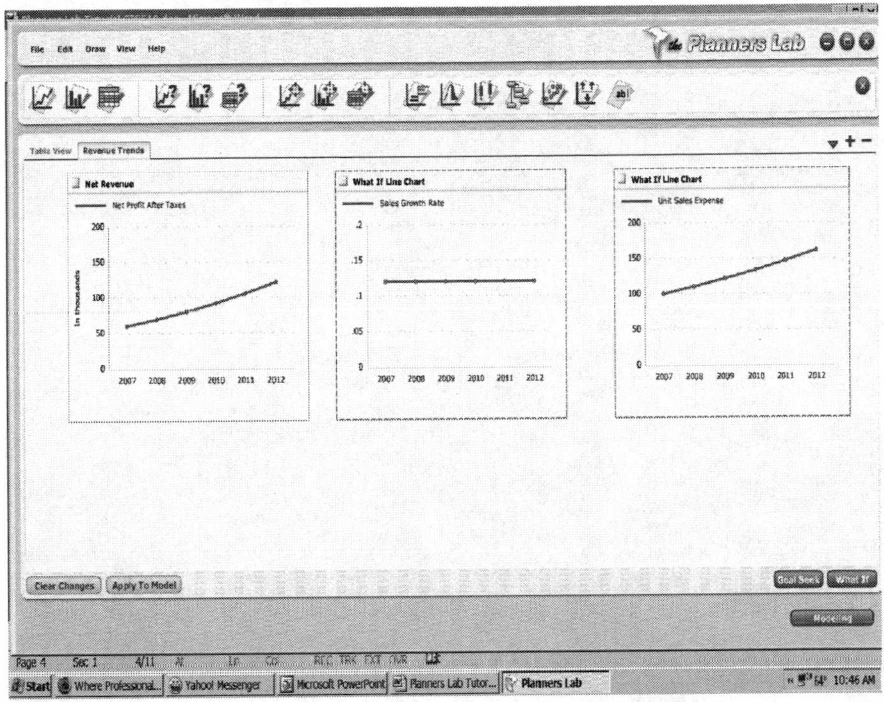

Fig. 10.4 Trend lines for net profit after taxes, sales growth rate and unit sales expenses

accordingly. In Fig. 10.5, the user has moved the line for Sales Growth Rate to a point representing 15% growth and Unit Sales Expense levels off at 128 in 2008 and beyond. It may be difficult to see in the screen print in Fig. 10.5, but the pointer has been placed on the point for 2010 on the Net Profit After Taxes line and the small pop-up window above indicates that the base value with the original assumptions was 120,818, and with the new assumptions is 165,005.

The next three icons in the chart window list that have circular target-like rings on them are for goal-seeking charts. In goal seeking, one variable is chosen as the target and another as the What If variable that will change. The difference is that the line for the target variable is manipulated in goal seeking and the What If variable changes in response to it. In Fig. 10.6, Total Revenue has been chosen as the target variable in the chart on the left. Sales Growth Rate is the What If variable on the right. This scenario assumes that we would like to achieve sales of about 1.1 million by 2012, and the What If chart shows that the Sales Growth Rate would have to be about 21% to achieve that goal. Only one What If variable may be active at any given time in goal seeking.

The next icon in the Chart Menu is for an Impact Analysis, which shows the impact of proportional changes in several What If variables on one selected target variable. In an impact analysis, all variables change by the same perchance. Figure 10.7 shows an Impact Analysis of the effects of a 10% change in Sales

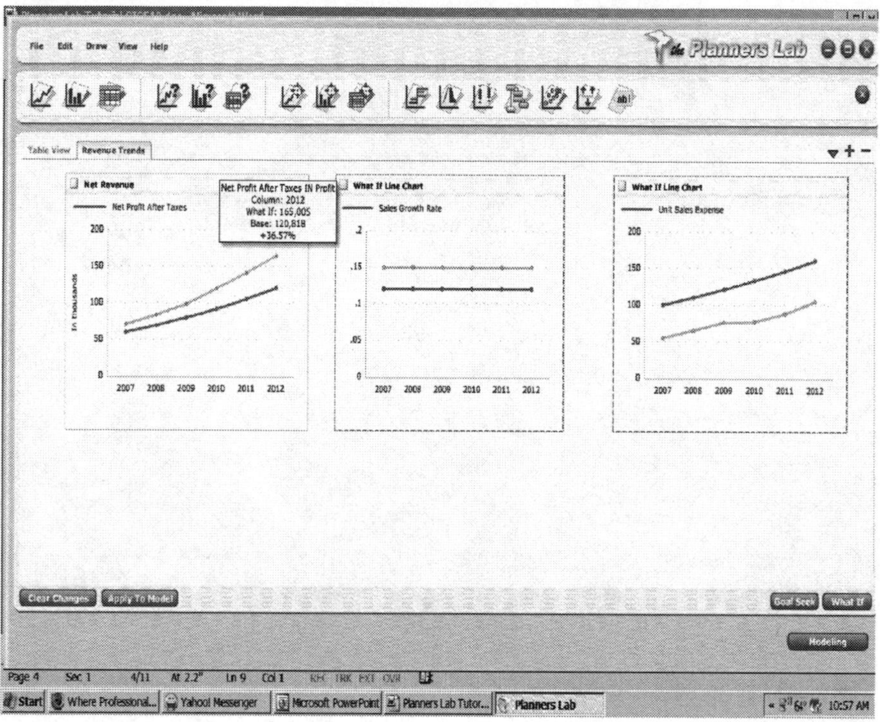

Fig. 10.5 Effects on net profit after taxes of expected sales growth rate increasing to 15% and lower unit sales expenses

Growth Rate, Inflation Rate and Unit Sales Expense on Net Profit After Taxes. The vertical slider bar on the right is used to select the percent change, and the horizontal slider bar at the bottom is used to select the time period. The pointer was over the bar for Unit Sales Expense when this screen shot was taken and the pop-up window above the bar indicates that a 10% increase in Unit Sales Expense results in Net Profit After Taxes dropping from 120,000 to 111,774 (5.64%) drop in Net Profit After Taxes in 2012.

The next icon is the typical bell-shaped, normal curve, which is used for a risk analysis, when a model contains random variables. Figure 10.8 illustrates a risk analysis with these assumptions using the random variable Sales Growth Rate as it affects Net Profit After Taxes.

To create a risk analysis chart, first its icon is dragged onto the stage. Then the desired variable to be viewed is chosen from the appropriate node in the model tree and dragged to the small window at the top of the chart. Here, Net Profit After Taxes has been chosen. It is partially a function of Sales Growth Rate, a random variable. Next the Simulate button is clicked and the number of iterations desired is selected (500 is the default). Click ok and the chart is created as shown in Fig. 10.8.

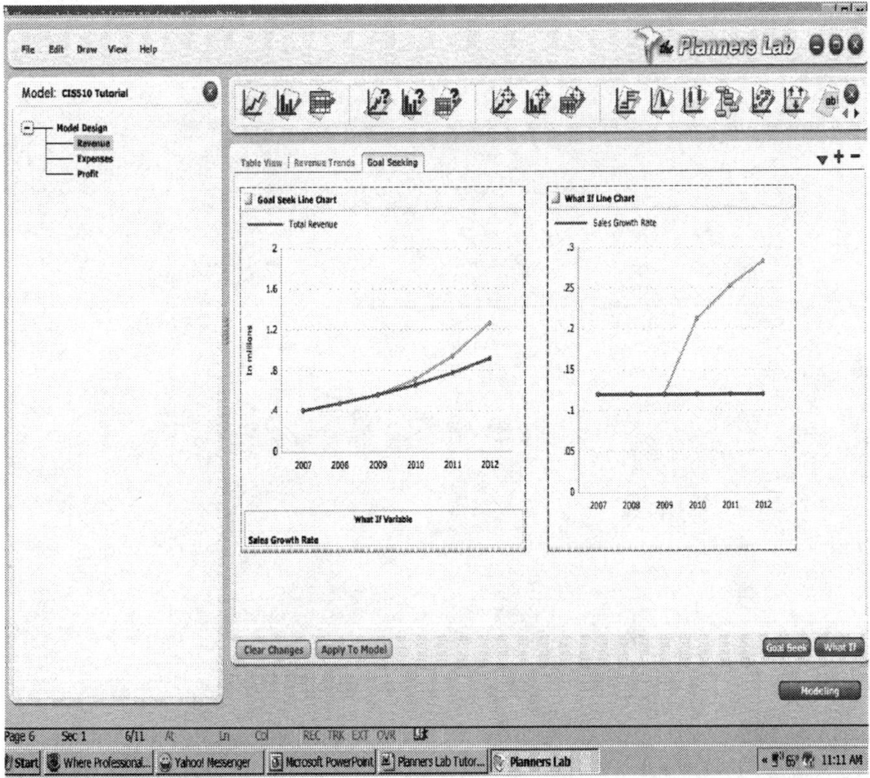

Fig. 10.6 Goal seeking with total revenue as the target and sales growth rate as the what if variable

Clicking the Simulate button on the lower right portion of the chart has generated the bar chart on the right. The slider bar below the chart is set on year 2012. The endpoints on the horizontal axis of the chart show that Net Profit may range from about 74,000 to 14,000 by 2012. This can be moved to any year we choose.

The pointers on the horizontal axis of a risk analysis chart indicate the number of observations falling in that range. For example in Fig. 10.9, the mouse has been used to move the left point to about 87,000 and the right point has been moved to about 122,000. By looking at the percentage above the highest bar, we can see that 90% of the observations lie in this interval, indicating that there is over a 90% chance that Net Profit After Taxes will be between 87,000 and 121,000

The next icon in the Chart Menu of the Playground is a Confidence Analysis. This function builds confidence intervals around the projected mean values of the chosen variable. In other words, if our assumptions are correct about the forecasted data, this feature produces a range of values that we should expect to contain the actual value, 1-α% of the time. Figure 10.10 demonstrates this feature using the variable Net Profit After Taxes.

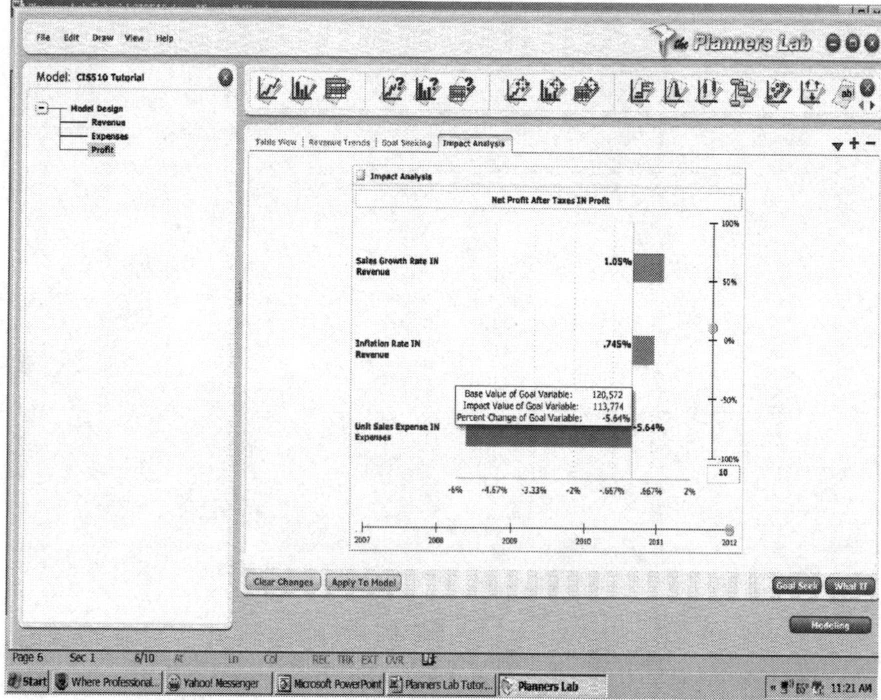

Fig. 10.7 An impact analysis of the effects of a 10% change in sales growth rate, inflation rate and unit sales expense on net profit after taxes

To create a new Confidence Analysis, simply drag the icon onto the stage. Then, drag and drop the desired variable from the appropriate node in the model tree into the small window at the top of the chart.

The intervals in Fig. 10.10 should appear once the variable is selected; however, if they do not, clicking the Simulate button on the lower right portion of the chart will do the trick. The slider bar below the chart automatically assumes $\alpha=0.10$.

Furthermore, you can adjust the level of "confidence" with which Planners Lab calculates the intervals, as indicated on the slider bar below the output. Simply drag the slider to adjust alpha (α). Ideally, the intervals should be wider when alpha is small, and more constricted when alpha is larger. Figure 10.11 shows the difference in output when 99% is selected as the level of confidence ($\alpha=0.01$).

Skipping over the Variable Tree icon for now, the fifth icon in the Chart Menu, the Correlation Chart, allows you to plot relationships between variables. Figure 10.12 illustrates an obvious relationship – Sales Price as a function of Total Revenue.

To generate a Correlation Chart, drag the menu icon down onto the stage. For this type of analysis, two variables will need to be selected. Select the appropriate

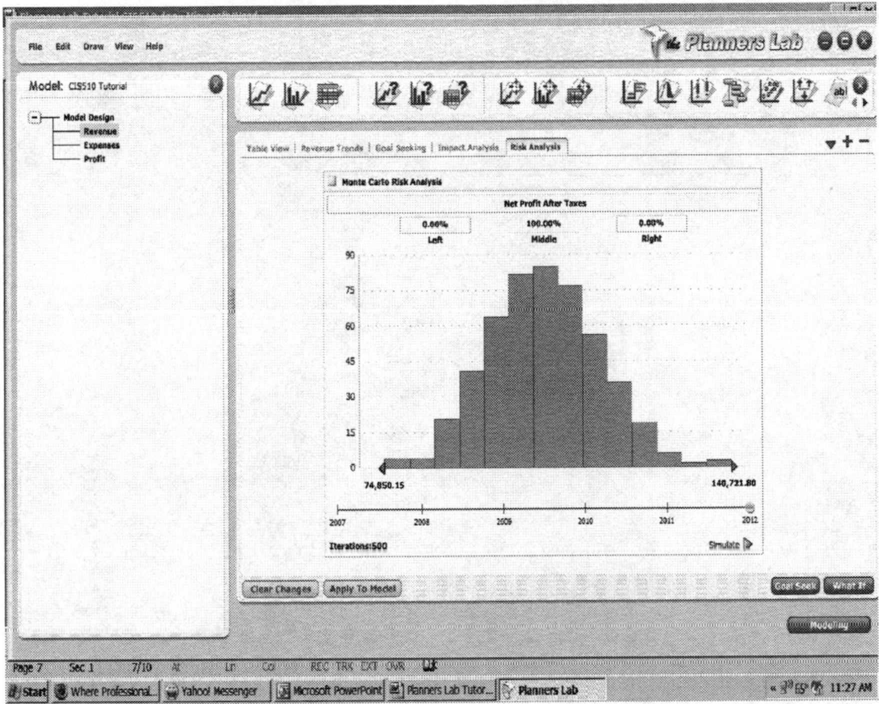

Fig. 10.8 A risk analysis with sales growth rate as a random variable

node(s) in which the variables are located, and drag/drop them into the small windows along the x- and y-axis. By default, all years of the analysis will be shown. As with several other of the Playground functions, you can adjust the slider bar along the bottom of the plot area to view different or segmented information – in this case, years 2007 through 2012 are available to select.

The final two icons that will be discussed in this tutorial are not for analysis but rather for debugging and documentation. The icon with the hierarchy chart is for a variable tree, such as the one for Net Profit After Taxes in Fig. 10.13. This shows all the variables having a direct or indirect effect on the selected target variable. The final icon is for a Sticky Note, which can be dragged onto the display to enter text describing a chart or table. Here the Sticky Note briefly describes what the Variable Tree does.

Other new chart types, such as the Variance Chart, are also available for further analysis.

Planners Lab models may be shared in a networked environment in which users are connected only occasionally, and it supports the use of mobile devices. Individuals may maintain their own personal versions of models, or may use a shared version, very useful features in current management era. It is also a simple

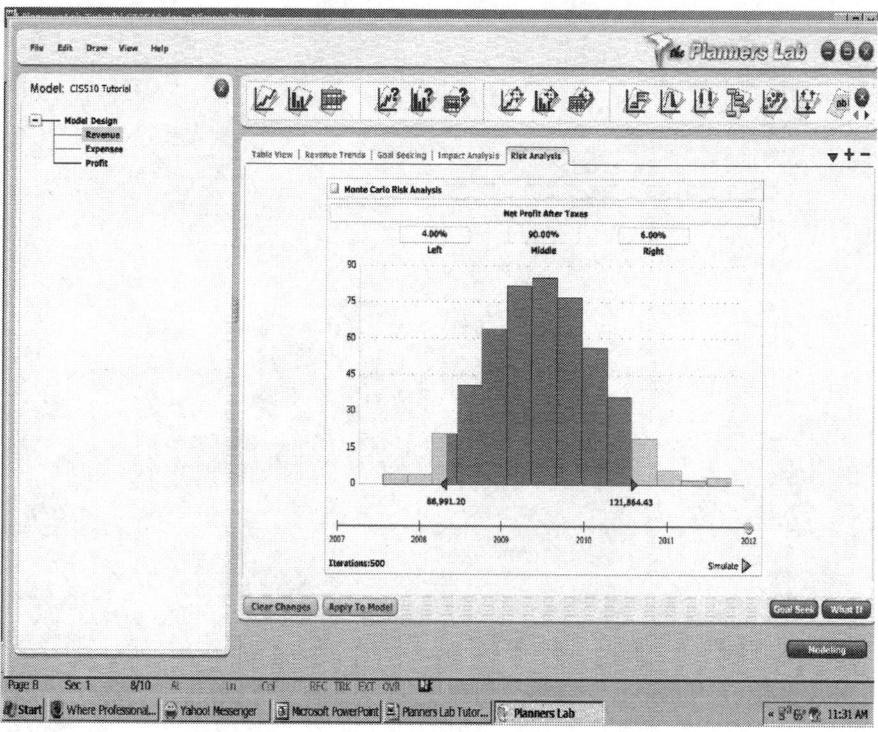

Fig. 10.9 The effects of moving the pointers on the horizontal axis of the bar chart

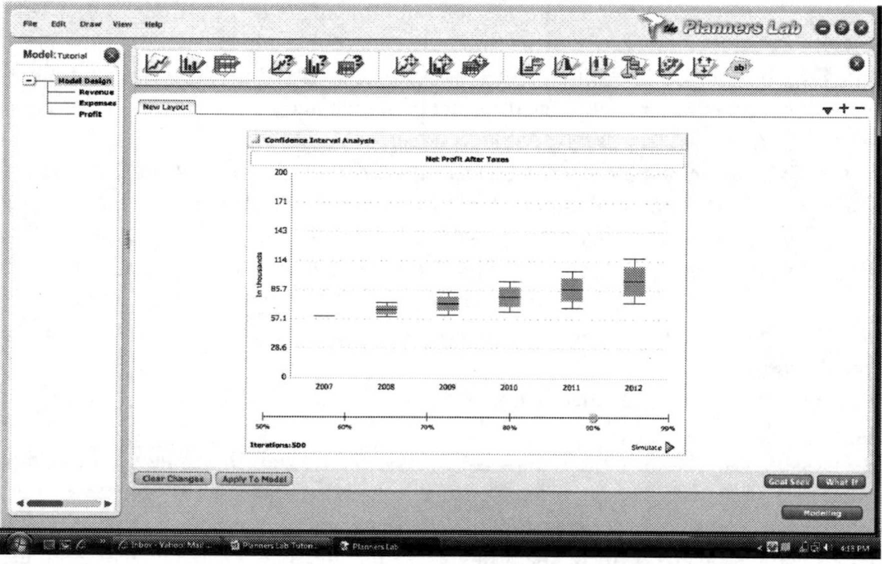

Fig. 10.10 A confidence analysis predicting net profit after taxes

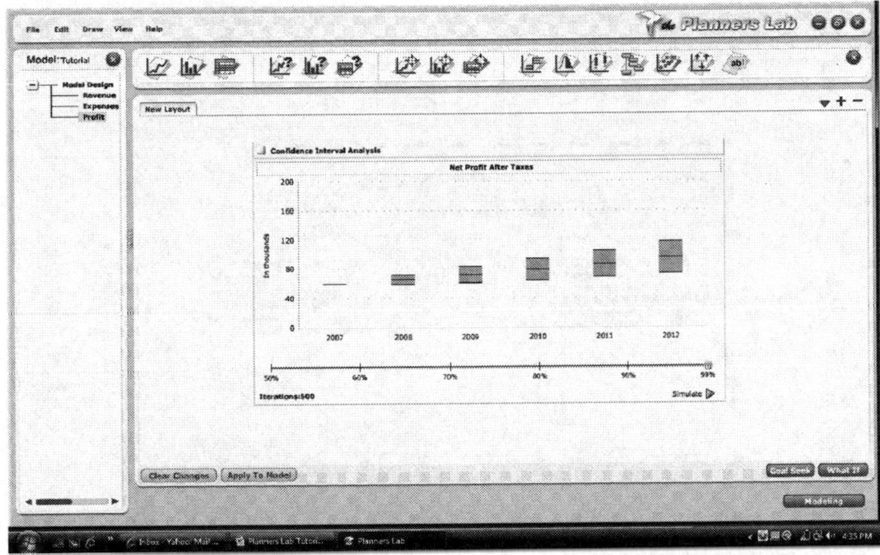

Fig. 10.11 Using the slider bar to adjust level of alpha

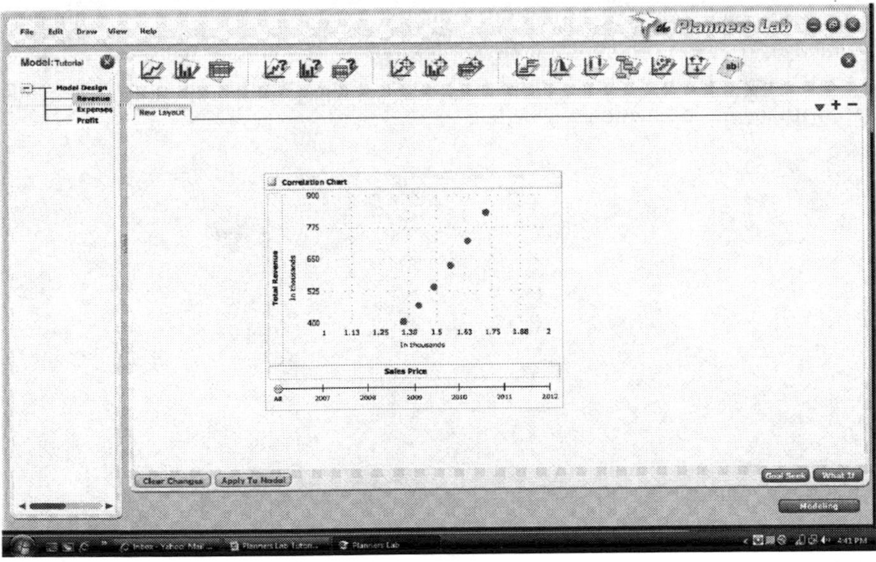

Fig. 10.12 Using the correlation chart to plot relationships

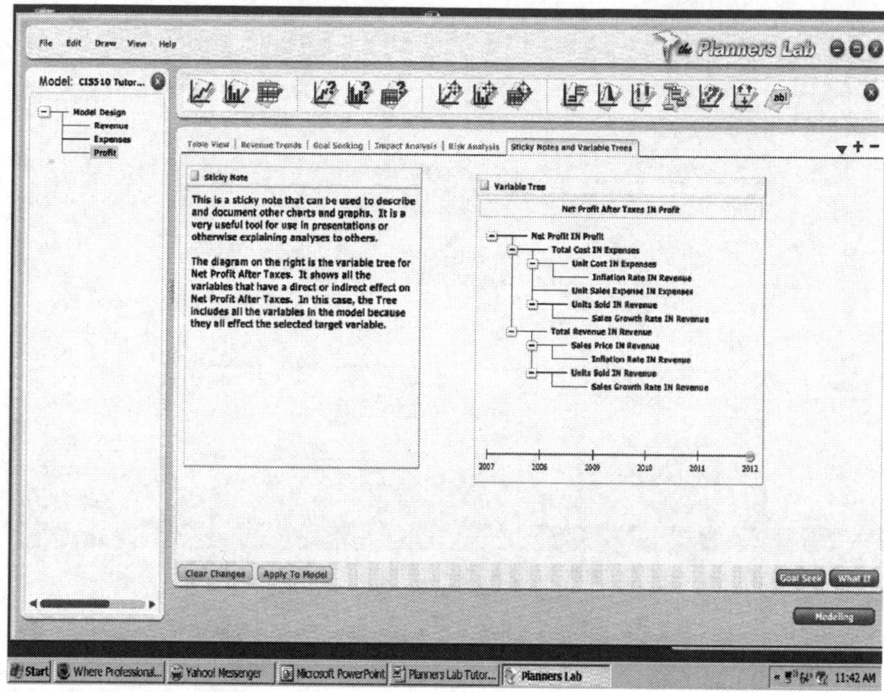

Fig. 10.13 The variable tree for net profit after taxes, with a sticky note attached to describe it

matter to import and export appropriately formatted Excel™ spreadsheets, as will be explained later.

Finally, as newer versions of Planners Lab are released, this information will need to be updated; however, this tutorial will serve as a starting point to familiarizing users with the basic functions.

Chapter 11
Assessing Today: Determining the Decision Value of Decision Support Systems

Gloria Phillips-Wren[1], Manuel Mora[2], and Guisseppi Forgionne[3]

[1] Loyola University Maryland, Baltimore, MD, USA, gwren@loyola.edu
[2] University of Aguascalientes, Aguascalientes, Mexico, mmora@securenym.net
[3] University of Maryland, Baltimore, MD, USA, forgionn@umbc.edu

11.1 Introduction

Decision support systems (DSS) have advanced significantly since their introduction in the early 1970s (Gorry and Scott-Morton, 1971). Modern DSS make use of distributed databases, real-time information, internal and external sources of data, sophisticated models, and intelligent techniques. DSS are essential aids to decision making in applications ranging from healthcare to operations to finance (Eom and Kim, 2006). Yet there is still no universally accepted measure of DSS value.

One of the early DSS researchers, Keen (1981, p. 1) proposed that decision support systems "by their very nature, make traditional cost-benefit analysis nearly useless." The reason is that the benefits from using DSS are often qualitative such as the ability to examine a greater number of alternatives, idea creation, improved teamwork, learning, and enhanced confidence in the decision. As systems have grown in complexity and cost, it has been argued that the business value of information technology (IT) systems in general is difficult to quantify, making IT investment decisions challenging (Kohli and Devaraj, 2003). In the case of DSS, one way to assess their value is to evaluate them on the basis of their goal, i.e. to impact decision making, or what could be called the "decision value" of the DSS. The literature proposes that the value of a DSS is its effect on the process of, and/or the outcome from, decision making (Forgionne, 2000). That is, the DSS can improve the way that the decision is made, and/or it can improve the outcomes from the decision. Both of these impacts have potential value to the individual decision maker.

Early studies focused on demonstrating that DSS have the capability improve decision outcomes. For example, Sharda et al. (1988) followed two groups of decision makers in a task environment for 8 weeks, with one group having a DSS and the other without one. Various measures of decision quality were tracked, and the group with the DSS made significantly more effective decisions. It is now generally accepted that DSS, properly developed and utilized, can improve decision making by assisting the decision maker to make better decisions. Shim et al. (2002) traced the development of DSS and looked ahead to the twenty-first century as being one of "active support" in which intelligent DSS and software agents interact with the

D. Schuff et al. (eds.), *Decision Support*, Annals of Information Systems 14,
DOI 10.1007/978-1-4419-6181-5_11, © Springer Science+Business Media, LLC 2011

user in a distributed environment over the Web. An example of such a system is provided by Silverman et al. (2008) in which a DSS assists in identifying potential terrorist activities. Modern DSS continue to demonstrate their value to improve decision making outcomes.

Pomerol and Adam (2008) proposed that a more useful model related to technology support for decision making is to consider the process of decision making. The best decisions are seen as coming from a largely sequential series of steps through a so-called rationalist approach (Pohl, 2008). Simon (1960) provided the most widely accepted process of decision making in the DSS literature as consisting of intelligence, design, choice and implementation. Decision making is seen to follow these steps, with feedback loops, in which the decision maker seeks information, develops a decision model, selects an alternative, and implements the decision.

Another way to assess DSS is on the basis of "what" characteristics lead to decision making improvement. In an early research paper, Sprague (1980) looked at attributes of DSS from the views of people at three organizational levels: the manager (i.e. user), the builder (i.e. developer), and the toolsmith (i.e. person concerned with the science needed to create the DSS). The manager sets performance objectives of DSS as: (1) addressing the decision problem: (2) assisting managers at all levels; (3) supporting interdependent decisions; (4) supporting all phases of the decision making process such as that characterized by Simon (1960); (5) not being dependent on a specific decision making process; and, (6) being easy to use. One possible way to assess DSS is against this set of criteria. Although a list of characteristics and capabilities can be developed, such a list does not have general agreement in the research and practitioner communities (Turban and Aronson, 1998), and, although descriptive, the elements are difficult to quantify.

We take a combined process-outcome approach to evaluate DSS in this paper by developing a framework on the basis of "how" DSS affect decision making and "what" decision is impacted. That is, we evaluate the impact of the DSS on the process of, and outcome from, decision making. We propose that DSS evaluation has not linked these organizational and decision maker benefits to the underlying technology used to deliver the appropriate characteristics. We address the gap in the literature by proposing an integrative framework that links the benefits of a DSS to the architecture used to deliver the DSS. The "decision value" reflects the value of the DSS to the individual user. The paper proceeds by first reviewing the underlying theoretical foundations of decision making. We then propose an integrative framework for assessment and apply it to an intelligent DSS application. We conclude with a summary and directions for future research.

11.2 Background on Decision-Making, DSS, and Evaluation

11.2.1 Decision Making Process

The decision making process is "fundamentally one of both recognizing and solving problems along the way toward the objective of producing a decision" (Holsapple and Whinston, 1996, p. 73). Structured decisions have well-known steps and measures to solve problems and reach the decision. Unstructured decisions have few if any known paths toward the solution. For example, Mintzberg et al. (1976) empirically studied unstructured decisions with a model of strategic decision making with substantial risk. They identified successful strategies by top managers that consisted of intuition, formal analysis and knowledge of organizational politics. A later study by Klein et al. (1993) explored the role of intuition in highly stressful situations, and decision making was called recognition-primed, emphasizing that the decision in such environments is highly individualized and not likely to be supportable with a DSS. In general, DSS are not needed for structured decisions, and supporting unstructured decisions is difficult. Between these two types of decisions is a wide range of semi-structured decisions for which methods exist to develop decision models, and DSS more commonly used, to improve decisions.

An early study of the decision making process well-known in military circles, but never formally published, came from air-to-air engagements in the Korean War (1950–1953). Colonel John Boyd noticed that US fighter pilots flying F-86 Sabre aircraft had a consistent 10:1 victory ratio over their opponents who were flying superior MiG-15 aircraft with wider turn radii and more manoeuvrability. He proposed that US pilots used a four-step decision making process shown in Fig. 11.1 that he called the Observe – Orient – Decide – Act (OODA) loop or four box method (Tweedale et al., 2008) that allowed them to achieve knowledge superiority to win a battle. Boyd presented his results to military strategists in a series of briefings and later applied his model to the business community and other conflict situations.

Nobel Laureate Herbert Simon provided a description of the decision making process that has been widely applied to DSS. He described decision making as consisting of iterative, but largely sequential, phases: intelligence, design, and choice (Simon, 1960) with an implementation phase added later. During the intelligence phase the decision maker observes reality, identifies the problem, gains an understanding of the problem and gathers information. During the design phase, the user develops criteria important to the decision, develops alternatives, specifies relationships between variables, and develops decision models. During the choice phase, alternatives are logically evaluated and selected, and the user acts on the decision during the implementation phase. Simon's fourth phase includes outcome review and feedback as starting points for the next decision. Mora et al. (2005) added an explicit learning phase to Simon's model during which outcomes are analyzed and

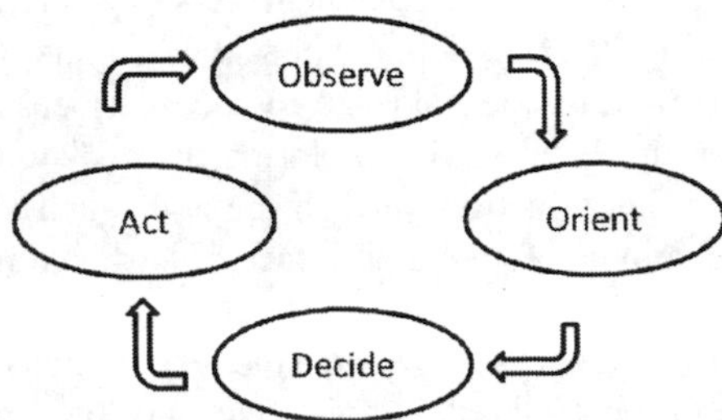

Fig. 11.1 Boyd's OODA loop

Table 11.1 Comparison of decision making process models

Simon	Boyd	Turban and Aronson	Mora et al.
Intelligence	Observe –Observe unfolding circumstances –Gather outside information	Intelligence –Organizational objectives –Data collection –Problem identification, ownership, classification, statement	Intelligence –Detect problem –Gather data –Formulate problem
Design	Orient –Perceive opportunities and threats –Focus thinking on particular direction	Design –Formulate model –Set criteria for choice –Search for alternatives –Predict and measure outcomes	Design –Classify model –Build model –Validate model
Choice	Decide –Make a decision	Choice –Solution to problem –Sensitivity analysis –Selection of best (good) alternatives –Plan for implementation	Choice –Evaluation –Sensitivity analysis –Selection
Implementation	Act –Act on the decision	Implementation –Implement the decision	Implementation –Present results –Plan tasks –Monitor results Learning –Analyze outcome –Synthesize process of making the decision –Determine what to change

synthesized. In all models the decision making process is iterative with feedback loops as decision making proceeds through the phases. A comparison of several decision making process models is shown in Table 11.1.

11.2.2 Decision Support Systems

In general, DSS are "interactive, flexible, and adaptable" computerized information systems to assist decision makers in primarily semi-structured decisions by incorporating "the decision maker's own insights" (Turban and Aronson, 1998, p. 77). They utilize data and models, provide interfaces so that the user can interact with the system in defining and exploring the decision space, and may provide recommended courses of action through methods such as intelligence or knowledge systems. A schematic of a DSS architecture is shown in Fig. 11.2.

DSS inputs include a database of pertinent decision data, a knowledge base of problem knowledge, and a model base that contains decision models and appropriate solution methods. Knowledge may be represented as production rules, semantic

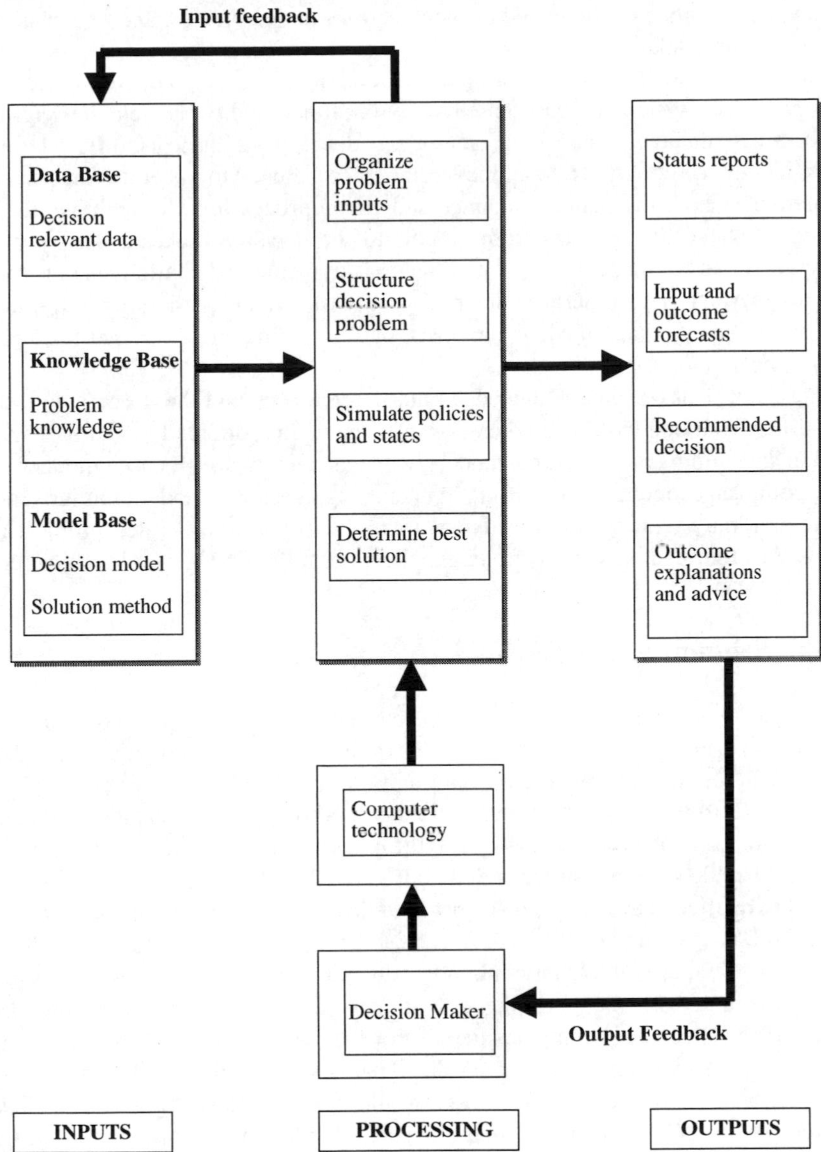

Fig. 11.2 DSS architecture (Phillips-Wren et al., 2009)

networks, frames, or in some other way. The decision maker utilizes information technology to access the various input bases and execute the processing tasks of organizing problem elements, generating ideas, structuring the problem, simulating policies and events, and finding the best problem solution. The DSS is interactive through a dialog management system that the decision maker controls. Processing generates status reports on the ideas generated and problem elements, forecasts of inputs and outputs, recommended decision actions and strategies, and explanations for the recommendations.

Processing can be assisted through artificial intelligence methodologies. For example, expert system and case-based reasoning functionality can help the decision maker access data and models, generate ideas, develop a consensus, infer relationships, and interpret outputs. Machine learning can be used to generate forecasts of problem elements, and natural language and vision processing can facilitate dialog management. Feedback loops from outputs to the decision maker and from processing to inputs indicate that DSS processing is dynamic and continuous in nature. Outputs may suggest further decision maker processing, and processing may create new or additional data, knowledge, models, or solution methods relevant for future processing.

The content of the data, knowledge, and model bases and the processing tasks may differ from one DSS to another. For instance, a data-oriented model base may contain data mining and statistical models, while an analytically-focused model base may require an economic, accounting, or management science model. Similarly, one application may require only a satisfactory problem solution, while optimization may be the dominant task in a different application of the DSS general architecture.

11.2.3 Evaluation of DSS

One way to evaluate DSS is in terms of business value generated from the inherent information technology. Measuring the value of information technology systems has proven difficult due to the intangible nature of many of the benefits. Evaluation criteria range from the "pay-off" from technology investments using capital budgeting methods to multi-objective assessment (Hitt and Brynjolfsson, 1996; Devaraj and Kohli, 2002; 2003; Kohli and Devaraj, 2003; Alter, 2004).

DSS have often been evaluated against a single criterion such as the cost of developing the DSS (Adelman, 1992; Akoka, 1981; Brynjolfsson and Hitt, 1998). Keen (1981) suggested that DSS should not be evaluated with cost/benefit analysis since the value is underestimated, and suggested that Value Analysis was more appropriate. Cost/benefit analysis computes the cost of the system compared to the benefit that one obtains by using the system. Value Analysis is a method in which the benefits are compared to the amount that one would pay to achieve the benefit without considering the DSS. The amounts are then added and compared to the cost of the DSS to determine if the value exceeds the cost. Money et al. (1988) determined the value of a DSS by alternative methods of utility generation, namely a direct self-explicated method and a conjoint measurement method. Their structured methods included intangible and tangible benefits of a DSS. Ahituv and Wand (1981) argued that the choice of an information system is based on more than utility since the decision maker may have multiple objectives and more than one outcome to consider.

Holsapple and Whinston (1996, p. 212) suggested that evaluation standards should be "coupled with setting objectives ... at the onset of development and clearly related to the objectives" and that "some benefits of DSSs are intangible, subjective, or difficult to quantify." Turban and Aronson (1998, p. 37) stated that information "systems are evaluated and analyzed with two major classes of performance measurement: effectiveness and efficiency." Effectiveness is concerned with outputs and measures the degree to which goals are achieved. Efficiency measures the use of inputs and resources used to achieve goals, with a more efficient system using fewer resources (e.g. time, human capital, computing power) to achieve the same output as another system. Clark et al. (2007) used the same two measures, effectiveness and efficiency, to evaluate management support systems as a broader class of DSS related to business decisions.

Many studies of DSS over the past decade focus on either effectiveness or efficiency as the system benefit, but not both at the same time (Forgionne, 1999; Phillips-Wren et al., 2006). These two factors can be related to what Forgionne (2000) called the process-to-outcome link. This is, assessment should include both the process of, and outcome from, decision making as multi-criteria to evaluate "decision value" of a DSS to an individual user (Phillips-Wren et al., 2004).

The use of multiple criteria to evaluate DSS has been examined in earlier studies. Chandler (1982) stated that the user and the technology should be considered as the system, and he developed an approach to compare goals and performance. Pieptea and Anderson (1987) proposed that DSS value was context dependent, that the gap between cost and value was correlated to the extent to which the supported decision was structured. Adelman's proposal (1992) was a comprehensive evaluation with subjective, technical, and empirical criteria. His approach integrated user and sponsor perspectives within the subjective criteria. Technical criteria included models, data and methods. Empirical criteria encompassed performance with and without the DSS. The three elements were combined to give an overall evaluation of the DSS.

Checkland (2000) used general systems principles and suggested one of the most encompassing schema by evaluating DSS from different "worldviews" including organizational, user and technical. The worldview was defined as a model of the relevant perspective, beliefs, and values of the part of the world being considered. Manyard et al. (2001) proposed an evaluation including the viewpoints of different stakeholders into a multi-criteria evaluation. Other combinations of evaluation criteria have been given by Chandler (1982); Kurikose, (1985); Sharda et al. (1988); Santhanam and Guimaraes (1995); Forgionne and Kohli (2000); Sun and Kantor (2006); Wang and Forgionne (2006).

Given the wealth of evaluation studies of DSS, one must ask what could be gained by yet another research paper in this area? We propose that DSS evaluation has not linked organizational and decision maker benefits to the underlying technology used to deliver appropriate characteristics. Previous studies by Jeffers et al. (2008) demonstrated that the availability of appropriate information technology resources is linked to process performance in an organization. In the case of intelligent DSS, in particular, such traceability between technology and process would allow the designer and evaluator to determine the precise contributions of different intelligent methodologies to the overall system. We address this research gap in the next section.

11.3 Integrated Design and Evaluation Framework for DSS

Benefits associated with DSS in the literature are often stated in terms of the improvement in the decision. For example, the decision with a DSS may result in improved profit, decreased cost, or improved accuracy in prediction. As DSS have incorporated more technology, they have also had more influence on the process of decision making (Jeffers et al., 2008). Modern DSS enable faster decision making to respond to changes in data occurring in real-time, personalization to support user satisfaction, time savings by using intelligent methods, distributed decision making though dispersed teams, and organizational learning by linkage to systems such as knowledge management systems. Our evaluation framework addresses decision value, and it is measured by the effect of the DSS on the process of, and outcome from, decision making. Simon's phases of intelligence, design, choice and implementation detail the decision making process We have included Mora et al.'s (2005) specific learning phase to explicitly incorporate features of modern DSS.

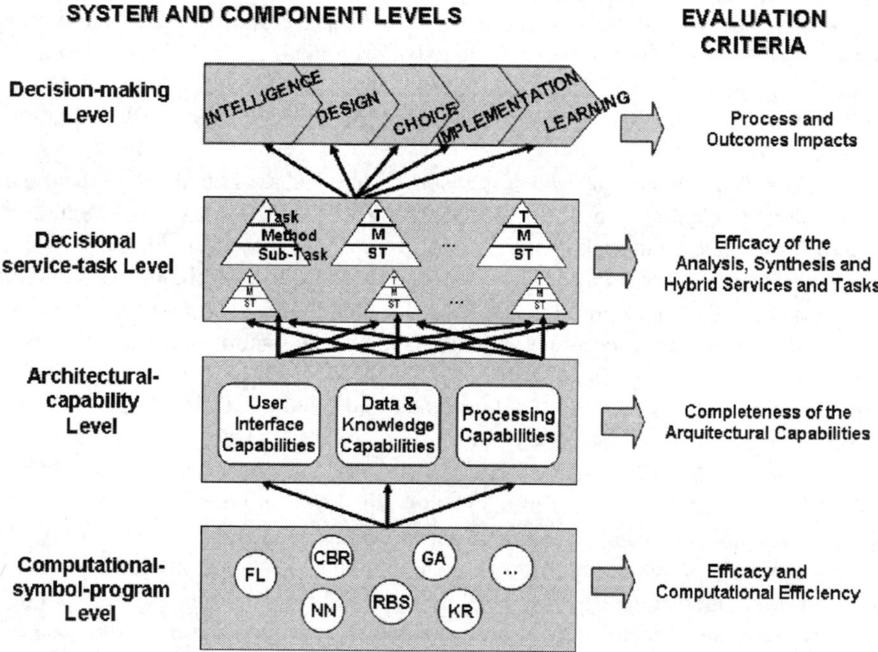

Fig. 11.3 Conceptual framework for design and evaluation of DMSS (Mora et al., 2005)

We now want to link the technical architecture of a DSS to the outcome and process elements at the top level. To do so, Mora et al. (2005) used a systems approach with four levels, as shown in Fig. 11.3:

- Decision-making Level – to account for Intelligence, Design, Choice, Implementation and Learning in the decision-making phases and activities to be executed by a decision-maker using a DSS;
- Decisional service-task Level – to account for the decisional support services of the DSS, e.g. Newell's Knowledge Level of Task, Method, and Subtask;
- Architectural-capability Level – to account for the user interface capabilities, data and knowledge capabilities, and processing capabilities provided by DSS architectural components;
- Computational symbol-program Level – to account for specific Artificial Intelligence (AI) computational mechanisms that implement the architectural components of the DSS such as Fuzzy Logic, Neural Network, Case-Based Reasoning, Rule-Based, Genetic Algorithm, and Intelligent Agents.

This architecture can be implemented with a multi-criteria model so that the "decision value" of a DSS is linked through process and outcome down to the computational symbol-program level. We illustrate the approach with an applied problem in the next section.

11.4 Application

11.4.1 Analytic Hierarchy Process (AHP)

The Analytic Hierarchy Process (Saaty, 1986; 1997; Harker, 1988) is a multi-criteria model that allows a comparison of alternatives by structuring criteria into a hierarchy. At the lowest level, alternatives are compared in pairs against a criterion by a user, and the AHP synthesizes the results according to the hierarchy to produce a single value for each alternative. The AHP has been used extensively in applied problems to support decision making (Saaty and Vargas, 1994), and more recently to evaluate intelligent systems (Ngai and Chan, 2005). The criteria can be weighted if desired, and an eigenvalue solution is used to reconcile the initial judgments. The AHP model for the application problem is shown in Fig. 11.5.

11.4.2 Description of Application

Alter (2004) proposed that decision support should be understood within the real world of the work environment. Thus, we apply our evaluation framework to an intelligent DSS published by Lee (2004) to illustrate our approach to design and evaluation of DSS. Lee's DSS is illustrative of "active support" as described by

Shim et al. (2002) for the twenty-first century. We describe the application and then apply our framework to determine the value of intelligence in the DSS.

Lee described an agent-based decision support system that elicits expert knowledge from a number of people and makes an optimal recommendation to an individual consumer. The system uses behavior patterns collected from previous consumers to guide the user to a decision. Lee pointed out that some commodities are not purchased regularly, such as home theatre systems, and that users have inadequate knowledge to make a choice. The user's past choices are not useful in predicting an optimal decision since the user has few or no instances of previously purchasing the product. In these cases, the advice of experts is particularly useful. The DSS collects information from multiple experts, and combines it with previous consumer behaviour to guide the decision choice.

The specific system makes recommendations about computer, communication and consumer electronics purchases based on preferences of the user. Knowledge is collected from domain experts and used to evaluate the quality of different products. A user is assisted in navigating the general features of the product space which embed multiple functions into one product. Social information is also used by comparing the user's behavior patterns when interacting with the system with other users. Choices made by users with similar behavior patterns serve as a guide to the system's recommendation. Rather than a normal case-based reasoning approach, the system takes a collaborative approach to decision making.

Four intelligent software agents are used to implement the system as shown in Fig. 11.4. The Interface Agent interacts with the consumer to develop qualitative criteria. It also interacts with experts and combines their opinions to calculate a composite conclusion. The Behavior-Matching Agent compares the user's behavior to that of previous consumers to reduce the effort of the Interface Agent. The Decision-Making Agent converts the user's qualitative criteria into product components. The Knowledge Agent mediates between the product components and the consumer's needs to convert them to a common form. Products are represented as a vector of ranks with overall rank measured by shortest distance to the best solution and farthest distance to the worst solution. The Decision Making Agent recommends products with top ranks to the user.

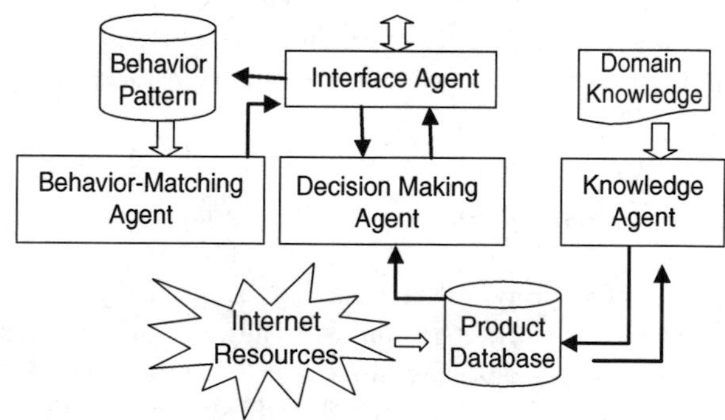

Fig. 11.4 Recommender DSS from Lee (2004)

The Recommender System is an intelligent DSS and supports decision making by a human user who needs to make a specific decision. The user is part of the system, and the system supports the decision making processes of intelligence, design, choice and learning. It is interactive, includes the decision maker's insights, provides a user friendly interface, allows the user to modify the recommendations, and supports analysis throughout the process. Intelligence is embedded in the use of agents that improve system performance and outcomes.

11.4.3 Evaluation of Application

Recommender DSS can be evaluated to determine the contribution of intelligent agents to the process of, and outcomes from, decision making. As illustration, we demonstrate proposed values for the comparisons of Recommender DSS and a DSS with no intelligence attempting to provide a recommendation to the user. The evaluation model, implementing the architecture from Fig. 11.3, is shown in Fig. 11.5.

The specific values used to weight criteria are unique to the user, and different users may provide different outcome criteria and weights. Our process alternatives are established by Simon's theoretical framework. Clark et al. (2007, p. 592) pointed out that "the difficulty . . . in establishing universal measures of decision quality lies in the difficulty of understanding human and organizational decisional processes (Simon, 1960; 1987; Newell and Simon, 1972)." We therefore provide a possible weighting for a potential user in Table 11.2. The values can be modified to reflect different priorities of different designers or users.

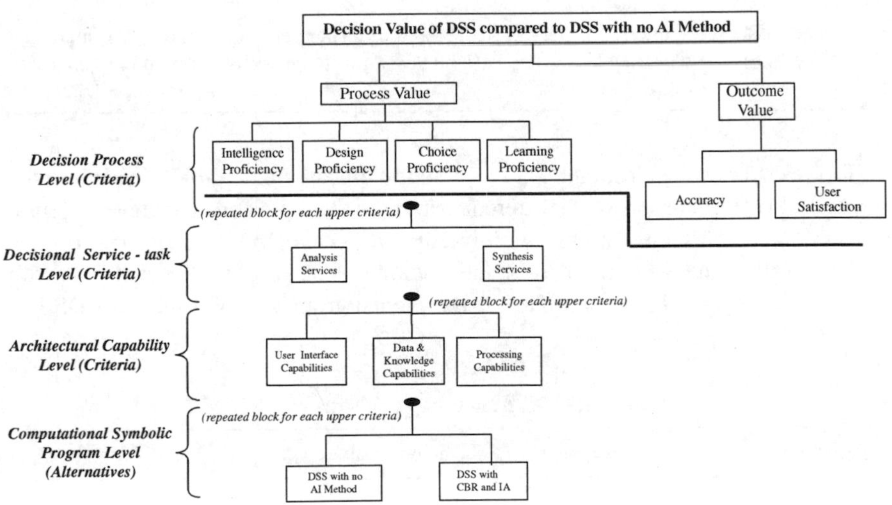

Fig. 11.5 Evaluation model for recommender DSS

Table 11.2 Weights assigned for the criteria in the AHP model for the components of the DSS

Level	Criteria by level	Weights	Comments
Decision-making	[Process | Outcome to decision value]	[0.65, 0.35]	Process considered more important than outcome
	[Accuracy | User satisfaction]	[0.25, 0.75]	Most important for the user to be satisfied with the recommendation
	[Intelligence | Design | Choice | Implementation | Learning proficiency to process]	[0.15, 0.45, 0.25, 0. 0, 0.15]	Design phase is most important since it specifies user preferences; Implementation not included; User learns during process
Decisional service-task	[Analysis | Synthesis to intelligence]	[0.65, 0.35]	For the Intelligence phase, the user considers analysis support to be the most important
	[Analysis | Synthesis to Design]	[0.15, 0.85]	For the design phase, the user considers synthesis to be most important
	[Analysis | Synthesis to choice]	[0.75, 0.25]	For the choice phase, the user considers analysis to be most important
	[Analysis | Synthesis to learning]	[0.85, 0.15]	For the learning phase, the user considers analysis to be more important
	[Analysis | Synthesis to accuracy]	[0.55, 0.45]	The user considers analysis to be somewhat more important than synthesis for accuracy
	[Analysis | Synthesis to user satisfaction]	[0.05, 0.95]	The user considers synthesis to be much more important than analysis for user satisfaction
Architectural-capability	[User interface | D&K | Processing to analysis services]	[0.15, 0.35, 0.50]	The user considers processing to be most important for analysis
	[User Interface | D&K | Processing to synthesis services]	[0.45, 0.35, 0.20]	The user considers the user interface to be most important for synthesis

The decision values from the AHP evaluation are shown in Table 11.3 and in the Appendix. Different users, with different criteria and weights, may achieve different results. As can be seen, the DSS with intelligent agents (IA) is superior in overall decision value, and on both process and outcome. The results are consistent with findings by Todd and Bensabat (1999) that decision makers will utilize a DSS to

Table 11.3 Decision values of alternate DSS

Alternative	Process value	Outcome value	Overall decisional value
DSS with IA	0.5982	0.5780	0.5911
DSS without IA	0.4018	0.4220	0.4089

lower their overall effort expenditure since intelligence in the DSS makes it possible for a user to more easily apply alternative strategies.

The AHP hierarchy results also can be used to trace the specific contributions of each alternative to all the upper level criteria. For example, as demonstrated through the AHP calculated weights in the Appendix, the AI architectural component makes the most substantial contribution to both process and outcome values in the decision making process. However, the results may differ if the DSS was evaluated by a different user who has different preferences. The benefit of using the AHP approach is manifested in terms of effectiveness (i.e., helping the user pick the one best suited to his need). The decision value is the value to the specific user, and the AHP model identifies the components of the DSS that deliver value.

11.5 Future Trends

Intelligent systems are becoming recognized for their potential to, for example, enhance business processes (Taghezout and Zarate', 2009), improve decision making in dynamic environments (Smirnov and Jakobson, 2009), and aid in healthcare diagnosis and care (Kodogiannis, 2007). These systems can process information faster than conventional systems, consider more alternatives, increase flexibility in responding to changes, coordinate multiple resources, learn patterns of behavior to predict future actions, maintain situation awareness in disaster scenarios, and resolve conflicts in complex situations. The designer of these systems must make a multitude of choices ranging from the specific intelligent technique to the specific user interface. It will become increasingly important to employ a systematic methodology to guide these selections. Criteria that link the upper level decision processes and outcomes to the DSS architectural characteristics will aid in design, diagnosis and evaluation of DSS to achieve the user's requirements.

11.6 Conclusions

Assessment of DSS has spanned the years since the origins of decision support systems. Early literature focused on demonstrating DSS benefits in order to obtain and maintain managerial support for systems development. Later research developed measures that evaluated the developed systems' contributions to performance specifications. Recent research has used evaluation to illustrate the benefits of DSS in specific applications and to incorporate stakeholder perspectives.

The unified architecture proposed in this paper contributes to the literature by linking specific technical DSS architectural components to the decision making process and outcome. The resulting comprehensive integrated decision value can be used to compare various DSS and to trace the specific contributions of individual system components. The architecture is general enough to be applicable to any problem domain. The user has flexibility in defining the specific outcome criteria for a particular domain as well as modifying the weighting of criteria as needed to reflect the priority of different outcomes or of decision making processes.

The implementation used to illustrate the proposed concept demonstrates that our evaluation framework captures both process, outcome, technical, and managerial considerations. As such, the evaluation identifies the specific links between DSS architectural and service elements, and managerial and organizational processes and outcomes. These specific links provide guidance for further DSS design, development, and implementation. For example, the evaluation indicated that the artificial intelligence provided through the system effectively guided the user's decision making process and led to an improved organizational outcome. Such information can be used to improve system support for decision making and to justify DSS expenditures by focusing attention on the value of process enhancements as well as outcome measures.

Acknowledgments The authors would like to thank the anonymous reviewers whose comments significantly contributed to the quality of the paper. We particularly appreciate the suggested references and the careful reading of the paper.

Appendix: Evaluation of DSS Compared to DSS with No AI Method – The First Value Is Calculated for the DSS with IA and the Second for the DSS Without IA

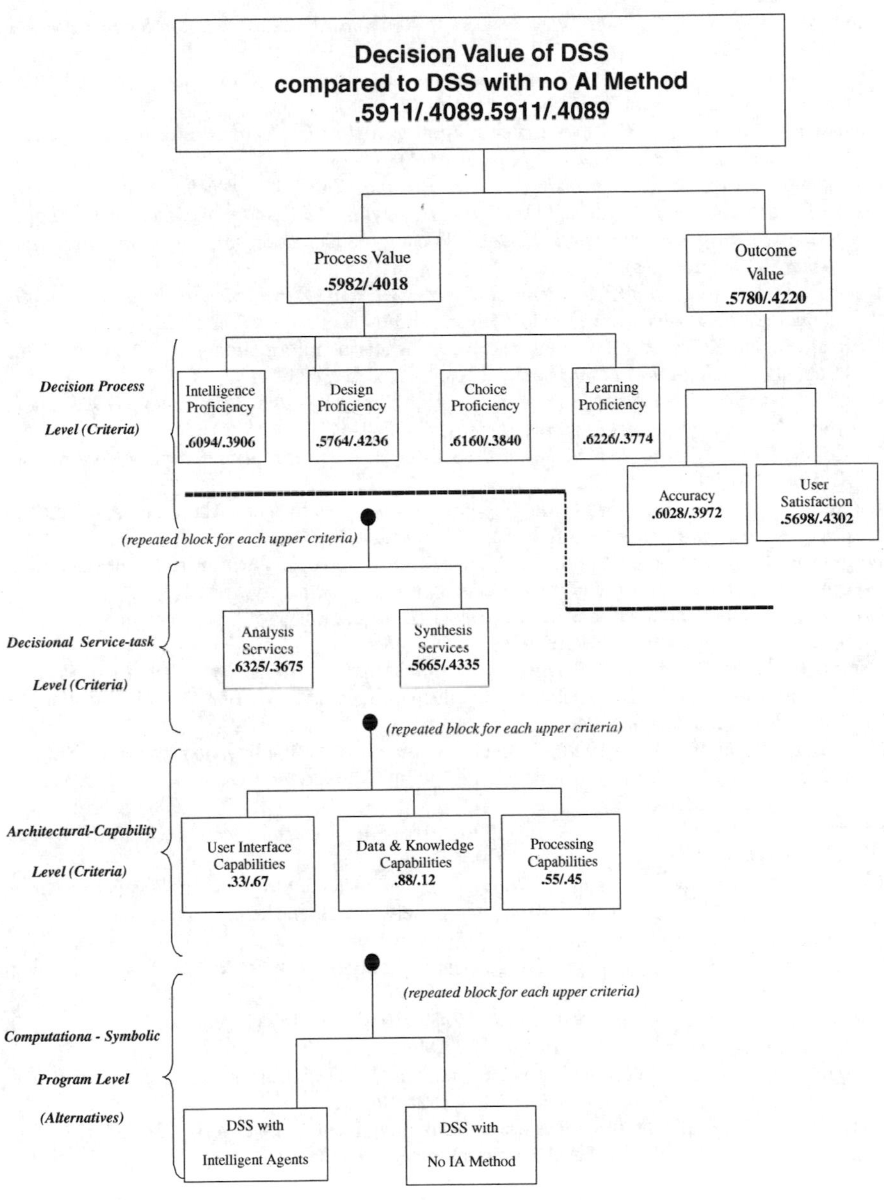

References

Adelman, L. (1992). *Evaluating Decision Support and Expert Systems*. New York, NY: Wiley.

Ahituv, N., and Wand, Y. (1981). Information Systems in Management Science – Information Evaluation and Decision Makers' Objectives. *Interfaces*, 11(3), 24–32.

Akoka, J. (1981). A Framework for Decision Support Systems Evaluation. *Information & Management*, 4, 133–141.

Alter, S. (2004). A Work System View of DSS in Its Fourth Decade. *Decision Support Systems*, 38(3), 319–327.

Brynjolfsson, E., and Hitt, L. (1998). Beyond the Productivity Paradox: Computers are the Catalyst for Bigger Changes. *Communications of the ACM*, 41(8), 49–55.

Chandler, J. (1982). A Multiple Criteria Approach for Evaluating Information Systems. *Management Information Systems Quarterly*, 6(1), 61–74.

Checkland, P. (2000). *Systems Thinking, Systems Practice*. Chichester: Wiley.

Clark, T., Jones, M., and Armstrong, C. (2007). The Dynamic Structure of Management Support Systems: Theory Development, Research Focus, and Direction. *Management Information Systems Quarterly*, 31(3), 579–615.

Devaraj, S., and Kohli, R. (2002). *The IT Payoff: Measuring the Business Value Information Technology Investments*. Upper Saddle River, NJ: Financial Times Prentice Hall.

Devaraj, S., and Kohli, R. (2003). Performance Impacts of Information Technology: Is Actual Usage the Missing Link? *Management Science*, 49(3), 273–289.

Eom, S., and Kim, E. (2006). A Survey of Decision Support System Applications (1995–2001). *Journal of the Operational Research Society*, 57, 1264–1278.

Forgionne, G. (1999). An AHP Model of DSS Effectiveness. *European Journal of Information Systems*, 8(2), 95–106.

Forgionne, G. (2000). Decision-Making Support Systems Effectiveness: The Process to Outcome Link. *Information Knowledge-Systems Management*, 2, 169–188.

Forgionne, G., and Kohli, R. (2000). Management Support System Effectiveness: Further Empirical Evidence. *Journal of the Association for Information Systems*, 1(3), 1–37.

Gorry, G. M., and Scott-Morton, M. S. (1971). A Framework for Management Information Systems. *Sloan Management Review*, 13(1), 55–70.

Harker, P. (1988) *The Art and Science of Decision Making: The Analytic Hierarchy Process*. Working Paper 88-06-03, Decision Science Department, The Wharton School, University of Pennsylvania, Philadelphia, PA.

Hitt, L., and Brynjolfsson, E. (1996). Productivity, Business Profitability, and Consumer Surplus: Three Different Measures of Information Technology Value. *Management Information Systems Quarterly*, 20(2), 121–142.

Holsapple, C. W., and Whinston, A. B. (1996). *Decision Support Systems*. St. Paul, MN: West Publishing Company.

Jeffers, P., Muhanna, W., and Nault, B. (2008). Information Technology and Process Performance: An Empirical Investigation of the Interaction Between IT and Non-IT Resources. *Decision Sciences*, 39(4), 703–735.

Keen, P. (1981). Value Analysis: Justifying Decision Support Systems. *Management Information Systems Quarterly*, 5(1), 1–15.

Klein G. , Orasanu J. , Calderwood R. , and Zsambok C. , (Eds.) (1993). *Decision Making in Action: Models and Methods*. Norwood, NJ: Ablex.

Kodogiannis, V. (2007). Decision Support Systems in Wireless Capsule Endoscopy: Revisited. *Intelligent Decision Technologies Journal*, 1(1–2), 17–31.

Kohli, R., and Devaraj, S. (2003). Measuring Information Technology Payoff: A Meta-Analysis of Structural Variables in Firm-Level Empirical Research. *Information Systems Research*, 14(2), 127–145.

Kurikose, A. (1985). Successful Decision Making Starts with DSS Evaluation. *Data Management*, 23(2), 24–29.

Lee, W.-P. (2004). Applying Domain Knowledge and Social Information to Product Analysis and Recommendations: An Agent-Based Decision Support System. *Expert Systems*, 21(3), 138–148.

Manyard, S., Burstein, F., and Arnott, D. (2001). A Multi-Faceted Decision Support System Evaluation Approach. *Journal of Decision Systems*, 10(3–4), 395–428.

Mintzberg, H., Raisinghani, D., and Théoret, D. (1976). Structure of 'Unstructured' Decision Processes. *Administrative Science Quarterly*, 21, 246–275.

Money, A., D. Tromp, and T. Wegner (1988) The Quantification of Decision Support Benefits Within the Context of Value Analysis. *Management Information Systems Quarterly*, 11(4), 515–527.

Mora, M., Forgionne, G., Cervantes, F., Garrido, L., Gupta, J., and Gelman, O. (2005). Toward a Comprehensive Framework for the Design and Evaluation of Intelligent Decision-Making Support Systems (i-DMSS). *Journal of Decision Systems*, 14(3), 321–344.

Newell, A., and Simon, H. A. (1972). *Human Problem Solving*. Englewood Cliffs, NJ: Prentice-Hall.

Ngai, E., and E. Chan (2005). Evaluation of Knowledge Management Tools Using AHP. *Expert Systems with Applications*, 29(4), 889–899.

Phillips-Wren, G., Hahn, E., and Forgionne, G. (2004). A Multiple Criteria Framework for the Evaluation of Decision Support Systems. *Omega*, 32(4), 323–332.

Phillips-Wren, G., Mora, M., Forgionne, G., Garrido, L., and Gupta, J. (2006). Multi-Criteria Evaluation of Intelligent Decision Making Support Systems. In J. Gupta, G. Forgionne, and M. Mora (Eds.), *Intelligent Decision-Making Support Systems (i-DMSS): Foundations, Applications and Challenges* (pp. 3–24). New York, NY: Springer.

Phillips-Wren, G., Mora, M., Forgionne, G., and Gupta, J. (2009). An Integrative Evaluation Framework for Intelligent Decision Support Systems. *European Journal of Operational Research*, 195, 642–652.

Pieptea, D. R., and Anderson, E. (1987). Price and Value of Decision Support Systems. *Management Information Systems Quarterly*, 11(4), 515–527.

Pohl, J. (2008). Cognitive Elements of Human Decision Making. In G. Phillips-Wren, N. Ichalkaranje, and L. Jain (Eds.), *Intelligent Decision Making: An AI-Based Approach* (pp. 41–76). Berlin: Springer.

Pomerol, J.-C., and Adam, F. (2008). Understanding Human Decision Making – A Fundamental Step Towards Effective Intelligent Decision Support. In G. Phillips-Wren, N. Ichalkaranje, and L. Jain (Eds.), *Intelligent Decision Making: An AI-Based Approach* (pp. 3–40). Berlin: Springer.

Saaty, T. L. (1997). A Scaling Method for Priorities in Hierarchical Structures. *Journal of Mathematical Psychology*, 15, 234–281.

Saaty, T. L. (1986). How to Make a Decision: The Analytic Hierarchy Process. *Interfaces*, 24(6), 19–43.

Saaty, T., and Vargas, L. (1994). *Decision Making in Economic, Political, Social and Technological Environments with the Analytic Hierarchy Process*. Pittsburgh, PA: RWS Publications.

Santhanam, R., and Guimaraes, T. (1995). Assessing the Quality of Institutional DSS. *European Journal of Information Systems*, 4, 159–170.

Sharda, R., Barr, S., and McDonnel, J. (1988). Decision Support Systems Effectiveness: A Review and an Empirical Test. *Management Science*, 34(2), 139–159.

Shim, J., Warkentin, M., Courtney, J., Power, D., Sharda, R., and Carlsson, C. (2002). Past, Present and Future of Decision Support Technology. *Decision Support Systems*, 33(2), 111–126.

Silverman, B., Normoyle, A., Kannan, P., Pater, R., Chandrasekaran, D., and Bharathy, G. (2008). An Embeddable Testbed for Insurgent and Terrorist Agent Theories: InsurgiSim. *Intelligent Decision Technologies Journal*, 2(4), 193–203.

Simon, H. A. (1960). *The New Science of Management Decision*. New York, NY: Harper and Row.

Simon, H. A. (1987). Two Heads Are Better Than One: The Collaboration Between AI and OR. *Interfaces*, 17(4), 8–15.

Smirnov, A., and Jakobson, G. (2009). Intelligent Decision Making in Dynamic Environments: Methods, Architectures and Applications. *Intelligent Decision Technologies Journal*, 3(1), 1–2.

Sprague, R. (1980). A Framework for the Development of Decision Support Systems. *Management Information Systems Quarterly*, 4(4), 1–26.

Sun, Y., and Kantor, P. (2006). Cross-Evaluation: A New Model for Information System Evaluation. *Journal of the American Society for Information Science and Technology*, 57(5), 614–628.

Taghezout, N., and Zarate', P. (2009). Supporting a Multicriterion Decision Making and Multi-Agent Negotiation in Manufacturing Systems. *Intelligent Decision Technologies Journal*, 3(3), 139–155.

Todd, P., and Benbasat, I. (1999). Evaluating the Impact of DSS, Cognitive Effort, and Incentives on Strategy Selection. *Information Systems Research*, 10(4), 356–374.

Turban, E., and Aronson, J. (1998). *Decision Support Systems and Intelligent Systems*. Upper Saddle River, NJ: Prentice-Hall.

Tweedale, J., Sioutis, C., Phillips-Wren, G., Ichalkaranje, N., Urlings, P., and Jain, L. (2008). Future Directions: Building a Decision Making Framework Using Agent Teams. In G. Phillips-Wren, N. Ichalkaranje, and L. Jain (Eds.), *Intelligent Decision Making: An AI-Based Approach* (pp. 387–408). Berlin: Springer.

Wang, Y., and Forgionne, G. (2006). A Decision-Theoretic Approach to the Evaluation of Information Retrieval Systems. *Information Processing and Management*, 24, 863–874.

Index

D. Schuff et al. (eds.), *Decision Support*, Annals of Information Systems 14,
DOI 10.1007/978-1-4419-6181-5, © Springer Science+Business Media, LLC 2011